# THE BEST SUNDAY TIMES TRAVEL

*Edited by*
RICHARD GIRLING

A Graham Tarrant Book

David & Charles
Newton Abbot  London  North Pomfret (Vt)

Cover illustration by Brin Edwards

**British Library Cataloguing in Publication Data**

The best of Sunday Times travel.—(A Graham
   Tarrant book).
   1. Travel. Personal observations –
   Collections
   I. Girling, Richard
   910.4

   ISBN 0–7153–9194–1

Printed in Great Britain
by Redwood Burn Limited, Trowbridge, Wiltshire
for David & Charles Publishers plc
Brunel House  Newton Abbot  Devon

Published in the United States of America
by David & Charles Inc
North Pomfret  Vermont 05053  USA

# CONTENTS

# EDITOR'S NOTE

This book lies at the end of millions of miles of travel by thousands of travellers. Only forty-nine writers are published in this latest collection, but they are the chosen representatives of a vast army of others. These are the pick of three previous collections – *The Sunday Times Travel Book* (1985), *The New Sunday Times Travel Book* (1986), and *The Sunday Times Travel Book Three* (1987) – which were themselves the selected best entries from the Sunday Times Travel Writing Competitions of their respective years.

Making an overall 'best' selection has been no easier a task than selecting the original three volumes. Again, the need to design a balanced book, without duplication of content, has meant that some excellent writing has not received the recognition it deserves. This is a matter of regret. But once again it is offset by the pleasure of presenting the work of a wide range of talents – some professional writers but mostly not – who continue to create astonishment both with their literary skills and their imagination as travellers.

*The Best of Sunday Times Travel* is a tribute to everyone who has been involved in the Travel Writing Competition over the years: the inaugural sponsors, Speedbird Holidays; the three distinguished panels of judges (Beryl Bainbridge, Robin Hanbury-Tenison and Paul Theroux; Dame Naomi James, Tom Sharpe and Jonathan Raban; Virginia McKenna, Dr John Hemming and William Boyd); but most of all to the 10,000 or so writers who entered their work. To all of these we offer our thanks and our congratulations. Nothing would have been possible without them.

RICHARD GIRLING
*The Sunday Times*, London

PETER MAYLE

# Two Hundred Metres
# of Burgundy

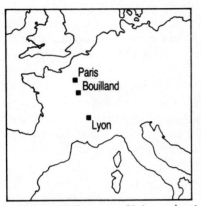

'Of course,' said the old man, 'since the telephone and mains sewage, one is as modern here as in Paris.'

He placed the last evil half inch of his yellow-papered cigarette carefully into the corner of his mouth. His hand, a freckled ham, was missing the top two joints from the index finger. A pruning accident. That and his nose, seasoned to a delicate pinky-purple by two litres of wine a day for sixty years, testified to a lifetime of labour in the vineyards.

He stood wheezing contentedly in the flat evening sun. In his brown canvas boots, faded blue trousers, checked shirt and frayed cap, one might have mistaken him for a man of no consequence instead of a senior member of local government. He was our self-appointed guide to Bouilland, population 136, sixteen kilometres from Beaune.

Our journey was to take us from one end of the village to the Bar-Tabac at the other end, a trip of some 200 metres down the straight street that led to the plump, vine-studded hills in the distance.

We started at the World War I Memorial, clearly the object of great respect and attention. The grass was clipped, and banks of flowers grew round the base, hiding some of the names cut into the stone slab. There were many names for such a small village, and the old man remembered most of them from his childhood. Fallen for the glory of France. It's a bad business, war. He shrugged and moved on.

We walked between two ancient plane trees which generations of hard pruning had reduced to bunches of arthritic grey knuckles, and arrived at Bouilland's 200-year-old launderette. It was the size of a double garage, open on one side, built of stone and roofed with tiles. In an English village it would have been converted into something quaint, selling teas and postcards. Here it was neglected.

The stone table once used by the village women to pummel their washing had patches of moss growing on it. The water trough was empty except for a layer of scum, a beer bottle and some sweet wrappers. A peeling notice warned us not to throw ordure. The old man flicked his cigarette end into the trough as we asked him when the laundry had stopped being used.

'The year electricity came,' he said, 'Madame Rivarel got a washing machine. Now the village has ten, maybe twenty machines.' He pulled the lobe of his ear reflectively. 'One must profit from progress.'

He seemed pleased to remind us of yet more evidence of Bouilland's humming modernity, and took us out into the sun again. At a slow but purposeful lurch, he led the way towards the Bar-Tabac.

The street was wide for an old village, and the houses were solid. The architecture was all of a piece; nothing recent, nothing flimsy. Wooden shutters of washed-out blue and green were folded back against the walls to show thick, beautifully patterned lace at the windows. Almost all the front doors were open, but it was impossible to see inside. Each door had its curtain – not the traditional strings of wooden beads, but bright strips of plastic or curious brown furry segments, like end-to-end caterpillars writhing in the breeze. Geraniums sat on the window ledges and oleanders grew from old Elf oil drums outside the doors.

And inside, unseen but definitely there, were the inhabitants. We felt them looking at us from behind the lace and from the shadowy hallways, peering through their caterpillar curtains at these strangers with clean shoes and light, impractical clothes. Tourists.

In a gap between two houses, an old wine barrel rested on its side doing duty as a kennel. A large mud-coloured dog was in residence, front paws crossed, the remains of a stale *baguette* within gnawing distance. He opened an owlish eye and barked unconvincingly at us before yawning and going back to sleep. We wondered if French dogs are taught in puppyhood how to cross their paws. It's not something English dogs do.

The approach to the bar's terrace was guarded by two old women taking the sun on a wooden bench. Black cotton dresses, ankle-height zippered carpet slippers, stockings like brown bandages, not quite thick enough to conceal the knots of varicose veins. We smiled and nodded. They nodded and smiled, exposing a total of not more than seven teeth between them.

'Sisters,' said the old man. 'They both lost their husbands in the war. Now they're losing their teeth. They can only eat soup.'

The bar was dim and neat, with a zinc counter and a fine rich smell of coffee and black tobacco. Taped to the mirror behind the bottles was a poster of the Lapierre of Dijon cycling team squinting into the sun, arms crossed, immense thighs bulging from long black shorts. Across the upper half of the poster, someone had scrawled, *'Un verre, c'est con. Trois verres, c'est bon'*, and drawn a crude wine glass balancing on the top of the team manager's head. Wine is more profitable than bicycles in this part of France.

At a corner table, three men and an ample woman in an apron played cards noisily, the slap of the cards punctuated by bursts of virtuoso coughing, that cavernous café cough which echoes up from the boots. The hand finished, Madame negotiated her bulk through the tables, wiping her hands on her apron. We ordered white wine. Did we want Aligoté or Chardonnay? Aligoté? *Bon*. The glasses were generous, so full that the surface of the wine trembled just above the rim. The old man dipped his nose and took a first careful sip. We followed him outside and sat at the tin table under the tree.

We were just in time to watch the evening rush hour. Led by a small boy in shorts and singlet and over-large wellingtons, a herd of cows was coming in from the fields. Buxom cows, creamy-white and clean, with proper horns that had somehow escaped the French passion for pruning. Twenty or thirty of them swayed past in dignified convoy, followed by the farmer and a matted dog of uncertain ancestry. He exchanged insults with the dog in the wine barrel and got a kick in the ribs from his master. The procession disappeared up the street as the old man sucked his glass dry and sighed hopefully.

Another? Well, since he's not pressed for time, perhaps one more. With the new round of drinks, he insisted that I try one of his yellow cigarettes. It was like smoking a bonfire rolled up in lavatory paper.

From the far end of the street came an irregular clanking sound, and a small, thin man in blue overalls appeared, carrying a handbell and a clipboard. He stopped outside the bar and rang his bell vigorously before reading the six o'clock news from his board.

'The Electricity of France wishes to announce a power stoppage due to work on the main transformer. There will be no electricity from seven until noon on the morning of Thursday, the 14th of June. Members of the commune are advised to arrange themselves accordingly.'

'*Merde!*' A deep voice from behind us. It was Madame in the doorway, loudly disputing the accuracy of the information and the need for a power cut.

The man with the bell glared at her. They were obviously familiar enemies. 'Thursday, the 14th of June. Seven till noon. *Pas de jus.*'

He flourished his bell and started back up the street before she had a chance to reply. Madame snorted and returned to her cards. The old man cackled.

'He is like the weather forecast, that one. Never correct. The noise of the bell makes an omelette of his brains. It is also my opinion that he cannot read. Not a man to rely on.'

The next day, Wednesday June 13, dawned clear and sunny, with the promise of more heat. There was, however, no electricity.

DAVID BRIERLEY

# QUESTIONS IN EL SALVADOR

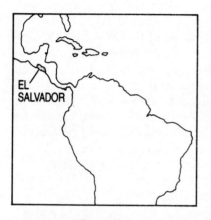

Where's the damn army? Why aren't they guarding the airport? At Belize, a twenty-minute hop away, there are camouflage nets and sandbags and RAF Hawks and squaddies with pink British faces. At El Salvador International Airport, not a single soldier, in a country torn by civil war.

Maybe the army aren't at the airport. They're everywhere else. So is the Guardia Nacional. Also the police. They all carry automatic weapons. The police patrol the capital in black and white gas-guzzlers, rifles poking out of every window. The army ride round in jeeps, rifles in the crooks of their arms. The Guardia Nacional wear jackboots and hook their fingers in their trigger guards.

Two blocks from the hotel is a McDonald's. It was blown up last year. Now it has two security guards. They carry rifles and check every car coming into the parking lot. This must be the end of civilisation as Americans know it.

Civil war has been eating up the country for five years. The army and the guerillas are not the greatest sufferers. Forty-five thousand (or is it fifty-five thousand – it's difficult keeping a body-count) ordinary citizens have been killed. The guerrillas shot some; most were murdered by the *escuadrones de la muerte*. These are the army and the police out of uniform. A night on the town for the boys.

The army is directing traffic at a crossroads. It's a job-creation scheme. One holds up the east-west streets. Another waves on the north-south streets. On each corner stands a pair of soldiers, rifles aimed at the lines of cars. You've never seen such careful drivers.

The National Museum has an exhibit that makes my eyes blink. A statue shows a priest dressed in the skin of a prisoner who has been flayed alive. Such sacrifices were common in these parts. Still are, when you consider the fifty-five thousand.

The victim has been scalped and the priest wears the hair. The skin is flecked with bits of flesh. It is in two pieces, like a pair of pyjamas.

It helps the crops grow, a museum guide explains to three teenage girls. They nod. Their faces show nothing. They express no horror. If I could understand why they accept such cruelty, I could understand why there is so much violence here.

The National University was closed four years ago by the army. Too many subversives, they said. The gates are barred, the grass grows long, the paint peels. It is completely deserted. Then, passing the Dental Faculty, you notice the rifles pointing at you.

I take the bus to Santa Ana, the second city of El Salvador. Its welcome sign says it has 90,000 inhabitants. It feels smaller.

The main square holds the three buildings of importance. One is the town hall, elegant with colonnades. Then there is the theatre, built in Jungle Opulent, with pillars and balconies and statues lifting off on wings. On the third side is the cathedral, which has its inspiration in Prague. It doesn't seem out of place because of the whiteness of the stonework, so brilliant in the sun it could be spun sugar. This is a facade. At the sides the cathedral is built of red brick and looks like the headquarters of some great insurance company before computers replaced clerks. Right and proper, I decide, for spiritual insurance is an urgent need here.

I'm called back by a member of the Guardia Nacional. They're the ones in jackboots. 'Where are you going?' To the square. 'Not to that building?' I realise I have been crossing the street towards an open door. A sign says it is the Governor's office. No, I insist, and bring out my passport. 'You're English?' Yes. He flips over the pages: US visa, Turkish stamps, Czechoslovak visa. He lingers over that and I wait for him to ask why I was visiting a Communist state. But he grins at me. I grin back. My cheeks ache with the grin. Okay, I can go. 'Hey,' he calls and I turn back. His hand is out to shake.

Another day, another bus. It skirts a smouldering rubbish tip outside Santa Ana. A man and a woman pick through the filth while cattle forage. The bus passes nameless villages. Posters hold the shacks together: *Coca-Cola es asi, Doberman Jeans – New York, Paris, London, San Salvador.*

The bus halts. It is an army roadblock and everyone gets out. The men stand with arms raised while soldiers search for weapons. A young conscript feels my back, my crotch, my legs. Nobody speaks. My passport causes excitement and a soldier thumbs through the pages. When he reaches the photo, he realises he's been holding it upside down. If they cannot read, why check papers? It's a ritual, showing who has power.

He goes off to report to the sergeant. We stand like cattle in the sun for a quarter of an hour while the sergeant clears me on his radio. Finally we climb back and the bus continues. Nobody comments on this check. Happens all the time. And so pointless: the soldiers never searched the luggage.

The land is dry and poor. The hills are tiny. They look violent, as if just made. Crows circle, looking for carrion.

Metapan is squalid beyond imagining. A two-storey building would be a skyscraper. The town centre is a huge jumble sale: combs, mirrors, ballpens, lipsticks, exercise books, clothespegs, Chiclets, knickers, buttons, baseball caps, sweetcorn, dried fish, the Encyclopedia of Sex (in eight Roneo-ed pages), belts, scissors, batteries, plates, machetes, crucifixes, razor blades, padlocks, strips of mango in plastic bags, everything well-fingered.

'Senor.' I turn back. There are three of them, Guardia Nacional. 'Your papers.' They inspect my passport and I do not find favour in their eyes. 'Why are you here?' To see the church and have a meal. 'Where are you from?' England. 'Where is your car?' I came by bus.

Behind them in a doorway is a man wearing plain clothes and dark glasses. Anger runs in furrows across his forehead. 'Why Metapan? Where are your companions?' I am alone. He wants very much to take me inside for further 'questioning'. It shows in his face. Reluctantly I am let go.

That pain in the back of my neck is four pairs of eyes watching every step I take to the church.

I have an introduction to L, an army conscript. He picks me up in his mother's car and we drive through Colonia Escalon to a roundabout where cars park beside snack stalls.

How long have you been in the army? 'Two years.' How much longer must you serve? He shrugs. 'Until this is finished.' Or until he is finished. He pushes back his sleeve to show scars where I have vaccination marks. A bomb blew up near his truck. Shrapnel wounds never look healed. The skin is purple and puckered.

How is the war going? 'It is getting worse.' The guerrillas are highly motivated. The conscripts have little stomach for a fight. If they surrender they expect to be stripped of uniforms and weapons and sent back naked. An officer would be tortured for information. Corruption is widespread. Wherever American aid goes, dollars stick. An officer becomes a colonel, moves into a mansion, buys a bulletproof Mercedes. He never goes on patrol. Instead he visits army corps with a photographer.

L drops me near my hotel. Perhaps he should have dropped me further away.

A man comes on to the terrace while I'm eating breakfast. When I finish, he walks over and sits down. 'Are you American?' British. 'I could have sworn you were American. What are you doing here?' Looking and listening. I ask what he does. 'I'm a businessman from Indiana.' Here on business? 'On vacation.' You must be the first tourist in years. 'Right.' Been here long? 'A couple of days.'

His tone is friendly but the questions are direct: where I've been, who I've talked to, what I'm doing that day. He calls for our bills in Spanish. I sign mine. He pays cash. When he leaves he doesn't deposit a key at reception. And his face is very tanned for a man two days away from an Indiana winter.

The coast is a different world, humid and lethargic. There's a shanty town built of flattened oil barrels and packing cases. People camp inside their shacks: a hammock, a bed made of driftwood, a Madonna, a machete, a doll, a dangling lightbulb. Outside children play among fermenting puddles. Why don't they run on the beach? Afraid of its freedom?

The beach stretches to the horizon. Coconut palms, bananas and papayas shade the edge. The sand is soft, the colour of old pewter. The beach is all mine but I cannot stay long for I lack a senorita to oil my back.

I walk into the village and choose a restaurant. A *mariachi* band approaches and launches into a lively lament on what it is to be alone and without love. I order a second beer. We are very macho about it here, drinking straight from the bottle. Pacific breakers curl in, the sun blazes, the prawns are amazing.

I leave and there he is, the man from breakfast, walking along the back of the row of restaurants. He carries no bag, such as might hold a towel and swimsuit.

'Hi,' he says, 'I see you made it.'

That night I ask the opinion of an American reporter. 'Paid cash for his breakfast?' Yes. 'Didn't leave a key?' No. 'Followed you down to La Libertad?' Yes. 'When are you leaving?' In the morning, I say, and order more drinks, doubles.

The taxi goes down Paseo Escalon. We pass the statue of Jesus standing on top of the globe. El Salvador del Mundo, the Salvadorans call it. Christ on the ball, the Americans say. We turn right and left and I check the route, just in case.

'American?' the driver asks. No, English. 'What is your profession?'

Questions, always these damn questions.

## DENNIS McDONNELL

# HEAD TRANSPLANT AND THE HANGING TREE

On a bend of the Colorado river we made camp for a month.

Well, to be strictly truthful, camp had already been made for us by some hi-tech realtors. And the mighty Red River, having been dammed six times for hydro-power, was actually the motionless mud-coloured Town Lake in the middle of Austin, the State Capital of Texas.

The University of Texas at Austin is very rich – it had the good sense to find oil on its own land. Some of the money has been spent on a great collection of literary manuscripts. We had come to study some of them.

**It's hard to be humble if you're from Texas**
– *car sticker*

**Not all Texans are true Texans
. . . send $18.95 for your Authentic Texan Heritage
certificate (suitable for framing)**
– *ad for The Association of Certified Texans*

To describe the 150 miles from Houston airport to Austin as un-dramatic would be to over-dramatise unforgivably. For the first sixty miles, State Highway 290 offered hardly a bend, hardly a hill: just dry pastures and an almost empty road. Once clear of Houston there weren't even many billboards, apart from those offering acreages for sale – some as 'farmettes', others as 'ranchettes'.

Every now and then a straggling two-dimensional township, with its sign: BLOGGSVILLE CITY LIMIT. Pop 912. Groggy with heat, Jackie wondered feebly if they changed the sign with every birth and death.

**LITTERING IS unlAWFUL**
– *highway sign*

Our rental car was called a Ford Escort, but you could have fooled me; somebody had smoothed off all the corners. Still, it went, and the air-conditioning worked.

After a long flight your perceptions are dulled, and everything is synthetic. But on Highway 290 unreality ruled. In the unchanging landscape we drove but we didn't get anywhere. In the October heat haze we sat in stately convoy among huge 5-litre cars – all floating like ships becalmed at a docile 54mph. I will never understand how a country that savagely defends the right of every citizen to carry a gun (and that won't enforce seat-belt laws because they interfere with the rights of the individual) meekly accepts the 55mph speed limit.

## CHILD RAISED AS CAT
– *newspaper headline*

Austin is a good deal smaller than Edinburgh, but has about as much motorway as the UK. We rolled recklessly down concrete channels, bombarded now by meaningless names and unfamiliar imperatives: E. NACOGDOCHES; R LANE MUST EXIT R.

'Look – Hyde Park!' shouted Jackie. 'Stella said that's near the campus – very posh.' But next to the Hyde Park Drug Store is the Hyde Park Tattoo Parlor, and The Texas Plasma Center ('Earn $$ in your spare time!') and the Wild Snail Pawn Shoppe.

But clinging to the numbered street grid system we found, and flopped into, our riverside home.

**All the frogs legs you can eat – Monday nite $7.95**
– *sign at Cactus Joe's Watering Hole*

The apartment was new, and cool, and decently furnished, and we liked it. We were appalled, though, at its appetite for electricity, even apart from the air-conditioning: the tiny kitchen had the water heater, the mighty cooker (with its spotlights and extractor hood), the fridge, the dishwasher, the waste disposer – and, already plugged in, the coffee-maker, the toaster and the electrical can-opener. A terrific place to have breakfast in, but hopeless to cook in: no strainer, no grater, and not a knife sharp enough to cut a lemon.

Little more than a century ago, when the river ran free, the Comanche would have taken our scalps for being here. Now the Indians are in their reservation, which you can visit like any zoo ('a special part of Texas' say the billboards tactfully). And our air-conditioned box is a stunning assertion of man's victory over heat and danger and wild country. It differs from a moon-shot only in degree. A power-cut, though, would leave us like stranded fish, unable to live.

**If you don't like the way I drive,
stay off the sidewalk**
*– car sticker*

'Hi, yo'll! I want you folks to have a nice day, now!' said an official in what was surely a parody of a Texas accent.

But *everybody* talked like that. And everywhere, even in restaurants, enormous men strode around in cowboy boots and 10-gallon hats. We weren't prepared for Texas to be quite so – er, Texan. It was as if all Scots wore the kilt, or all Cockneys dressed as Pearlies.

**Passer-by weds jilted bride**
*– newspaper headline*

The official was helping us get a parking pass from the Campus Police. The university has 50,000 students and 20,000 staff, and parking is a serious business. There are Campus Police roadblocks as you go in, and parking in the wrong place gets you a $12 fine. We heard that some rich kids just ignored their fines; theirs will have been the Porsche 928s we saw about the place. The university's smart answer has been to withold their degrees, but a law student is currently taking them to court, claiming violation of his rights.

*Theatre tour of London*
**If you love the theatre, here's a tour you must act on.
You'll be treated to four of the hottest plays in London:
CATS    SINGIN' IN THE RAIN
THE MOUSETRAP   NO SEX PLEASE WE'RE BRITISH!**
*– British Caledonian ad in Texas paper*

At first we thought we had no neighbours down by the river: nearly all the picture windows were blank. In fact people kept their drapes drawn as insulation. Practical, but eerie. Most of them looked to be students, but in a month we never managed a longer conversation than 'Hi! How are *you* today?' Then they vanished into their square caves.

**'V–P Bush utilised his sense of humor by laughing'**
*– University of Texas speech coach, adjudicating on V-P TV debate*

I noticed a job ad which ended 'an equal opportunity employer: m/f/h'. But on Channel 21 (of our 42!) when a Baptist minister was asked about homosexuality he almost frothed at the mouth: '. . . an abomination . . . Leviticus . . . a nation shall vomit them forth . . . We get 1,500 homosexuals a week who come to us, glad to give it up and turn to Jesus!'

In this land of big boots and Stetson hats, it's probably hard to be (m). Or (f). Or, particularly, (h).

**'I'm a firm believer in the old hanging tree'**
*– Stuart Huffman, Sheriff of Johnson County*

Austin didn't exist until 1846, when some prominent Texans decided it would be a good place for the new state's capital. Antiquity is in short supply, and over-valued. We felt almost guilty that our unremarkable house in Edinburgh would have been one of the dozen oldest buildings in Austin.

And we didn't know what to make of The Butler Window, a landmark in Zilker Park. Mr Butler, it seems, was a prosperous merchant who supplied the bricks for some of Austin's main buildings earlier this century. He died, and when the time came for his house to be demolished, a window from it was preserved and rebuilt in the park on a pedestal. Through it you can look out on some trees.

## HUMAN HEAD TRANSPLANT
*– newspaper headline*

Though nobody knew we were there, our phone rang quite often. Usually it was someone congratulating us on having won a free dancing lesson or test drive; but there were quite a few grumpy wrong numbers, which made us feel at home. (Scots get very querulous if you're not the person they thought they were ringing.)

I read in a paper that in some states more than 50 per cent of subscribers are now ex-directory. This must make it hard for the agencies who undertake to deliver telephone sales messages. If the trend goes on, their teams of congratulators will be calling fewer and fewer people, more and more often – until the remaining subscribers are always engaged, because they are always being congratulated.

> **'This is a dry county, very dry . . . the beer drinkers here carry posthole diggers in the backs of their cars. They don't throw the beer cans out; they bury them'**
> *– Dan Saunders, Sheriff of Martin County. (Quoted, like Sheriff Huffman, in **Texas Monthly**)*

Some of the campus buildings have unnervingly jocular names, like the Sid Robertson Building, or the Harry Ransom Center. We make condescending jokes about Johnny Balliol College and the Bert Sheldon Theatre. We're wrong, of course. Paying public respect to eminent people is a good thing; and using the names by which they were known is direct and refreshing. (All the same, we mumble, we didn't call it Winnie Churchill College.)

We work in the Harry Ransom Humanities Center, where the

facilities for study are magnificent and the people very helpful –
though we had to get used to being greeted each morning with loud
cries of 'Hi, you guys!' from the librarian. Not at all like the National
Library of Scotland.

The building itself, though, worried us. It's new, a massive seven-
storey cube, with only a few, irrelevant, windows. Inside there are
spacious archives and art galleries, but you have no sense of the form
of the building, or of which part you are in. The lifts are scattered
about, and each one serves only selected floors. Ours went, I think, to
2, 5 and 7; the other floors might have been in another building, or
another town.

One morning we went in out of blazing sunshine. Four hours later
we came out to find that three inches of rain had fallen, creeks had
burst their banks, cars had been swept away, and people were injured
and homeless. Up in the vast cool reading room, none of this had
happened.

A few days later we heard a reading room receptionist telephoning
the ground floor police desk to ask if she needed her umbrella to go to
lunch.

> *(film of ambulance; male voice over)*
> **'. . . it's nice transport – even sleeps two . . . but it's
> never saved a life on its own! Our trained people do
> that! We don't only get you to the hospital – we get
> you there *alive!*'**
>          *– commercial for private medical firm*

Dept of Coy Euphemisms: Austin is, of course, a very proper city.
But less-than-proper advertisers offer real dollar notes to Yellow
Pages, so an accommodation has to be reached. This must be why
Abracadabra Nude Modeling and Midnite Cowboy Exotic Massage
both solemnly undertake Outside Calls to Residences and Nursing
Homes. ('Nurse . . . nurse . . . Aargh!')

> **If guns are outlawed, only outlaws will have guns**
> *– car sticker (Is this the silliest piece of circular logic ever?)*

During our stay there was a two-day symposium about 'The Texas
Myth'. Much high-powered theorising and introspection. We smiled
our superior Old World smiles, of course. But we couldn't think of
many states with a strong enough identity to have a symposium
about. 'The Idaho Myth'? 'The New Hampshire Myth'? No. We
were, after all, visitors to the most interesting state in the union.

ROBERT TASHER

# A Day in Narnia, A Night in Phang Nga

On the village green in front of the Chinese Bhuddist temple a fairground was being erected. The skeleton of a Ferris wheel loomed; shooting galleries and hoopla stalls were being knocked together.

The purpose of the structure immediately outside the temple was not so obvious. The men hammering it together had beckoned us, beaming, inviting inspection. A raised wooden runway, carpeted with the pin-sharp points of six-inch nails hammered through from the bottom, ran out 50ft and ended in a bed of nails laid on the grass. At the foot of the bed, guyed by wire ropes, a forty-rung ladder rose vertically. The rungs were steel knives, blades up.

The message was clear – 'Come back at nine this evening' – though they spoke no English, we no Chinese and no help was to be had from the Thai phrasebook.

We had come to Phang Nga to visit the limestone islands that rear in their hundreds from the bay. These natural wonders occur only here and in the gulf of Tonkin: connoisseurs rate Phang Nga. A day-trip from Phuket had only whetted our appetite and we had left that tourist ghetto by local bus and moved into a hot and grubby Chinese hotel in Phang Nga town.

The boy who had carried our bags up to our room so eagerly was of course a boatman. Would we like to sail out into the bay? As a matter of fact we would, tomorrow. He would take us all day for 1,000 bhat. We threw up our hands and bargained, and agreed that he would find two more travellers and we would each pay 200 bhat. That settled, we wandered down to the river looking for food and natural wonders.

The limestone scarps that rushed down to the sea and broke up into islands hung over the town, dripping green and yellow trees. Women sat under carved wooden verandahs preparing vegetables, fish and chicken. Children abandoned their play and pointed at the Farangs.

We had travelled only forty-five miles and had moved into a culture completely different from that of Bangkok, Chiang Mai and Pattaya. Everything was in Chinese. The banners of yellow paper hanging between the bright silk banners and red lacquered columns in the temple by the village green were covered in lists of Chinese characters. The advertisements for Coca Cola were in Chinese. The three dozen life-size turtles, made of dough and coloured red, standing on racks in the temple forecourt, had their names, perhaps, painted in gold Chinese ideograms on their crusty shells.

After dark we followed the smell of sizzling meat down to the fair-ground. Families eating candyfloss under strings of coloured lights, crowds of bikers guzzling frogburgers, country music wailing from loudspeakers; we could have been on Hampstead Heath on Bank Holiday night. Except for the drumming and chanting coming from the temple, and the photo display of the horrors of VD which had attracted a huge audience of twelve-year-olds.

We found a tent where they were cooking omelettes filled with clams. Two huge frying pans were being wielded on charcoal fires by a pair of vividly made up girls in blue jeans and flowered blouses. But a few sidelong glances revealed them to be He-Shes. The Thais are very keen on transvestism; way off any tourist route we would find them, making up and giggling, modelling clothes for each other and generally being girlish. Nobody seems to mind; as an aberration it rates low, on a level with Christianity or driving carefully. We sat down and gorged.

Sharp at nine a conch shell sounded and the temple courtyard filled up with Thais, dressed in white trousers with embroidered aprons, chanting and shaking in time to gongs. The first one mounted the runway and briskly walked its length, barefoot on the nail points. Stepping down at the end, he lay on the bed of nails and rolled across it to the foot of the ladder, which he climbed, pausing on each blade to detach a yellow paper prayer flag and send it fluttering to the ground.

For those unmoved, the Ferris wheel spun its neon lights and the shooting galleries popped. But as more young men, then older men, then women, came forward to walk the nails and climb the knives, so the general air of fun increased. Spectators eating ice cream crowded round the performers thirty deep, and cheered and clapped. As the only Farangs there, we were drawn by friendly hands to the best viewing spot, and beamed at and invited to climb the ladder. But still we could not discover the why of this ordeal by steel.

Next morning in the market, shopping for a picnic, our struggles with the phrasebook brought an English-speaking Thai to our rescue, explaining that the quail eggs we had bought were raw, but could be cooked for us in the soup cauldron wherever we took breakfast. And the performance with the nails and the knives? A thanksgiving. All those who went through the ordeal had at some time survived an accident or illness when their lives had been despaired of. In gratitude they undertook to walk the nails and climb the knives every year until they died. They spent the day chanting and dancing, and when they came to walk and climb they could be heard speaking Chinese, a language none of them could speak during the rest of the year.

Sapan, the boatman, had found two other tourists to share the fishtail boat and the cost. Peter was from Germany, and Helga was from California: they were solo travellers looking for entertainment, travelling together for her convenience. Sapan had brought along a couple of passengers too. Mike was from Phang Nga town, back from studying economics in Bangkok; Strawberry was from Panyi Island, like Sapan himself. We had a momentary chill when they climbed aboard . . . piracy? Would we ever be seen again? But when Strawberry reached under the seat and produced the first bottle of an apparently endless supply of Star Tiger rice spirit we realised it was not going to be that kind of adventure.

The islands rose sheer out of a millpond sea, pillars of white limestone with ochre splotches capped in crinkly green. Rank on rank they stretched to the horizon, their reflections shimmering towards us on a blue mirror. The coast dropped away into mist and we nosed into a world of fantasy. It bore no resemblance to our map.

Getting closer we saw that the islands rose more than sheer, their bases eaten away by the sea. Sapan sailed in beneath the overhang of limestone. He leapt up on to the ledge of rock which ran around the whole island under the overhang like some inside-out cloister, and tied us up. From the cool of this cloister the island-dotted sea shimmered in the sunlight. We found our torches and entered the caves beneath the island.

Later we drifted and found: a beach, 20ft of yellow shingle under a dozen palm trees; a grotto more lurid than Lourdes, every glittering bowl crying out for a plaster Madonna; a lagoon in an island's heart reached through a rock tunnel. In a gallery of stalactites, baobab roots seeking water winding down from the roof, we asked Sapan what the island was called.

'It has no name,' Sapan said, 'but when I told some other people I brought here that it had no name, they said to me that it was called Narnia.' He looked puzzled.

We ate quails' eggs, drank Star Tiger, swam in the warm sea floating from sun into shade and back again under trailing vines. The sun tumbled the islands' shadows on the sea.

Panyi island, where Sapan and Strawberry lived, had only enough room on it for the mosque. The rest of the village was on stilts, a Southend pier of teak, and we stopped there for petrol and beer. Oily water glittered through gaps in the teak boards as we climbed the gangplank. A plump old man sitting in a wooden scaffold on a marine building site sawed the top off an immense teak column to make it flush with the decking. The village was expanding. Seen through the lacy walls of the village pool hall the polystyrene floats of the fish farm bobbed busily.

While Sapan found the petrol we strolled the boardwalk where ladies sold shells and coral jewellery. One in jeans and blouse laid a hand on Ann's arm. Despite the nail varnish, it was a man's hand.

'What's your name?' He-She asked huskily.

'Ann. What's yours?'

He-She simpered prettily. 'My name is Linda.'

Sitting in a bus next morning, eating pineapple and waiting for the driver, we heard that the survivors were going to walk on fiery coals that night down on the fairground. But we were bound for Tekua Pa, and rumours in our guidebook of an ancient city.

## D. A. CALLARD

# THE DRUMS OF NEFTA

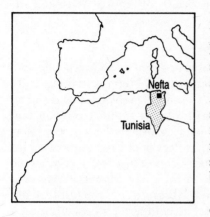

It is late evening and Marianne, Walter and I have just finished a large *couscous* washed down by several bottles of heady local wine. My companions start talking in Arabic again and I have the depressing sense of being a hick tourist fallen among real travellers. Wine-numbed and bloated, I lapse into silent recapitulation of what has brought us here.

I met Marianne on Jerba, an island claiming mythic status as the place where the Sirens held Ulysses. I too was becalmed, though the Sirens were inaudible. I would take bus trips from the island to towns in southern Tunisia but they never lasted longer than a day. Their chaos and squalor did not compare well with the pristine beauty of Jerba and, as a lone male out of season, I was prey to a horde of street hustlers. On Jerba I had made it clear that I was not in the market for anything and they left me alone.

Returning on the bus from Medenine I noticed a solitary blonde whom I assumed was a stray package tourist from one of the hotels on the west of the island. I asked if she was lost. She was not. She had just arrived and was looking for a cheap hotel. I suggested mine which was cheap, central and practically empty. So our friendship began, and the Siren spell was broken.

Her story is barely credible. She is Dutch, in her late twenties, and she has been in North Africa for one-and-a-half years. During this time her sole contact with a European has been a fortnight with a German woman in Algeria. She has almost always travelled alone and has lived with very poor and very rich families, participating in the most private aspects of Arab family life. At times she has dressed as an Arab woman, worn the *ha'ik*, looked at the ground as she walked, among women only. At other times she cut her hair short, wore a *djellaba* and travelled as a man. In relatively Europeanised Tunisia she has shed these disguises. She is fluent in the Moroccan dialect of Arabic, to the amazement and amusement of the Tunisians.

She has penetrated other exclusive worlds before this. In spite of the slimmest Jewish credentials, a surname inherited from a non-practising father, she spent six months at a *yeshiva* in the ultra-orthodox Mea Shearim quarter of Jerusalem. By virtue of her fluent Hebrew she once led prayers at a Passover feast of wealthy Moroccan Jews – the only one present who could read them in the absence of a rabbi. She had no ideas of conversion since she previously spent six months in an ecumenical Christian community in the South of France. Why had she done these things?

'How else do you find out?'

I have no answer to that.

A trail through several Saharan oases brought us to Nefta, close to the Algerian border. If Jerba was picturesque, Nefta is magical and I regret that I must fly home in a week. Our hotel in the medina is run by an amiable eccentric whose vagueness probably results from constant imbibing of palm wine and smoking *harar,* a local herb similar in effect to mild hash. Last night he claimed that President Bourguiba used his hotel before he came to power and that Brigitte Bardot, accompanied by a canine entourage, stayed there in the early Seventies. He produced newspaper cuttings proving that BB came to Nefta but I am not convinced that she stayed in the Hotel de la Liberté, whose plumbing leaves everything to be desired.

But little would be surprising in Nefta. It is on the edge of the Chott el-Jerid, a saline depression in the Sahara once part of the Mediterranean. From late morning onward the combination of sunlight, heat and the reflective properties of its salt surface throws up a host of mirages. Seen from the hills above the town the Chott becomes not an arid wasteland but a phantom sea, piercingly blue.

Dominating Nefta is another extraordinary feature, so incongruous that at first sight it might well be a mirage. It is the Sahara Palace Hotel, the most luxurious in Tunisia, a cavernous, currently near-deserted edifice with all the charm and intimacy of an international airport lounge. Below it is the old palmerie, the Corbeille, nourished by channels of water running from a hot spring poetically named The Source. In the heart of the palms is a pool credited with miraculous curative powers where the Neftis come to bathe: women in the morning, men in the afternoon. Looking toward the town from here, the sky is dominated by the seat of a religious brotherhood from whose minaret a human muezzin, instead of the usual loudspeaker, calls the faithful to prayer. Nefta has more than sixty places of worship and is a centre of Sufism, but there is no fanatical edge to its people. Once, being led by a boy through the maze of the medina, Marianne asked our guide if the people were religious. He laughed loudly. 'No, we are not religious. Nefta is a town of drunks and revolutionaries.' I was heartened by this news though Marianne, who has experienced the unpredictable effects of alcohol on the North African male to her cost, was less amused.

We both met Walter a few days ago. He is a German working at a doctorate on the post-colonial development of the region. He has lived here for eight months and knows more about the town than the Neftis, who are infuriatingly vague when it comes to giving directions. He knows nothing of Brigitte Bardot's visit but confirms that President Bourguiba used to stay at our hotel, though he now spends two months every year at the Sahara Palace.

Mercifully Walter and Marianne soon exhaust their mutual stock of Arabic and, in the silence that follows, we all become aware of a faint constant drumbeat in the medina. Walter says that it is probably a wedding but suggests that we investigate. We leave, and Marianne stays behind picking at a fruit salad.

The drums lead us through the warren of narrow alleys to a courtyard whose entrance is blocked by a knot of people. Walter sees a friend among them and asks if this is a private wedding party. He is told that it is a ceremony connected with Sidi Bou Ali, a long dead Sufi mystic whose precepts many Neftis follow. The friend is an invited guest and asks us to join him.

The courtyard is illuminated by a single light and against the far wall five drummers keep a constant rhythm, breaking into occasional chanting. Beside them a group of older men sit impassively, eyes closed, listening intently to the music. To the fore of the courtyard about twenty male, mostly young, dancers shake their bodies rhythmically but independently as a man carrying a pot of burning incense weaves among them. A larger group of people stand on the outskirts surveying the spectacle and we join them. In two rooms off the courtyard are women, children and a few greybeard patriarchs.

Walter's young black friend serves us tea. Drinking it, I wonder what to do about Marianne since this is an all-male affair and I am reluctant to leave. Walter solves the problem by volunteering to report back to her and I am left alone, highly conspicuous but undisturbed and ignored by the crowd.

There is a sudden scuffle as one of the dancers collapses, delirious on to the stone floor. Two spectators jump in, seize his trembling body and carry it away from the dancers. I watch as the convulsions subside, the delirium leaves his eyes and he returns, slightly dazed, to normality. Then it happens to another dancer and, as I am watching the same pattern of recovery, the man next to me throws his arms into the air, totters forward and begins to experience apparently involuntary spasms. Two other watchers take hold of him, lift him up to remove his shoes and thrust him into the dance.

The drums and the chant continue. Others join the dance in the same way and others collapse. To dance, it seems, is not by choice: you dance when the drums call you and you stop when whatever moves you to dance ceases. For a supposedly religious ceremony there is a very secular feel about the whole affair. The spectators smoke and laugh among themselves: near the doorway a youth records the drumming on a cassette recorder emblazoned with a Rolling Stones decal. Many of the men are black or half-caste descendants of freed Saharan slaves and I feel that what I am watching is not Islamic at root but a practice brought by their ancestors and grafted on to the religion.

From the corner of my eye I see Walter return and realise with a start that the person accompanying him enswathed in a black *bournous* is Marianne. Fortunately all eyes are elsewhere and no-one seems to notice. However, Walter's friend is not fooled and, drawing a seat and offering tea, whispers pointedly, *'Bonjour Mademoiselle'*. He seems very amused by the subterfuge.

The drumming and dancing continue for another hour, reaching no climax and no greater or lesser degree of intensity. Suddenly it stops and, it seems within seconds, drummers, dancers and audience disperse. As we leave someone tells Walter that there is a later, private part to the ceremony.

Back at the hotel we hear the drums begin again and continue long into the night, past the time when exhaustion overcomes the excitement which keeps us from sleep for many hours.

# MODERN HISTORY

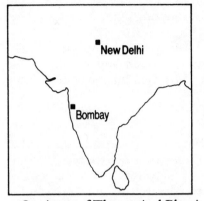

Mohan Lal was waiting for us when we came out to breakfast on 31 October. We decided to hire him for the day, and negotiated a price. Before we set out, he showed us his letters of recommendation from delighted tourists. But with Mohan Lal this went a bit further. We were to ride in a rickshaw which was itself a gift from a delighted tourist. The name and occupation of the donor were painted on the back: Professor x, Institute of Theoretical Physics, Stuttgart.

He dropped us in a short street which led to the entrance to the Taj. We bought our tickets and went through into the grounds, sitting down just inside to admire. The building was so perfect that it became fantastic, and we imagined a huge finger coming from the sky and pressing on the dome. The minarets would start to revolve, and organ music would strike up ('Oh, kiss me my sweet, it's the loveliest night of the year'). We explored, we gazed a bit more, and I discovered the pleasures of walking barefoot on marble. The world's greatest monument to the exploitation of women had its appeal, I had to admit.

On the way back to Mohan Lal, we stopped for soft drinks. The pips of a time-check echoed across the street. 'Funny,' I said, 'that's the first time I've heard the pips this trip.' A boy rushed up with a transistor radio. '. . . attempt on the Prime Minister's life. Leaders of all opposition parties have condemned the act. The President is flying home from his visit to the Gulf . . .' and on, with statements from every leading politician but no hard information till right at the end. 'A bulletin on the Prime Minister's condition is expected shortly.'

There were seven of us round the radio, English, Hindu and Sikh. One of the Hindus asked, smiling, 'Prime Minister gone out?'

'Not yet, I don't think,' said Ruth. We all laughed.

We walked back to the rickshaw, saying 'well' to one another, not knowing what else to say.

We spent the middle of the day at the red fort, returning in the late afternoon to catch sunset at the Taj. We arrived again at the street where we had heard the news of the assassination attempt. Men were pulling down the shutters of the gift shops. It was five o'clock.

At the Taj, Indian families were grouping themselves for the professional photographers who swarmed over the central platform. Tourists of all kinds wandered by. A plaque beside the empty reflecting pool and its silent fountains explained that the water system which filled it had become 'obsolete' in the nineteenth century. The sun set behind us, reflecting gold on the building. The Taj turned silver, and then a late pink. The light went. It was getting cold. The dogs were appearing.

Back at the Agra Hotel we ordered coffee to warm up and started a game of Scrabble. Some Indian guests arrived and sat under the portico. The manager joined them. 'Mrs Gandhi died today.' We froze.

'She's actually dead,' said Ruth. 'There'll be riots everywhere.'

November 1. We sat down to breakfast in the garden, and listened to the World Service news. There was mention of trouble in 'some areas'. The next programme started – an analysis of political and social life in Cedar Rapids, Iowa. As we heard a description of a day in the life of the mayor, a Sikh in a green turban wandered out into the garden, brushing his teeth.

The car which we had ordered to take us to the station never appeared, and we travelled instead in a dilapidated tonga. We arrived at 9.30, went through the usual contortions to buy a ticket, and were told to expect a train at 10.30. We sat down to read. Ruth constantly complained about the fidgeting child next to her. Ten-thirty came but the train did not. We wandered up and down to the inadequate refreshment kiosk, drinking soda and eating buns. Up the track came an engine pushing a blazing box-car. It seemed odd, but not remarkable. I looked at our fellow passengers. There were two men in identical fawn clothes. One was short-haired, dark and fat. The other was a Sikh, very small and slim. They looked like a comic turn. There was a tall Englishman, dressed in white, with silver and turquoise earrings and a beard down to his waist. There was a young Sikh in a red turban, wearing a blue quilted jacket despite the heat.

At one there was an announcement. The train from Bangalore would soon arrive. We leapt into a carriage at the end of the train. We were followed by a family – mother, father and daughter. The mother, large and jewelled and forceful, was determined to let us know she spoke English. 'So this is a second class carriage. It is not bad.' They ate an elaborate snack. 'You might as well get as much pleasure as possible out of every situation,' she said, packing the dishes away.

Ruth and I played a spiritless game of Scrabble. We dozed. When we woke, the light was low and yellow. We passed a sign saying 'District of Delhi'. Ruth was by the window. She turned to me as the train slowed, her hand over her mouth and her eyes wide. 'There's a dead body out there.'

We are on a train, I thought. This is what they did in 1947. They stopped trains.

'A body? What do you think's happening?'

'I don't know,' she said. 'It's just someone's body.'

Through the window I could see a group of men walking away. One was carrying a crash helmet. They cast long shadows. They started to run. The train moved forward a few yards and stopped.

'What the hell's happening?' asked Ruth.

I knew what was happening, and my voice expressed the knowledge. 'Shut the windows!' I shouted.

On the other side of the train, the mother protested. 'They will think we have something to hide.'

'But you have already got your windows down,' we shouted back, as we pulled at ours.

Young men walked through the train, looking under seats, looking hard at faces.

'They are looking for someone who is hiding,' said the mother.

'Who?'

She leant towards us and whispered, in dramatic tones. 'A Sikh.'

A large group of men passed through the carriage. They were carrying bamboo poles. They were intent on murder. The mother told her daughter to get on a top bunk. I said to Ruth that we should do the same. I did. She did not. She sat with the mother on the station side of the train. She took her earrings off.

'What the hell's happening?'

I had read about 1947. Now the same thing was happening only yards away. More groups of young men pushed through the train. Just out of sight, someone started to shout. The mother shushed them.

Scuffling outside. Another train passed, going the other way. The mother said something to Ruth, which the daughter repeated to me. 'You know the young man on the platform in the red turban and the blue jacket? They are burning him now.' 'But why?' 'Because he is a Sikh, and they have killed Mrs Gandhi.'

I wanted to express my fear and my horror. I wanted to drum my heels and wail and be comforted. But how could I seek comfort? I was not central to this drama. I lay peripheral, uncomforted, afraid. Time passed.

'Here are the police.'

'A bit late,' said Ruth.

There was running and shouting outside, then a long wait in silence. There was nothing more to comment on, and no comment to be made.

The train started to move. Everyone was climbing on to the top bunks. 'What's happening?' I asked Ruth as she joined me.

'The train which was coming the other way had all its windows broken.'

'Protect your face,' cried the mother to the daughter.

From where I lay I could see the repeated pattern of the sleepers slowly passing beneath the train. Again and again we slowed, almost stopped. We drew into the suburban station where the train terminated.

We were advised to catch the local into New Delhi. As we tried to calm ourselves with sweet coffee, a Swiss traveller appeared. 'There are a group of us just down the platform, come and join us.' Twenty tourists of all kinds had huddled together. Among them was the young man I had seen earlier. 'Look,' said Ruth, 'his beard's gone.'

A few minutes later we were in Delhi. We crossed the footbridge and went out into a silent forecourt. To our left were rows of deserted taxis. Straight ahead, the motto of the Indian Railways was written, seven feet high, in English, on the wall. PUNCTUALITY, SAFETY, SECURITY.

## STAN GEORGE

# ONE MORE BURMESE DAY

At five in the morning Rangoon shakes off sleep. Paraffin lamps cast pools of sputtering light on the wet streets. After a night of drizzle, the city murmurs as though sound, like the dust, has been cleared from the air by the rain. The lamps wheeze. In a café doorway a man slaps chapati dough on to a board, and stacks the rolled balls into ranks. A boy yawns and adjusts his *lunghi*. He oversees a water tank parked in the road. Water splashes from a faucet into a jerrican, and when it fills the boy sluggishly replaces it from a line of empty ones. A truck, far off, grinds gears and whines, coming slowly closer.

At dawn the city has a somnambulant purpose. Gaunt men emerge from doorways, and proceed, swinging rolled umbrellas down the street. The city is empty. Traffic lights blink impotently at the odd cyclist who now, as later, ignores them. And in the soft light which permeates below the cloud cover, the city is familiar. Awash in greys and blues, the Victorian tenements melt into the dawn mist, reminiscent of Glasgow or Liverpool, once grand, now in decline. Except that here the foliage is more determined.

Rhizoids of jungle creep between the paving stones. The buildings weep ironwork. Gutters, overhung with herbaceous toupees, wave dangerously from the rooftops. Balconies cling to walls like frightened climbers. Stucco lies in drifts of powdered plaster. Street lighting is spasmodic and piped water comes in sluggish fits and starts. Blocked storm drains flood the streets. It seems as though a slammed door would level the city.

Writing in 1934, George Orwell feared that modernisation would sweep aside Burmese culture. He needn't have worried. The Burmese are truly living in the past.

The country goes its own way. Even in the capital, life ticks by with the rhythm of the rice-growing cycle. There are no slums, and no discernible wealth, just an equal distribution of what looks like poverty. Yet a scorn for materialism, the measurement of wealth, is fundamental to Buddhism which is rooted in the national psychology. Because life is an illusion, what is the significance of development? Why worry about efficiency? Of course the buildings decay, and so must everything!

This fatalism lends itself to the infamous Burmese bureaucracy, partly because bureaucracy looks like efficiency, partly because bureaucracy fits so neatly into the unchanging Buddhist worldview. And inevitably a static officialdom leads to corruption. Yet, as an ageing journalist in Rangoon explains, corruption is a Western value judgement. Bribery, familial influence, the black economy are endemic in Asia. Because Burma is not a rich country the potential for racketeering is limited, and shrugged off. For those Burmese who want one foot in the material world, at least so far as the occasional bottle of Scotch is concerned, the black market exists. At times in Rangoon it seems that the second economy is all pervasive, and gaps in conversation are filled by discreet requests to change money.

Rangoon airport is the first contact with the workings of the second economy. Guidebooks advise travellers to bring their fully duty-free quota, to offset the official rate of exchange. Moving through the customs shed, itself a film set from *Casablanca,* new arrivals encounter a pantomime. On one side of the desk officials leisurely scrutinise and catalogue every marketable item, and on the other, baggage handlers maintain a cacophony of stage whispers, demanding 'Johnny Walker'.

Yet even the black market in Burma has an ease unknown in the rest of Asia. Hustlers are polite and accept refusal amiably. Apart from a few pickpockets in Rangoon, street crime does not exist. It is a remarkably well-adjusted society where the alienation of adolescence, universal throughout Europe and Asia, is unheard of. The largest identifiable youth group are the monks.

Although Burma is an oil producer, national lassitude and the lack of a desire for 'development' ensure a leisurely extraction, and petrol is rationed. A lack of foreign exchange means that, apart from a few Toyotas, there are virtually no new cars in Rangoon. Overladen buses trundle about the city, and a taxi fleet pensioned off in colonial days still plies its trade like a permanent veteran car rally. What rush hour exists is merely a breeze of bicycles.

The Schwe Dagon Pagoda on the edge of Rangoon is a religious city. Armies of monks in blood-red robes hang around the place. They stand about chatting, smoking cigarettes and chasing dogs from the temple grounds. Some monks sweep the long expanses of the stone plateaux; some carry offerings of donated food; some undertake pagoda business, receiving visitors in drafty offices where money is handed over. For Burmese, the upkeep of religious centres is a way of acquiring merit for a future incarnation.

The main courtyard is a jumble of shrines and small temples. It is a mixture of the spiritual and the profane. Yet an unexpected feeling of fun and clutter pervades the complex. Children daubed with circles of yellow ochre offer tiny figurines and toys for sale. Old ladies peddle incense. Child monks play in the alcoves. There is even a sideshow where a large gilt *stupa* rotates on an electric motor. Punters throw coins, trying to score a hit in the tin trays. When they are successful a bell rings and a mechanical buddha lights up and makes a creaky obeisance. The prize is the motto printed next to the tray: 'Freedom from Five Enemies', 'May you be Well and Happy'.

A couple of English-speaking students explain the hold of religion on the populace. All young boys spend time in monasteries. They grin at the idea, crinkling their noses in mock distaste, suggesting that the monastic life holds no attraction for them. There is no dividing line between the pagoda and life outside. Recently when a gang stole some large buddha images from the temple complex at Pagan, the whole country was outraged. There were no 'safe' houses for the thieves, who were quickly apprehended, and the images were returned.

The students mention the seventy-year occupation of the Schwe Dagon by the British army, and the devastation they left behind. They relate the story in a hushed tone, watching carefully for a reaction. And then to dismiss any embarrassment they laugh. The history of Burma has been one of imperialism. The Burmese are descendants of the Mongols, and now they try to dominate the Shans, the Kochins and the Karens. The students shrug; that's life, they seem to say.

Pools of rainwater collect on the uneven pavement. Tiny gilt bells record the passage of the wind, and an amiable buddha expresses a worldly, less than tranquil smile on the bustle around his feet.

The Strand Hotel, near the waterfront, was the Imperial equivalent of the Schwe Dagon. Like Raffles in Singapore it holds in amber a record of the past. Yet, whilst the Burmese retain a grudging respect for the British, they exact a characteristic vengeance upon the sanctified edifice of their former masters.

The palm court, both vegetation and orchestra, has long since been repossessed. Only the clank, clank of the wrought iron lift cage provides a kind of background music, echoing through the empty building. Damp stains creep down the walls to join in sombre triumph the black fungi ascending from the floor. Cadillac cockroaches, friction-driven, ply the roadways of the corridors. Cigarette burns lacerate the teak furniture.

In a far-flung foyer three Burmese officials drink in silence, as though in respect for the spirits of the departed. There is no barman but the hotel receptionist, under duress, rummages a bottle of beer from a tin box and wanders away in search of a glass. Above, in the gloomy upper reaches of the hotel, a lavatory cistern clangs. Dust-wreathed propellers turn overhead, twisting and turning the grime of centuries into the crannies of the moulded ceiling.

Beside the reception desk there is a large glass cabinet, labelled 'Lost and Found'. It is one of the sights of the city. A time capsule containing the personal effects of a long dead civilisation: the pince-nez of an extinct dowager, a tarnished cigarette case, two withered clasp handbags, indeterminate items of jewellery, and the desiccated remains of insects. Each item is separately labelled and lies on perpetual display, reducing all the pomp and ceremony of Empire to a few mute and pathetic items. On the last silvered patches of a fading mirror, the ghost of Orwell smiles.

CAROLINE DILKE

# A VISIT TO DOMINICA

A strange thing happened this year. A man I'd met only twice, a bit of a loner, invited me to go with him to the West Indies. I fancied him so I said yes.

I knew of Dominica only as the birthplace of Jean Rhys, a writer I deeply admire. Now when I read about the island I discovered that it is volcanic and mountainous and is the last refuge of the Carib Indians, the descendants of proud cannibals who starved to death rather than accept the fate of slavery. It is one of the wilder places on earth and contains rainforest, and boa constrictors.

The Caribbean is a vast sea, the islands so small. From the air they all look different. We flew over dry, brown Antigua with its ruined sugar mills standing solid as castle puddings; butterfly-shaped Guadeloupe with city boulevards; green Martinique and Marie Galante. Then sliding reluctantly over the ocean came a thunderous grey cloud, and under it was the crumpled, dark green lozenge of sulky Dominica.

There wasn't much of an airport: just a largish shed with a corrugated iron roof, open at the sides like a cattle shelter. Roseau, the capital, had primitive street lighting, no smart shops, and nowhere to post a letter. Concrete drains ran down the sides of the streets, with a bridge across to each house. In the botanical gardens a huge tree had fallen and crushed a bus. It looked startled and bedraggled, like a rat in a trap.

The town ended sharply, and we were driving along a bumpy lane through the jungle at reckless speed. It began to rain. In the porch of a wooden shack a small boy dangled a land crab on the end of a makeshift fishing rod; it clawed the air, defensive and gaudy.

When we arrived at Papillote, which had advertised itself as being 'in the rainforest', we found that its flimsy buildings were half engulfed by the surrounding forest. The owner of the guest-house, Mrs Anne Baptist, was a small, shy, American woman. She greeted us guardedly, smoothing her wispy hair. She urged us to order supper straight away from a painted board which said:

KINGFISH
FLYFISH
CRAYFISH
CHICKEN
MOUNTAIN CHICKEN

'Mountain chicken is not available,' she added, 'because the frogs are still in their breeding season.'

We sat in the open-sided restaurant and saw forest all around. There was a pressing, gently swaying wall of vegetation in a thousand shades of green. Beside the kitchen a communal bath, fed from a hot sulphur spring, was built into the wall. A whole family sat in this, nattering and chuckling in the brown steam. They had walked up the road from Roseau. With a tinkling sound, the spring emptied into a shower basin at the edge of the jungle. Fowls stalked out of the vegetation, looking incongruous: geese, peacocks, guineafowl. Mrs Baptist grumbled, 'The snakes are very unpopular here. Boa constrictors. However you build your henhouse they'll sneak through a crack. Then of course, when they've eaten they can't get out again.'

Our room was tiny and wooden. Through the slats of the shutters we saw the high, green sides of a ravine and a solitary tree fern growing luxuriantly, a living fossil from the coal forests of the Carboniferous.

'I'm sorry I don't love you,' my friend said.

'Don't be sorry.'

We heard a chorus slowly start up and deepen, far back into the forest night. Something high in a tree clinked sharply, over and over again like a coin thrown into a metal dish. Other voices mewed, rattled, croaked, quacked and barked. They were frogs. One of them was the mountain chicken, emitting a discreet 'woof'.

I lay in the cacophonous darkness thinking about magic. There was magic here. Even in our short journey the taxi driver had spoken of the *soukoyant,* the witch who takes off her skin at night and flies about like a bat. Magic: it lubricates the gap between what we can see and understand, and what unhappy feelings haunt our dreams.

Anne Baptist joined us as we explored her jungle garden before breakfast. She showed us trees with calabashes and wooden fruits, and a thicket of juicy ginger stalks which sheltered huge, pink plastic blossoms. She pointed out tiny, delicate orchids growing on trees, and the dammed ponds in the river where she planned to breed crayfish.

Some way below the garden a man stood quietly washing himself in the hot water from the spring; it was channelled down there in a home-made aqueduct of halved bamboo stalks resting on forked twigs. 'For every improvement to the guest-house, I make something for the local people,' Anne said. 'It's their island.'

I wanted to see the rainforest I'd read about, a place where vast trunks rise up like the pillars of a gloomy cathedral, where lianas hang down, where bright parrots chatter in the sunlight of the tree canopy.

'Before the hurricane we had rainforest everywhere,' Anne said. 'Now it's just jungle.' The hurricane struck in 1979 and blew the roof off Papillote. A wall fell across Anne and her Dominican husband and protected them. All over the island tall old trees crashed down, and less tall trees whipped about and were filleted of their leaves and branches. 'Trouble is,' Anne said, 'hundred-year-old trees take a hundred years to grow.'

We hired a truck and a driver and explored the island, jolting along rough wet roads through an endless banana plantation. Yard-high walls of bananas waited at road turnings for the Geest lorry to collect. We saw the pale brown, almond-eyed Caribs spiritlessly making baskets for tourists. We saw dead volcanic lakes, grey under the grey sky. We picnicked on beaches of jet black sand under windy coconut palms, where surf rolled in from Africa. We swam in the chilly river of the Titou Gorge where it winds through caverns underground.

On our last evening in Dominica the weather was clear, after days of rain. Anne's husband, Cuthbert, said there'd be fireflies tonight. He asked, with relish, 'Ever seen mushrooms that light up in the dark? Like to see them?'

He led the way up a path through the jungle. We saw the moon appear and disappear, veiled by clouds. Gradually we could make out the shaking fronds of the trees, the thick herbs at the side of the path.

'Fireflies!'

The small, brave lights wandered among the trees, keeping together for comfort. They were like tiny aircraft following a demented flight-path, having lost their way.

Something else was alight in the undergrowth. Cuthbert drew out a damp stick on which were two pale blue, phosphorescent toadstools with delicate gill clefts, glowing like the harsh strip lights in a modern kitchen.

By the time we reached the airfield next morning a tropical storm was raging. We waited in the shed while rain boomed and clattered on to the metal roof, and no aircraft took off or landed for hour after hour. When we realised that we'd missed our flight to London from Antigua, my friend said,

'Let's find where Jean Rhys lived. We could stay the night there.' Anne had told us it was in Cork Street, Roseau, and had been converted into a sleazy guest-house.

It was a two-storey building, rather flimsy-looking, not old. The courtyard behind was now a restaurant, and had a tree which Jean Rhys might have remembered. Inside, Vena's guest-house was certainly sleazy. The small lobby had a high plastic desk at which the manageress sat. She demanded payment in advance.

'It's like a brothel in a French film,' my friend muttered.

From somewhere *inside* the house came the loud, curlew-like cry of a tree frog. There was no character to the room we were shown into. It was impossible to tell what part of the house it had been. A pantry? A slice of a larger, more commodious room? Cheaply varnished, huge furniture leaned into it. The shutters were wedged shut behind a carelessly installed washbasin. When it came to sleeping on the horrid, plastic bed in the sultry room we had the choice of suffocating in the heat or enduring the groaning clatter of an electric fan, which sounded like the *soukoyant* flapping her leathery wings, rattling at the unopenable shutters and trying to get in.

It was a relief to get a flight the next morning, yet I felt I'd been dragged away from Dominica: I had not explored its dangerous magic as I ought to have done. The island had cheated and spared me, like a love affair where there has been no delusion, no passion and no remorse.

Since we returned, I've seen my friend twice. He is a bit of a loner.

## ELIZABETH A. McCORMICK

# BIG GAME IN THE OKAVANGO SWAMPS

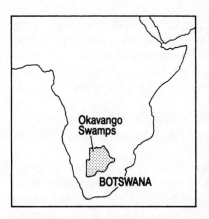

Okavango Swamps

BOTSWANA

Stranded in the Kalahari desert we had no water and half a packet of Marie biscuits. The bus from Francistown had broken down again and the passengers disembarked, squatting in the cumbersome shade of a baobab tree. They, like us, were shifty-eyed; there had been no rain in Botswana for four years and the lions of the Kalahari were getting hungry. In Gaborone, a week before, we had watched the mauled body of a German girl carried into the hospital. Her death reminded us of the dangers of complacency in Africa. In the shadow of the bus, a vulture wheeling overhead, I kept my eyes fixed on the bush behind us.

The driver and friend tinkered with the engine which had burst into flames twice, and been push-started once by the passengers. Nobody seemed in any great hurry. Perched on the step of the bus, circa 1935, an old man in a military coat fished a handful of polished knucklebones out of his pocket. He rattled them between cupped hands and threw them into the dust. He stared hard at the pattern, gathered them up, threw them down again. He raised his eyes from the pattern and stared a long time at my friend and I – the only two white people on the journey. The wings of the vulture rustled over our heads. Feeling uneasy, we turned to our *Africa on a Shoestring* handbook, learning that the Kalahari consists of some of the most arid and remote land in the world. We realised that only two cars had passed us all morning. By midday we realised we had finished our water and were sweating profusely.

The driver whistled through his teeth. Nuts, bolts, a broken fan belt dropped from the engine. It was 40°C in the shade and so quiet that all we heard was dust settling, the rattle of bones and the rustle of wings. A spring fell out of the engine. But it coughed, wheezed, and shrieked into life. The driver cavorted round the bus, beaming – no less surprised and pleased than we were.

After 100 miraculous kilometres we met the other bus returning to Francistown. Discretion erring, our driver announced we would swap buses. There followed much confusion. Passengers were still climbing off while the second load of passengers were scrambling on. Rugs, clothing, mielies, were tossed on top of the buses while the first load of passengers were still trying to reach their luggage. Finally, each bus made a three-point turn in a cloud of dusty exhaust, and off we went; 300km to Maun, on the very edge of the Okavango Swamps.

I woke, cold and stiff, at 4am as the bus lurched into Maun. The heat of the day had been replaced by searing cold and the bus was nearly empty. I dimly remembered having watched the sun set, copper orange over a colourless world. Then I had slept and awoken as the bus stopped amongst a scatter of mud huts. Somebody told me we were halfway to Maun and gave me some water which I was too thirsty to sterilise.

Sitting up in the cold morning light we could have been sprayed by a fine grey snow as we slept – dust from the Kalahari which I can still smell in my clothes.

The Okavango river flows across the desert to form a huge swamp-land, a watery jungle where animals roam; a fascinating, dangerous place. With a friend we visited the local hospital and saw victims of crocodile, hippo, and lion attacks, and a man blinded by a spitting cobra. The patient with the hippo bite told me that hippos have become the most dangerous animals in Africa.

'Once they were shy,' he told me, 'but now they attack because the white man . . .' he pointed an imaginary rifle at the window and pulled the trigger. Using exceptionally sharp teeth, the hippos can crunch up both dugout canoes and their occupants. Indeed, the injured man did not even know he had been bitten until the water turned red as he swam to shore. I found this vaguely reassuring; a short, sharp death seemed preferable to a long, slow chewing underwater. However, as if this excitement were not enough, we were warned against malaria, bilharzia, and tsetse fly, all of which flourish in the swamps.

The following day we flew into the swamps in a six-seater plane. Dry desert gave way to blue lagoons full of water lilies, palm trees, islands and deep blue lakes. Herds of giraffe and waterbuck raced across the swamps in our shadow as we swooped on to the sandy airstrip.

A 15-foot canoe waited along with our poler for the week, Matata. As he pushed away from shore, the reeds of the swamp parting before us, I asked him what his name meant in Setswanan. 'Problem,' he translated with a very disarming smile. Did it mean he was a problem, or could he solve problems? We did not dwell on it.

We slid through the swamps while animals criss-crossed our path before and aft; kudu, zebra, buffalo, impala, and a herd of fifteen giraffe, splashing through the water with feet big as plates. Matata poled gracefully; he could have been punting down the Cam as his pole pushed blue and white water lilies aside. His ears were sharp as a jackal's and he could spot the tracks of a hippo from an extraordinary distance. The lilypad sized footprints, at least one foot across, sank deep into the mud – heavy, purposeful tracks.

We camped on an island of palm trees. Matata built a fire over which we cooked a supper of beans and rice while he caught a fish with a piece of string and what seemed very little else. The night air amplified the snort and splash of animals and I was very grateful for the orange glow of the fire through the canvas walls of the tent. Matata slept outside and promised to keep the fire burning; I hoped he was a light sleeper.

When I awoke it was very dark and the fire had gone out. I lay very still, the hair rising on the back of my neck as something nudged me through the canvas. There was a snuffle, a grunt, followed by the sound of chewing. It started to rain. The animal pushed against the floor of the tent. The German girl killed by a lion had been sleeping in a tent like ours. I screamed.

'Matata!'

My friend, slumbering fitfully by my side, awoke with a yell. Matata's voice said in my ear, 'Let me in, please. Quickly. It's raining.'

For an hour the three of us crouched inside the leaking tent. When the rain eventually stopped Matata crawled outside to relight the fire. I closed my eyes but seconds later there was a scream and the sound of crashing undergrowth; Matata had found a snake curled up in the warm ash of the fire. There was only one thing to do; light another fire to drive the snake away. We spent the rest of the night collecting wood, examining each piece by torchlight before touching it.

We soon learned to give animals the right of way in the swamps, sitting for hours at a time in the dugout, watching elephants plod by. Our unwound watches lay in our rucksacks and when they stopped we followed the pattern of night and day instead. Eating supper early, we were asleep by eight, before waking at five for the dawn.

In spite of Matata's shock-horror tactics, he was the most wonderful guide, in tune with the swamps by some atavistic sixth sense. After we woke, he would take us on to the bigger islands, known as the 'Big Bush'. Here he tracked animals, and we followed, wading waist-deep through swamp water, crawling on our stomachs to be as close as possible.

The brooding atmosphere of the swamps accentuated our smallness and vulnerability. Even sounds at night dominated us, as the firelight picked out bright eyes, blinking through the darkness. I was comforted when Matata showed me a Boer war rifle wrapped in rags in the bottom of the canoe. I doubt whether it could have found its target but the very shape of it in my hands was reassuring. A very small pocket penknife (with hoof-pick and corkscrew) hadn't been lending me much courage.

We told Matata we wanted to go further north still, into the Chobe and Moremi game parks. He missed a beat with his pole and muttered the word '*Caprivi*', shaking his head. He told us his cousin was a game scout in Moremi, employed in order to prevent poaching. He was the only man for hundreds of miles, without radio or vehicle. He saw no more than four people a year, and was given three bullets a month with which to catch his food. Matata shook his head again, as if we were fools.

After a week in the swamps he left us in a camp at the north end of the Okavango. We drank from the crocodile-infested river, and lions visited the camp every night. I missed Matata's sixth sense and the Boer war rifle. I missed the wet, swampy jungle and the snort of the hippos. I found my penknife and kept it close as the shadow of a vulture wheeled over the tent. I remembered the old man in the military coat and knew I would have felt safer with a handful of dry knucklebones in my pocket.

# A SECOND SHUFTI AT JORDAN

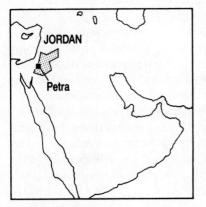

The Queen beat me to it – she got to Petra first! But I doubt if she had as much fun. There was she, a horse-loving woman, bumping through the Siq in a Land Rover, wearing a skirt and hat. Whereas touristy me – town-bred and with no more knowledge of nags than a few donkey-rides sixty years ago – I rode high and proud on Suzy, a two-year-old Arab who was full of wind and nervous at moving so slowly.

Holding my back straight and clutching the plaited strings that had once been reins, I felt as intrepid as Stark, as hardened as Lawrence, as much the explorer as Burckhardt. I was there – at last!

Petra to me had been listed with the Pyramids, Timbuktu, Venice, Hadrian's Wall and Troy as places that I had to visit before I died. Some of these have been 'ticked off' and none has failed me. But *Petra!* Petra surpassed anything that I had visualised in my kitchen fantasy-life. That 'rose-red' cliché rang true but Burton hadn't gone far enough in hyperbole.

Here were all the colours of the pink-side of the palette, from blush-veined ivory to the deepest purple. Layer upon layer of shot-silk sandstone soared skywards in the warmth of the sun.

However, not everyone sees Petra so romantically! Edward Lear's Albanian cook declared – 'O Master! We have come into a world where everything is made of chocolate, ham, curry-powder and salmon!'

Well, we can't all be poets; some of us get no further than alliteration!

I'd done my homework in advance. I knew I'd see the facades of Nabataean temples chiselled into the rock and that the cliff-walls would be riddled with empty tombs. But I hadn't realised that there were extensive Roman ruins as well, and that the wide valley waited for archaeologists to dig deeper.

At this *karavanserai* merchants had bartered Damascus brocades for Chinese spices; camels and goats for slaves; thin, brittle pottery for water or weapons. Only when Red Sea dhows replaced camel-trains did Nabataean prosperity diminish.

Nor had I expected to see people living in this city of the dead. As we climbed up the crags of Petra, black goats eyed us warily from black holes. Donkeys saluted our passing with those howls of anguish that had made maiden ladies establish animal sanctuaries in Cairo between the wars. Tiny children, barefoot and dirty, tried to generate enough courage to touch us for a few *'fils'*.

The caves gave shelter to a new generation of troglodytes – European nomads, Australian girls ending their 'Grand Tours' by going native, those few English women who had felt the lure of the desert so intently that they now nursed fair-haired, olive-skinned babies and hung their washing-lines from one eroded pinnacle to another.

Another day I went into the Siq when the sun was setting and the air was already chill. Smoke from charcoal fires swirled from these windowless dwellings. Birds argued sleepily in the thornscrub. The older children were back from school in Wadi Musa, the village outside the Siq where water bubbles from the rock once struck by Moses. Here the nomads water their flocks and the horses drink their fill when the tourists have dismounted.

Wadi Musa has electricity, provisions, a mosque, teachers, police, a doctor and cultivated terraces of crops, the only green in that wilderness of tortured stone. Petra is parched and primitive. Those who choose to live there keep it undefiled. Perhaps they feel an affinity with its ghosts.

If this is so, time is *not* on their side. Soon simplicity must give way to sophistication. Petra's new hotel, built outside the Siq, is run by an Englishman who cut his catering teeth in the palaces of Saudi Arabia. He has the personal directive of the King to develop the tourist-appeal of the site and already talks of a helicopter pad and a VIP's 'cave' on one of the mountain summits.

So the Queen and I just made it before the deluge! If you have the same urge for desert places – go *now*. The pioneering days are all but over.

Jordan has no oil. It has very little that anyone covets, so the Hashemite Kingdom has no choice but to woo the traveller; to see that he has ice for his drinks, a soft bed, a flushing loo and a dash of Bedouin mystique to add zest to his package-deal.

Let's have a 'shufti' at this kingdom. Do you know this word? If you do, you give away your age. Shufti was Desert-Rat slang in the Forties. To 'take a shufti' was to explore a new posting. To find a girl was to 'shufti bint'. For me, this was a second shufti, for I had visited Jordan almost forty years before.

I was working then in Palestine, a territory torn apart by Arab and Jew, held together by the British Mandate. A boyfriend offered me a weekend in Amman, with no strings attached. A chance to buy presents in Amman's bazaar to take home to 'utility' Britain.

We left Jerusalem and breakfasted in Jericho! The Middle East is like that. Bible stories of Sunday-school days become reality. The 'Land of Milk and Honey' shimmers on the far side of the Dead Sea, when seen from Mount Nebo; from 'the Place of Sacrifice' in Petra, the white tomb of Aaron is a gazelle's leap away. Such sightings prove that those ancient wanderers actually lived. And what hardships they endured! For this is a land without water in the desert. Only around Jerash and Amman in the north is there the year-long green of vegetation. But when rain *does* fall, then the desert blooms and the parched earth sings, as the shepherd-boys sang in the Psalms.

On my first visit Amman was an overgrown, untidy Arab village, surrounded by seven hills. The palace of 'Black Ab', the grandfather of King Hussein, overlooked the mosque, the bazaar and the huddle of insanitary buildings that made up the capital. Only the musty Hotel Philadelphia was considered fit for Europeans. Opposite the Philadelphia was an almost perfect Roman amphitheatre; other Roman ruins lay scattered on the hills, barely investigated by the experts. Camels, goats, pye-dogs and donkeys scavenged the verges of the dusty, rough roads.

The British officers of the crack Arab Legion entertained us for our weekend. Off-duty, the subalterns took to their Jeeps and accelerated into the desert to shoot antelope. Their Arab legionnaires galloped behind, firing their rifles exuberantly into the sky like extras in a Beau Geste film.

Today, that 'sport' is banned. Conservation is 'in' and wildlife protected by order of the King. Oryx and ibex are scarce, but they are there. Rare blue lizards scurry among the rocks of Petra; clumps of black lilies grow beside the King's Highway; the few oases teem with birds.

Now the old Philadelphia is to become a Museum for Antiquities and Amman has superb hotels offering all the amenities of our TV culture – but, beware the muezzin at 4am. I flung open my double-glazed windows before I went to sleep and the first call to prayer of the Muslim day was a strident awakening.

The hills are built over with Royal Palaces, villas and apartment-blocks. The civic services work, the new trees and flowers are well tended, the Greek and Roman remains are catalogued and cared for. Jordan's airline is reliable, the medical services are efficient and the government rest-houses are clean. Within five years, it is claimed, every house in Jordan will have electricity. And the nomads are not overlooked – Jordanian army officers try to bring a smattering of schooling to the children who live in the goat-hair tents. Jordan is catching up with the Western world.

The Crusaders also left a legacy to the Arabs, as did those other invaders who came and went. Crusader castles cling to jagged crests or rise up from barren plains. The bones of Christian soldiers who did not return home lie beneath the stones of the desert, sometimes disturbed by the foraging goats.

T. E. Lawrence was a hero to my generation – a hero who is debunked today. A railway line, built by the Turks to link Muslim pilgrims with Mecca, parallels the asphalt of the Desert Highway. As the Turks cut down the oak-trees to fuel the trains, so Lawrence blew up the track. This line is to be reopened soon for tourists and again the steam-trains will chug to Aqaba on the coast.

Shanty-towns of refugee Palestinian Arabs keep the King's Army on the alert. 'Peace' is a fragile word, but the King has said – 'I want to hear the tracks of bulldozers, not tanks . . . the footsteps of travellers, not troops.'

He is a man of vision, whose Bedouin roots give him respect for tradition and the belief that the pursuit of peace must come through diplomacy.

His countrymen show a natural courtesy. Their hospitality is genuine. Their food is good, their coffee, spiced with cardamom, is delicious. And they laugh, so that you laugh too.

See for yourselves, and when you leave Jordan it will be with the words – 'Go in Peace, with God's protection' following after you. Jordanians mean it.

## RICHARD WARD

# MANI

Five hundred drachmas for the room: the matter was soon settled. Just over £3 for a generous bed, a vine-clad balcony with a splash of bougainvillea, two lemon trees in the garden below, and a view over olives to the sea – not a bad deal. Then the old lady took me firmly by the arm and led me into the bathroom. She pointed to a large hole in the ceiling. The sight of it seemed to provoke in her a torrent of recrimination. She spoke fast, too fast for my rudimentary Greek. What was she trying to convey? 'You can't get a plumber these days, not for love nor money.' 'You simply can't trust the workmen any more, can you?' Together we contemplated a knotted cord dangling from the black hole. *'Ipárhi neró zestó?'* I persisted tiresomely, 'Is the water hot?' *'Zestó, zestó,'* she echoed shrilly, irritated by a fatuous question, and launched into another dramatic monologue with a wealth of expressive gestures. Then suddenly she was gone, leaving me to ponder along the unpredictable and intractable nature of language as a medium of communication.

Well, the water wasn't hot, then or at any time. And indeed, who cared? Outside were the mountains of southern Greece, and in the days that followed there were more important considerations than hot water.

I was in Kardamíli in the Mani. A year ago the name Mani meant nothing to me. Then I read Patrick Leigh Fermor's classic and felt an overriding desire to follow in his footsteps. *The Blue Guide* too was encouraging: 'The predominantly mountainous region south of Sparta is seldom visited by foreign tourists . . . superb scenery and unexpected traces of the past.' How much had the Mani changed since Leigh Fermor, that most distinguished of scholar gypsies, explored it in the late 1950s? I intended to find out.

Kardamíli seemed a good base, since the author himself writes of it with such affection. Arriving on a hot afternoon in October this year I found a pleasant but unremarkable village spread along a bay. What sets it apart is its situation, with the massive range of the Taygetus mountains towering above. It is reached by bus from Kalamata through scenery of Arcadian gentleness. Then, for the last twenty minutes, the road snakes down the mountainside. Mountain, plain, sea and sky – the scale has grown suddenly grander. Yet there is nothing gentle about these scorched mountains. The traveller is moving now through terra incognita. You enter Kardamíli full of expectation.

The first thing you hear on leaving the bus is German: *hochdeutsch, plattdeutsch, schwitzerdeutsch*. There are German speakers everywhere, of all ages, from strident young back-packers to the discreet elderly, all deeply tanned, moving with the assurance of long-standing expatriates. These German tourists pervade the Peloponnese and the islands. There seems to be a seasonal mass migration from the Rhineland and the Ruhr, extending well into October. No corner of southern Greece is immune – not even, alas, the Mani.

There is one escape: take to the hills. This never fails. During five weeks in Greece I met four other walkers, all British, two of them women.

The hills above Kardamíli are a good place in which to loosen up. I followed the main road up the mountain leading west, then struck off along an old mule track. The goat bells receded and I seemed to be moving through even deeper layers of peace. There was stillness, an immense blue sky and only the olive trees for company. These olives – their trunks warped, gouged, carbuncled, abrasive to the touch – seem indestructible, as if they could survive even a nuclear winter. The trees gave way to scrub and there was little shade. I was sorry I hadn't brought more water. Even in an October sun one can get quickly dehydrated on these exposed slopes. I headed for the white gleam of a village in the distance and was grateful to find that the one and only store sold iced drinks. The storekeeper asked if I was German. When I said 'English' he started on some obscure anecdote in which I could make out little except the name 'Margaret' and the repetition of *'kato, kato'*, 'down, down'. Days later I realised he was trying to tell me about the Brighton bombing; it had occurred the same morning.

Another memorable walk was the nine kilometres from Yeroliména to Vátheia. This is the deep Mani, almost as far south as one can go on mainland Greece. The road passes through a landscape dotted with crumbling towers, those 'brooding castellations' which are the most striking feature of the region. It was from their gaunt tower houses that the feuding Maniot families of the eighteenth century bombarded each other with musket, cannon and rock, while a cowed population of serfs crept from their semi-troglodyte hovels between the fusillades.

From a distance Vátheia looks like a stricken Camelot. The towers seem grey at first, but grow golden as you approach. Most of them are in a ruinous state with their upper storeys missing, shattered by earthquake, war, neglect. The Government is restoring several of them as holiday flats, a slow process but tastefully done. An odd experience it will be to sleep among these spooky and decapitated towers.

In fact, as I soon discovered, these ruins are inhabited. I met the old lady as I was walking down a steep path out of the village. She was struggling up, bent under a heavy sack. We greeted each other. The skin of her face hung in purple folds and the old eyes were blurred with cataract. When I offered to carry her sack she waved me aside. Who was this impertinent stranger eyeing her baggage? We moved on up to her tumbledown tower on the last crag of the village. At the base was a terrace with one stool on it. Before us stretched an enormous view of mountain, promontory and shimmering sea. From my pack I offered her an apple, the only food I had. She dismissed it with a regal gesture. Then I saw her toothless gums. I left her in peace with her bundle, her stool and her majestic view.

Like so many villages in the Mani, Vátheia is a ghostly relic. Life has receded from it. When Leigh Fermor passed this way and was quizzed and befriended by the fair-haired girl Vasilio with the lamb slung round her neck, it was still a living community. No longer. If renaissance comes it will be in a new form: foreign tourists in holiday flats.

The road continues south, though not much further. The enterprising walker could reach Cape Matapan and look for the cave entrance to Hades. For those like me who fail to make it to the banks of the Styx, there is compensation at Vlykhada to the north, near Areopolis. Here is one of the finest cave systems in Europe. It is in fact an underground river so extensive that the trip in a flat-bottomed boat lasts twenty-five minutes. You glide through endless caverns of gleaming stalactites and stalagmites and all this time the boatman, dour Charon, speaks only once: 'Mind your heads.' The passengers first whisper, then fall silent. And still you glide. The Mani, which offers many curious experiences, has none more bizarre than this.

Yet the Mani is not for all tastes. It is a place apart, the last bastion. To this bleak peninsula the Spartans came as refugees. The Maniots, who trace descent from them, boast of never having been subdued by Slav or Turk. The ruggedness of the terrain was its safeguard: an arid mountain region peopled by warring clans in a perpetual state of anarchy. No-one coveted it.

Where the Ottomans failed, the travel agencies are succeeding. Coastal towns with beaches are succumbing to the fat profits of the tourist trade, while the hill villages become ever more depopulated. Greece has changed immeasurably in recent years. Many of these changes are for the better: accommodation is much improved, the roads now are good. Even Greek food – previously lumps of meat and veg afloat in an oil slick – has acquired an unexpected finesse. But the impact of six million tourists on small vulnerable communities has been profound. The human landscape so lovingly evoked by Leigh Fermor, Lawrence Durrell and others is now a wistful memory.

But the hills remain, for these mountain ranges of southern Greece do not lend themselves to the blandishments of the travel brochure. The Mani above all is not cosy; this is no man's dream of Arcadia. It is harsh and scarred and full of ghosts. Yet as you walk these hills you feel that nothing has changed. Goat bells, the smell of thyme, a path winding among olive trees, and the hot sun on your back: this is the Greece that endures. It is enough.

# Gypsy Serenade

By the time the train arrived in Madrid the Arabs had stolen my coat. I had not been long in the restaurant car: ten minutes, the length of a cognac. I was coming south from England; they were returning home from a factory in Germany.

On the way to the hotel I stopped the taxi to have a drink in a bar. Outside it was winter and raining. He was standing inside, an old brown overcoat and a white shirt buttoned without a tie, around forty. One of his sons was dancing in worn-out boots, the other singing for him, to the clapping of hands without a guitar. They looked about ten, with long hair, both so brown and handsome I could have hugged them; if I were a woman I would have made a date with them for ten years' time. The hair of the third son was cropped almost to the skin. He neither sang nor danced, but with his six or seven years could already dominate both the public and his brothers. When they had finished he ran round with a hat and allowed none of the audience to escape, saying:

'Gentlemen, for our art.'

Afterwards he brought the hat to his father, who counted the contents then placed it empty among the shrimp and peanut shells on the floor.

'And the rest,' he said.

His son swore there was no more.

'And the rest.'

The boy remained silent. After a moment he dropped some coins from his pocket into the hat and stepped back.

'Now the other pocket,' said his father.

He hesitated, then did the same and withdrew into a corner. The father looked stern for a while, but soon went to him and, whispering something into his ear in gypsy, gave him a kiss.

I too had put money into the hat. The father drew me aside and we exchanged names, Nicholas and Gonzalo. He discovered to his surprise that I was English, not American. Then he invited me to a gypsy baptism which was to be held that night in the suburb of Vallecas.

When I accepted he suggested I might like to give him a certain sum to help the wine flow. I hesitated. He turned to his sons demanding to know whether there was or was not to be a baptism party that night, and whether or not I would be the only white present. They told him. The sum changed hands, but underneath the table because it embarrassed him to receive money in public.

On our arrival the bar was full of hopeful faces, most of them gypsy ones. Gonzalo introduced me. When I inquired after the baptism he said he had been mistaken, it had been yesterday, but that there would be another in a few days and, anyway, who needed a baptism to enjoy themselves? We ordered Jerez wine and he presented me to his wife. She was the only woman there. She looked forty but must have been younger, and was dressed entirely in black – for her brother who had died three years ago, they said. She held a sleeping baby in her arms. When I asked how many there were in her family she said seven, but that the young ones were at home, and did not mention her pregnant abdomen. She was very polite and, like the rest of her people, never laughed if an outsider said something coarse. When her husband began to sing a little, snapping his fingers in rhythm, she smiled and for a moment looked like a young girl again; but the barman came immediately and reminded them that singing was not permitted. Then he said the father ought to be ashamed of himself, using children who should be in school to make money, and that one day the police would find him. So we moved to another bar, remarking how times had changed.

There in a tiled room in the basement the pleasure began: Gonzalo's daughter danced for us. She was fifteen, lithe, conscious of her own body and beautiful in her art, and all the while as the spectators' enthusiasm grew her father watched her, drinking Jerez, nodding his head and smiling.

Presently he drew me aside to suggest that if I would like to give him a certain sum his wife and daughter would go immediately and prepare a gypsy supper. He explained that their house down under the railway by the Bridge of Three Eyes had only one room, but his own eyes shone as he described the delights of a gypsy supper. When I said I did not have the sum he drew me even further into a corner. From somewhere upstairs came the sound of a group of people singing songs from their own province. He cleared his throat and laid his finger along his nose. It seemed as if the world had stopped to listen.

'You,' he said, '. . . that is, you . . . are my friend. I . . . that is I, my wife and my children . . . we, I, do not like to invite a friend to a party and not give him the best. Do you understand? Like this I can't treat you as I wish to.'

But I said it was impossible. I could not afford more of his hospitality.

We returned to the centre of the room. Gonzalo poured more Jerez, coughed and examined his throat in the mirror. Then he turned to his son and told him to sing *fandangos* in the way he had been shown. The guitarist began the familiar descending cascades and the boy entered. But after a while his father stopped him to say he was not singing what he had been taught. The boy looked at the ceiling. He had big eyes. His father told him to listen now to the way he himself was going to sing them. We all listened. Afterwards the boy tried again but was stopped once more. Suddenly a fat gypsy stood up. A few years ago he had been one of the best-paid dancers in Flamenco. There were several rings on his fingers and his shoes were still beautifully polished.

'Listen,' he said to the boy. 'I am only a dancer, and I'm too old now even for that. But I know more about singing than your father will ever know. You go on as you yourself are and one day you'll be good.'

'And you,' he said, turning to the father, 'should talk less. The kid isn't singing badly. He's just singing a style you don't know.'

The guitar was playing again, this time in slow rhythm, and after a while a voice broke in. It was an elderly gypsy who had been sitting silently all evening, and the voice was as rough as the open road but when it sang the room became quiet. The singer loosened the collar of his shirt and let his voice flow out as turbulently and tranquilly as he desired. That night he had reached a moment of feeling no-one else had, and his cigarette burned unnoticed in the fingers of his hands which stretched out parallel like mute ghosts. He did not sing for long because he was old, but it was enough.

After that we went up. As we passed out of the bar it was raining again and all Madrid's lights were swimming before my eyes, reflected on the street. Stepping carefully over the gutter, Gonzalo remarked that I ought to wear a coat like he did. When I explained what had happened on the train he shook his head and said one should never trust the Moors.

It was midnight. As we were giving our hands he looked up at me intently and told me that in two days there would be a gypsy wedding.

When I told him I could not come he turned up the collar of his coat and walked away, looking at the pavement beside the unlit shop windows, hands deep in his pockets, and passed into the night going towards the Bridge of Three Eyes.

By now the Arab with my coat would be in Malaga waiting for the boat across to Africa. Twenty-four hours earlier, we had both been in Paris.

# WOMEN AND SOCKS

Once Europeans had become accustomed to flip-flops, it wasn't all that difficult to get used to mitten-shaped socks, each holding the big toe in its own little pocket and letting the other four doss down together. But the very first visitors to Japan assumed, from the local socks, that the Japanese had only two toes. And the Japanese, on the basis of the visitors' socks, thought that Europeans had none.

Well, that's the essence of Japan: mystery and misunderstanding. You can't understand what people are saying, you can't read the street signs, and you can't find out where the buses are going to. Nor can you read the Tokyo tube map. Even if the trains are coloured according to the line they run on, the map itself is like an action painting by a hyperactive centipede.

But the compensations for being unable to read or carry on a casual conversation are overwhelming. The sight, for instance, of a fat wrestler dressed in a bright open kimono and what appears to be a black chastity belt sitting on the train reading a comic book. Or the children from primary school on an outing, dressed in sailor suits like Victorian children on their way to the seaside, snaking behind their teacher in twos, each round head and pair of button eyes topped by an identical pudding basin of black hair and blue sailor hat.

The cafés provide a nice easy introduction to the delights and puzzles of Japan. Avoid the hotel restaurants, and beware of Colonel Sanders. His larger-than-life statue with its slightly oriental cast of features serves as a warning that you are approaching the junk food area.

The most intriguing cafés have steamy windows filled with plastic replicas of the real food inside. It is certainly a better way of choosing food than trying to read the menu. The displays clearly represent food. The question is: what food? You can't go wrong with anything shaped like a noodle. It is almost certainly a noodle. But look out for those exquisite confections that look like liquorice allsorts. About the size of matchboxes, they are perfectly symmetrical – some tubular, some round, and some square, with black and white patterns relieved by little buttons of green or red. They are not liquorice allsorts. They are

fish; that is, they are made from fish. There's nothing wrong with the taste, but it's a culinary shock if you order one or two for dessert under the impression that you are about to eat some oriental sweetmeat.

If you see something that tickles your fancy you'll have to force yourself to bring the waiter outside and use sign language. But it's less risky than pointing to totally unknown items on a menu.

Sign language is almost essential in shops too, but it's a little less embarrassing because you can be more discreet. A tiny gesture towards a desired item and a slight flick of the eyebrows is almost enough to complete most transactions. Not like dragging a waiter out of a warm café into a cold street while you point at plastic puddings.

Paying for your goods will lead to further mysteries. In this country of robots, minuscule calculators and pocket TV, they use little wooden abacuses to add up your bill. You can, for instance, buy a computer, a digital watch and a transistorised tennis game, and the shopkeeper will reach for his abacus (called a *soroban* in Japan) to calculate the cost. In the upmarket shops they'll use a calculator to start with and then check the answer with a *soroban*.

It's obvious that in their heart of hearts the Japanese don't really trust calculators.

The same uneasy juxtaposition of man and technology is evident if you take the lift in a department store. Two uniformed girls will bow you in and another two will bow you out. They will also say something to you. Could it be: 'Did you have a nice trip?', or: 'You're looking well today'? Whatever it is, they say it hundreds of times an hour with endless patience and cheerfulness. The lifts of course are automatic and run without attendants.

Another way to get the flavour of Japan, but requiring a little more courage than merely eating in a local café, is to stay in a Japanese-style hotel. There are five or six in Tokyo and many more throughout the country. You can get a list from the Japanese Tourist Board in London, which for some inscrutable reason gives only half of them. You can get a full list in Tokyo.

In this kind of hotel you will sleep on the floor, wear a kimono (provided by the management) instead of pyjamas and share a bath with strangers. You'll also be given a new toothbrush every evening. Of course, if you're more comfortable in a lounge suit or twin-set and pearls, prefer eggs and bacon for breakfast, insist on using the same boring toothbrush day and night, and like to take baths alone, then you can go to the Hilton. There's one in London too.

In the Japanese hotel your bed is a comfortable mattress on the floor. In the mornings the chambermaid will roll it up leaving the floor space free. This is covered in rush mats which is why they ask you to wear slippers, not shoes, when you go into your bedroom. The surface is quite delicate.

Whatever breakfast consists of, it is brought to your table arranged so exquisitely, and with each dish packaged so cunningly, that you cannot refrain from tasting. You'll discover mussel soup and pickled plums among other unknown delicacies, and you can find out what those liquorice allsorts taste like. You can always fall back on good old rice and tea if the aesthetic qualities of the food are not enough to overcome your apprehension. But persist! After a while you'll find yourself beginning to enjoy breakfast.

As for the communal bath: it's not really for washing. This is Japan after all; part of the mystery, and so on. If you want to wash yourself you can go to the real bathroom, usually en suite. In there you'll find a sink on the floor, just large enough to stand in, and you can have a good long soak up to your knees. You'll have to wash the rest in air, as it were. Then, when your're really clean, put on your kimono, drape a bathtowel over your shoulders and join the other guests in the big bath.

There are Western-style concerts in Tokyo; if you're brave about food and hotels, I reckon you can treat yourself to a bit of Bach or Mozart, usually played with maturity and feeling by six- or seven-year-olds. Don't forget: this is where Suzuki started. At a recital I attended, when an elderly twenty-one-year-old was performing, the first two rows were taken up by tiny children watching the performer's every move like little sparrows watching their mothers bring in the worms. And God help the little sparrow that dares to close its eyes or shuffle its tiny feet during a performance. Mums and dads in the rows behind will soon give a practised twist to its ear.

I saw so many of these earnest young hopefuls that one day, I'm sure, we will be invaded by battalions of these *wunderkinder* descending by parachutes above the Royal Festival Hall, violins strapped to their backs.

The nice thing is that, at least in music, the girls are on par with the boys. Not anywhere else. The Japanese male seems to think that women have only recently developed skills and abilities they never had before.

'Women and socks,' the men say, 'have greatly improved since the war.'

DIANA PHILLIPS

# IN NORTH BIHAR

We knew the train would take at least four hours to cover the sixty kilometres from Raxaul to Dhang. The journey was meant to last three hours, but the train always left at least an hour late. We knew it would be late but we still hurried through the waking village, across the fields, past the hospital and along the railway track to Raxaul station. One morning, after heavy rain, the field by the hospital was full of giant yellow frogs; no-one paid them any attention.

Although it was one of the train's first stops and there were never many passengers on board, the people waiting at Raxaul always crammed around the doors, clambering up and forcing themselves in. Why didn't they wait for the passengers to get off first, instead of squeezing themselves, their sacks of wheat and bicycles on at the same time that others were dragging their possessions off? They pushed and shoved, reaching through the carriage windows to reserve places by laying their scarves along the bench.

At stations all was noise: bells ringing; people clamouring to get on and off; men walking up and down beside the train shouting mysterious cries, selling food and cigarettes from trays around their necks or from baskets on their heads.

As we prepared to get off, our fellow passengers tried to tell us we were making a mistake. There was nothing for white people in Dhang: just a cluster of shops and shacks; stalls at the side of the road leading from the station; a bicycle repair shop; little wooden shops on stilts which sold biscuits, cigarettes and sweets. And lots of lean-to teashops with their sticky mud floors, mud walls with greasy pictures of gods and film stars; the hole in the ground at the back where plates and glasses were washed and mouths swilled out; grimy tables with uneven legs; ants and wasps crawling around on the food displayed in front of the shop. Hardly a tourist trap.

It takes forty minutes to walk from Dhang station to the farm along a road which starts as a stony track then turns to mud. There is a short cut across the fields, zigzagging along the boundary banks. There are always people on this land: a boy sitting on a grazing buffalo, a girl cutting short, dusty grass with a sharp hand-held hoe, filling a basket to take home for the oxen. They are there; they have been there for years. For hundreds of years it has all been exactly the same. Walking along the tracks and paths between the fields, it feels as if thousands have walked there before you. A security.in the ground felt through bare feet: warm, hard ground, smooth and dusty. Guidebooks say the Bihar plain is barren. For them it is: there are no temples or museums, only people living by and for the land. Every scrap is owned, small banks separating each field. On the map it is divided up into feet. Every inch looks well used, whether by a girl foraging grass for oxen or by people resting at the side of the road.

The farm has nine acres of land, including the ruins of an old British indigo factory – a long redbrick wall with trees and bushes growing on the old factory floor, weeds climbing along the bricks. Children played there instead of minding their animals which would then wander out on to planted fields. A road runs in front of the farm, its tracks worn deep into the ground. Three crops a year are grown and the earth looks pale and tired in the hot sun. Buffalo dung is the only thing put back into the soil.

We started at five and worked until eight when we had breakfast, saved from the previous evening's meal. After breakfast we continued working until eleven, then returned to the long hut. Each of the men had his own lunchtime routine. Some washed under the pump before cooking rice and vegetables, while others seated by the heat of the cooking fire then washed before eating.

When there was water in the pond behind the hut, Goshai used to go fishing, damming the pond in the middle and scooping the water over to one side, leaving little fishes panting on their sides in the mud. He liked fish.

Work started again at three; we rested until then. At one time the big tree was where we all lay on our scarves and mats. Then the men took to lying under the mango tree, away across the fields at the crossroads of several paths. There must have been a better breeze there.

The sun should have paled slightly by three. But, carrying baskets of buffalo dung from the pit by the cattle shed, along the road and down towards the mango tree to put it on the furthest field, my nose was burnt before I'd walked twenty yards.

I remember the hottest day. One of the fields had been ploughed and our job was to weed out the wiry roots and tufts of grass that the wooden ploughshare had failed to dislodge so that the field could be smoothed out ready for flooding. That morning it was hot by six. After breakfast one of the men returned with an umbrella; everyone else worked with scarves draped over heads and necks against the sun. It grew hotter all the time. At eleven the earth was dry and thirsty, the field baking: it was like being fired in a kiln. At three it was no cooler. Moving from the shade to the middle of the field seemed sheer madness. The weeds that we'd uprooted in the morning were shrivelled and brown; the earth looked as if nothing had ever lived in it. It was still too hot so we all left the field for the shade of the big tree.

This tree is holy. There is a platform around it, natural on one side, made from the tree's roots, and built round by brick on the other. Where the roots stick out the bank gives way to a hollow where the buffaloes are tethered during the day.

At the time of weddings, a group of women and children came across the fields with baskets and scarves full of sweets and rice which they touched down under the holy tree to be blessed, before going back the same way they'd come. The men didn't like us to sit on the platform.

Evenings were beautiful when work was finished and the sun had gone. The land became active at dusk: oxen appeared in their fields, and buffaloes having their last feed before being led home after the day's grazing. All day long, boys and girls sat on the buffaloes' backs, lounging in expertly comfortable positions.

I remember one evening when we were returning home from Sitanarhi in the bullock cart. At dusk, passing through the countryside, everything was slowing down for the night. Everywhere there were children, crouching by the roadside, minding goats in the fields, cutting a last shaving of grass. In the dimming light the men were sitting together outside their hut, small children playing between the crouching forms. Away across the fields was the train, steam drifting out from the engine, people spilling out from inside and on top.

The bullock carts were empty, the oxen eating from huge shallow dishes raised up from the ground on stands made of branches. The threshing floors lay bare, pale, trodden and packed down in a circle around the post where the oxen had circled. As the cart passed, frogs jumped into pools made under pumps, women with bundles of twigs and leaves on their heads stepped to the side. Oncoming carts appeared in the gloom, the drivers calling to each other, one moving over for the other. The bamboo leaves bending low over the road whisked us as we passed and birds called in the mango groves.

When we got back, some of the men were asleep and some were finishing their supper. Each slept in a special place: one group in the shed where the chaff for the cattle was stored, some in the main room of the hut beside the cooking fires and others outside under the porch.

The nightwatchman sat on the bamboo bench at the side of the road as everyone else went to bed. He made rounds throughout the night, checking on the oxen and buffaloes tethered in the field. After the wheat harvest, there were two nightwatchmen. The men told us that the area was dangerous, that robbers used to hide in the mango tree at the crossroads and jump down on people returning home to their villages.

After the wheat had been harvested and the rice transplanted we were no longer needed, and took the same train back to Raxaul, leaving the buffalo grazing, Goshai fishing and villagers making their offerings under the holy tree.

ROLF JOHNSON

# FLYING HORSES

Whenever I've been asked to take a sponsored parachute jump I've declined, giving the excuse 'fear of flying'. Of free will I chose to fly to India, taking as my travelling companions a stallion and two mares, in the back of a decrepit Boeing 707 on its third time round the clock. The interior was like a dingier station on the Northern Line, complete with peeling, dripping walls. Outside, the Flying Carrot, as this airline's cargo planes are affectionately known to the handlers at Heathrow, has peeling orange and green livery. She'll be all right when she's finished, said one. Finished what?

The first leg of the first occasion I had flown horses from Heathrow was made bearable by a bottle of whisky and a regular itinerant groom. His responsibilities were for a single grey pony bound for a Kuwaiti Sheikh. They said *au revoir* at Beirut, the first port of call, having given me a crash course in survival.

We were jammed unceremoniously among sinister-looking unmarked packing cases, obviously best left alone. Compared with our own disembarkation, when the all-change was announced at Beirut they were unloaded with a certain amount of deference. Beirut! What could they do with more weapons that hadn't already been done? Rising columns of smoke from the ruined city, shell craters and baggage handlers with machine guns gave the airport the appearance of M6 Bank Holiday roadworks. After five hours (feeling a bit over-exposed) parked on the tarmac, flying off towards the Gulf was an appealing prospect.

The experience of travelling with horses need not be unpleasant. Horses won't be airsick all over your lap; they don't drone on about overbooked hotels, or insist on playing Scrabble to pass the time. Ideally a canopy should separate the beasts, and ideally a stallion should not accompany two mares on a pallet the size of a diving board. They should be let down properly before the flight and not, as in the case of one of the mares, introduced to racing a week previously in a Windsor selling hurdle. No-one accompanying thoroughbreds expects to glide along aisles adjusting headphones, providing pillows and dispensing drinks, other than the odd bucket of water. Then again the most beleaguered hostess would not swap a cantankerous granny on a Poundstretcher for a panicking mare trying to lie down in her stall at 30,000 feet.

The mare alongside the stallion rubbed her hip to the bone attempting to do just that, while we took turns swinging from her head and tail as a preventive measure as turbulence upset the flight across Europe. A hay net can be improvised as a seat belt, especially if there is nothing else (no seats either). Meanwhile the stallion's attentions were diverted by his own terror, and mine. The other mare obligingly took little interest in the proceedings – until the Beirut-Sharjah leg. By this time the new cargo of contraband televisions for India was tumbling about our ears. This threat posed less of a distraction to the horses than I would have hoped. When both mares began aiding and abetting one another to increase the confusion and alarm, somewhere high over the Gulf I made for the cabin to solicit help.

There I found an Australian pilot, German co-pilot and Lebanese navigator arguing above the noise of the engines, which sounded as if their exhausts had blown. These cargo planes are the modern equivalents of the tramp steamer. They flip from one airport to another collecting and dumping in remote corners, removed from passenger terminals. The aviators who fly them, while not (generally) sporting eye-patches, are particularly hard-baked salts. The exchange which I began, 'Could one of you give me a hand with these lunatics?' went as follows:

'Sorry sport, international regulations; can't leave the flight deck.'

'If you don't leave the flight deck at least one of these horses is going to be joining you on it.'

'You know what to do – shoot the buggers.'

'Where's the humane killer then?'

'Under the coffee pot.'

'There's only an old fire extinguisher here.'

'Use that then.'

When I got back to England, someone commented on my bravery in the crisis. What else could I do, I replied – bale out on the Iraqi trenches? Fire the extinguisher? Pray? Well, as I explained to the Almighty, at 30,000 feet I was much nearer to him than ever before and, shouting to make myself heard above those damned engines, perhaps there was an even money chance of being heard. I was certainly sincere.

When we landed at Bombay (for the story has a happy ending) I asked to be shown the piece of tarmac pasteurised for the Pope to kiss on his recent visit, so I could bless it too (poojahs is the Hindi word) and give thanks for deliverance. That's when I noticed oil dripping from the fuselage.

Whether or not horses understand landing procedure (they don't smoke or have to cope with seat-belts), it occurred to me that we had taken a couple of bites at the cherry on our approach – I could only guess how near we came to dismantling the gateway to India, for there are no windows in those vehicles.

There is a sweet old chestnut about the JAL jumbo mistakenly landing on a tiny nearby private airfield in smog. On that occasion three miles of slums were levelled as a pathway along which the stranded plane could be dragged back to the International Airport runway. Only from here could it be reasonably expected to take off.

Our problem had been landing at all. The hydraulic lines had burst and the wheels had to be lowered manually. The crew hadn't been able to knock in ('locate', for the purposes of the Captain's log) the nose-wheel pin. They took near-disaster as an everyday occurrence, which it probably is. In fact, the Captain, miffed that there was no hotel taxi waiting, was preparing to return to Abu Dhabi with his leaking plane when I left. I'm sure he did.

Deposited on the runway, horribly close to the fast lane, we must have been an unusual sight for incoming international passengers, gazing at a three-horse traffic island. The horses oggled back, equally bemused – especially the stallion, who would have failed dope tests for the next six months. At Heathrow I'd been asked specifically not to tranquillise him in case of the possibility of side-effects which could have seriously affected his future stud career. As he reared and kicked all those miles above the earth, the decision narrowed down to him or me. He had three syringes administered to him. The last one I saved, just in case, for myself.

To be brave, or blasé, was not my ambition. Having worked in racing stables for a number of years, I went to India with every prospect of enjoying racing despite the absence of luxuries like *The Sporting Life*. When we landed, the problems weren't nearly over. All the paperwork seemed correct, except that most important paperwork of all – the baksheesh. There weren't enough rupees to oil the wheels for those 'whose hands are greased not from honest toil', as an Indian newspaper euphemistically described sticky palms.

Two pretexts were given for the failure to release us from the airport: that one of the mares wore a head-collar with an obviously masculine name embossed, and that one of the fillies' passports was stamped GONE TO STUD. India has a number of diseases all her own, but if there is any suggestion that a foreign filly has been on the loose in a British stud she is rejected as unclean. So my first act on Indian soil was to telex a friend at Weatherbys, the British racing bureaucrats, to get them to explain the facts of life to the Bombay Turf Club.

After three days – as Indian delays go, lightning – the caravan moved to one of the best-run studs in India, in the grounds of the Maharajah of Mysore's Palace in Bangalore. Here I encountered some of the problems indefatigable Indian breeders deal with. In the middle of Bangalore, as you thread through a jungle of exotic trees and over-grown ornamental gardens, cross long neglected croquet lawns, ten-nis courts and disused summer houses, you are confronted with Windsor Castle, or at least a very passable facsimile locked up and in pawn to the Government to pay Royal debts. This is the Palace. There was no water, though, for an artificial Thames; and the whole relic, presently used as a backdrop for the film of *A Passage to India,* is patrolled by a pensioner who served the last war in South Shields.

The stud occupies the old cavalry stables and, imaginatively, the elephant houses. Nowadays it is run by an Englishman who arrived in India forty years ago with his billiard cue and eight shillings. He went on to become leading trainer in Madras for eighteen years and is set to retire to his property in Cheshire, which is fenced by the running rail from Castle Irwell, Manchester's racecourse.

The traditions of the British Turf, like the last Englishman, are safely enshrined in Indian racing centres like Bangalore, where scribes still describe jockeys as 'knights of the pigskin'. Horses with names meaningful to English ears have passed this way: Lance Corporal, Red Indian, King Midas and now the stallion I had delivered, Pink Tank. An effort was made to set up the stud in a more favoured, not to say more conventional, site in the foothills of the Nilgiris. This was de-feated by panthers who ate the foals, and by wild elephants on whose walk the buildings were sited. Now the Palace Stud lives on borrowed time as Indian racing moves up a gear. Apart from delivering Pink Tank and the two mares, and six foals in the stud season, my contribu-tion to the future of Indian breeding was almost certainly sacrilegious. Snakes abounded in the palace grounds, as did ants. They, and all of life in India in its own way, are sacred, but the holes bored by the former and the mounds erected by the latter in the paddocks were a threat to the horses. Occidental logic demanded that the one could best be filled by the deposition of the other. This was achieved but the worst was feared.

In my book, more danger would come from the vet, whose tetanus syringes were kept in his bicycle puncture outfit. But he meant well, and the place and his practice thrived in the way that life tends to in India. Fecundity and infinity make happy bedfellows: there are proba-bly 1,000 million Indians and – who knows? – the only impossibilities in this country are finding a size-three horseshoe nail and a bath plug that fits.

Given the chance, I suppose I'd take the Flying Carrot to Bombay again, though by that time I'd have taken parachute lessons.

CAREL TOMS

# TO THE MIDDLE OF NOWHERE

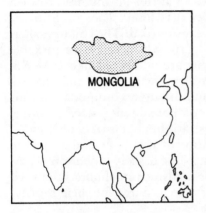

MONGOLIA

The train from the Back of Beyond is about to arrive at the Middle of Nowhere. A week out of Moscow across Siberia and five time zones later you somehow land up in land-locked Mongolia.

Galloping horses, endless deserts and grassland steppes. People with faces like unworked mahogany stand around in their tunic-like cos-tume and ill-fitting boots with turned up toes. All are heavily wrapped against searing Siberian winds which bear the ghosts of Genghis Khan, Marco Polo and 'living' Buddhas.

A flat-faced, slit-eyed courier smiles from her yellow moon face and says the baggage will follow on a lorry. It did and was dumped outside Hotel B, one of only two in Ulan Bator, capital of this People's Republic. Built just a few years ago it looks battle-scarred by usage and needs a good smartening up. The bedroom lock is insecure and only one hot tap on a swivel trickles into both bath and basin. Mongolia is remote, not easy to reach and feels like it.

Everyone is out to please and eager to show off their millions of desert acres. They have not long entered the twentieth century and in many ways still live in the past. Remnants of their old ways still abound. When you have shown your disguised appreciation of the country's monuments to the 1921 revolution and to the Great Patriotic War against Fascism and seen the palace where the last king lived, you will be taken to a Buddhist lamasery. There you are advised to hold your nose as you egg your way through groups of shuffling, shaven-headed and saffron-robed monks amid a stifling mixture of stale incense and body odour.

This is the country's one remaining lamasery and its last vestige of Buddhist splendour. There are sounds of tinkling bells and subdued, mumbling voices as the monks, sitting in the lotus position on wooden benches, turn the pages of their scripture books. Outside they prostrate themselves on wooden prayer beds. They call this enlighten-ment.

Sixty miles east of the capital is Terelj. It's a village of felt and canvas tents called yurts. There are also some wooden huts and everything is fenced in to keep out the wolves and curious locals. It's a kind of health farm and you go there to sample a simple lifestyle which Mongolians have been enduring for about 3,000 years and you are going to put up with for twenty-four hours.

To reach this desolate spot you set off at sun-up and head toward mountain ranges which scarcely ever get closer. The coach driver weaves his way through washed-out bits of road. The countryside is deserted but for groups of distant yurts which resemble pickable mushrooms. The rows of white tents are numbered like a council estate. A gravel path wanders between them. Here and there a duckboard keeps your feet off the mud. If yurt accommodation runs out, then there are the chalets. In the compound centre stands a model of a Buddhist temple and a prayer bed. It's fun but utterly phoney.

They say 40 per cent of the population of about one-and-a-quarter million Mongolians still live in yurts. None has any sanitation. They are designed to be portable and enable herdsmen and hunters to move around the countryside in search of new pastures for their camels, sheep and yak.

A rickety building called a 'hotel' is where you eat on the site. The washroom is outside, where there is a smell of scented Russian soap and bad drains. Mongolians, of course, use the steppe.

We share our yurt with an Australian couple. He snores and she complains about the lack of a good cup of tea. Because of our 'unex-pected' arrival the restaurant can summon up only tinned salami, half cold packet soup and some dry cake. Americans in the group flee for their vitamin pills and demand hot water to make coffee.

A yurt is comfortable and a wooden floor raises it from the ground. Lino and thick carpets cover the floor. Exposed woodwork of the roof struts and main pole are beautifully decorated. It's all rather like an old-fashioned gypsy caravan. But six-foot Aussies and Englishmen have to jack-knife their bodies at the four-foot door which leaks sub-stantial amounts of air – as does the roof where the stovepipe pokes through.

A 'chambermaid' who looks about eighty goes from tent to tent with a wheelbarrow full of logs and lays all the fires in the dustbin-like metal stoves. We put a match to ours and it goes up with a rocket-like roar, heating the yurt in a flash. The reconditioned air attracts the flies so we wander round like lost nomads thinking about the next meal. There is not even a postcard to buy, let alone a stamp.

If you follow the electricity poles over the steppe to the next village, the people there are partially settled inside bricks and mortar. Down by the river the boys fish with rods cut straight from the surrounding forest and grill their catches on an open fire.

No-one asks for a re-run of this one night stand. 'Scenery great, food awful' is the consensus. The traditional beverage here is *kumiss*, a thick curdly drink made from mare's milk which has been allowed to ferment. They say it contains eight per cent alcohol, and the locals down it by the gallon. You need an iron stomach as it tastes like some awful medicine.

We return to civilisation after a wash in cold water, a breakfast of buns and sour cream and a ride through knife-sharp mountain air. This is the stuff of travel.

## J. W. ACTON

# NOT ON THE ITINERARY

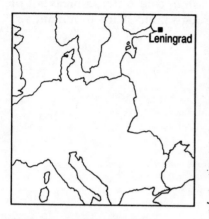

Although my churchgoing is confined usually to weddings and funerals, there are times when I am certain that one guardian angel at least has been detailed to watch over my welfare.

Such an occasion occurred halfway through my holiday in Russia. I had taken a package tour to Moscow and Leningrad primarily for the White Nights Festival of the Arts in June – an annual event of Soviet cultural life when the sun hardly sets for a fortnight and old men sit in the public gardens for half the night playing speed–chess.

One normally expects to see all the best opera, ballet and musical talent on this tour, but our group had arrived at the tail-end of a meeting of Comecon heads of state, the National Gymnastics Championships were in full swing and quite unexpectedly, a British delegation led by Sir Geoffrey Howe had arrived for peace talks. The net result of having so many favoured people around was that tickets for the Kirov and Bolshoi ballets were obviously rationed, and we had to be content with second league fixtures of circus and puppet shows to fill any gaps in the programme.

Five days of sightseeing in and around Moscow passed quickly enough. One marvelled at the two-mile-long queue for Lenin's tomb, and the loving care with which the Russians have restored the winter and summer palaces of the Czars after the destruction of World War Two.

But Leningrad is far more artistic in every way, and there is the strange experience of emerging from a theatre at eleven o'clock at night to find the sun still shining brightly. Now, on the Tuesday evening, I had obtained a ticket to the small Philharmonia Hall, where two of Russia's most distinguished musicians were to give a recital of classical favourites for violin and piano.

I left the hotel early and in pleasant sunshine, wearing a light jacket and bow tie, but alas did not bargain for a sudden change in the weather. After fifteen minutes on the Metro to Nevski Prospect I was met by a teeming downpour, heavy enough to keep me holed up under cover until ten minutes before the performance was due to start, and with the hall some hundreds of yards away along a back-street. At five to eight, the deadline, I decided to make a run for it, and was within sight of the doors when, without any warning at all, my stomach muscles suddenly began to roll up like a shop blind and I was violently and horribly sick. Doubled up with pain, I found support between two Lada cars (what else?) and emptied my insides with great gasping spouts. I was carrying a good supply of handkerchiefs and managed to keep myself clean, but it was ten past eight before I had recovered sufficiently to move, with attendance at the concert now out of the question.

My next problem was how to get back to the hotel before my stomach gave a repeat performance. Public transport was definitely out. In Leningrad's crowded streets a tram or bus ride is a virtual eyeball-to-eyeball body massage with the natives, while on the Metro, with the escalators descending at breakneck speed, there is little chance of a retreat and no toilets.

Bleary-eyed, I staggered back to Nevski Prospect, and there I spotted a dejected-looking husband sitting in his car outside a supermarket, obviously waiting for his wife to emerge with the shopping. It's the same the whole world over. Taking a one rouble note from my wallet, I tapped on his window. He looked me over before winding it down.

'Taxi?' I enquired, hopefully.

'You wish to ride?' he countered.

'Hotel Moskva,' I said. 'And quick!'

He snapped up the rouble and with a few deft movements had me seated, safety-belted and away. The drive would have done credit to a New York Yellow cab, and in no time at all I was being dumped at my hotel – on the blind side but within reach of my room and some assistance.

A young white-coated medico was called in, with an even younger sidekick to carry his bag, and a lady interpreter. Between them they took my pulse rate, temperature, and a decision that I was not, nor had been, blind drunk on vodka. There were other suspicions, though.

'You must come to hospital for correct medicines,' announced the lady. 'What have you eatings today?'

'Nothing but hotel food, nothing,' I replied most emphatically.

'Der best fodder iss domestic fodder,' said the medico darkly, as we descended in the lift. There was a red-crossed Land Rover waiting, and nothing more was said until we reached the hospital. On the outside it looked like something left over from the siege of Leningrad in 1944, but inside everything was in immaculate white, including a large wrinkled matron who proceeded to give the medico a verbal roasting, followed by expulsion from the premises. I learned later that, in the presence of a superior officer, he had wrongly suggested that I might be returned to the hotel after treatment.

'You cannot return,' said this matriarch. 'The 'otel has got thousands people. I must find what is your illness first, yes?'

The cross-examination which followed was alarming, and interspersed with words sounding like hepatitis and malaria as she filled in a long questionnaire with a series of *Niets* and *Das*.

By this time I was sorely in need of a toilet, and it was her turn to be alarmed when she suddenly grasped the meaning of my frantic gestures. We rushed along the corridor to a small private room with a bathroom en suite, and as the door slammed shut behind me a virtual volcanic eruption shook the other end of my torso . . .

Now I felt well under par. Lying on the bed, which was very old-fashioned but deliciously comfortable, I thought of my home, my Queen and my country. The time was now about nine-thirty, and I must have looked ghastly, for a young nurse who popped in with a set of pyjamas sized up the situation in a second and popped out again, running down the corridor calling for help.

Alarm bells rang. A kindly looking lady doctor arrived, followed by a porter towing a saline drip apparatus. After listening to my heart and extracting a syringe-full of blood from an artery, they connected my right arm to the drip-feed. A bustling staff-nurse washed my face and hands. A little ward-maid appeared at the bedside with an enormous vacuum flask of Georgian tea, refusing to leave until I had downed every drop.

They fussed around until the doctor left, when everything went deathly quiet, and I slept like a log until morning. I had come from the hotel expecting to return, and was quite unprepared. I had no razor or toiletries, but made the most of the bathroom shower and hot water and began to feel better. As I was about to get dressed, however, the doctor reappeared and began to administer the most thorough medical check-up I have ever experienced.

Apart from being pressed, prodded, tapped and manipulated whilst lying on the bed, I was cardiographed, x-rayed, blood-tested and biologically examined in a series of walkabouts and strip consultations. I was to be incarcerated for another two days and nights on a diet of three assorted pills and a curious fizzy powder in a paper wrapper, presented every few hours with instructions in mime.

The room was spartan and the furniture basic, but to my surprise there was a large colour television in perfect working order. So, as my whiskers grew, I settled down to watch France beat Brazil in an exciting football match, and enjoy one channel entirely devoted to children, where understanding was universal despite the language.

But I was to discover another facet of Soviet hospital life when, after the last meal of the day at six o'clock, I became aware of a plaintive female voice outside my window.

'Andrea! Andrea!' she called. I crept behind the curtains and looked out. The woman was middle-aged and handsome. She was scanning the windows of the ward above, and holding up a plastic shopping bag, through which I could discern two bottles of wine and several cartons of cakes and other goodies. Presently, her worried look changed to a broad smile as a hook on the end of a fishing line was lowered past my window. She attached the bag and it was swiftly hoisted aloft. After a brief conversation she said goodbye, blowing kisses, and immediately her place was taken by another hard-working housewife calling 'Victor! Victor!'

I began to think that I was in an isolation hospital, until I realised that nothing at all happens after six o'clock until breakfast next morning – not even a hot drink except in emergencies. And with hospital food also being the same the whole world over, I could have done with my own wife appearing outside with a food parcel. But she was not on the tour, so I had to grin and bear it.

As a final gesture of international goodwill, I was given a massive injection into my rump, before being released on Friday morning. Vitamins, they said it was, to build me up for the flight home on Saturday.

Those kindly people also provided a full written report on my state of health, with a diagnosis of gastro-enteritis, the tests and the treatment.

'You will present this to your doctor in England, please,' said the Matron at the door. 'It is something unfortunate on the table, goodbye.'

'*Do svidaniya,*' I answered, and kissed her on the cheek. She was built like a javelin thrower, but she blushed and I knew I had been in good hands. The medical report is written in Russian, with even my name translated into Cyrillic, so I've had it framed to save my local GP from having a brainstorm.

Yet my fate could have been infinitely worse. Much, much worse. For had it not been raining so hard on that Tuesday evening I would have arrived at the Philharmonia Hall in good time. Seated in the midst of an elegant and well-informed audience, my stomach would have erupted during the opening bars of Dvorak's *Humoresque* . . .

EMMA BROOKER

# A SLICE OF THE BIG APPLE

New York

Six gritty months of fumbling with biros and over-read text books in A level tedium were wiped out. Wiped out by a five-hour flight to a city where riding the subway is an act of hedonism, and where the pollution on the streets works on the brain like speed, driving people scrambling to the summits of New York City's towers of granite and power.

'The movies are true,' screamed my eyes from the back of the yellow can which I took from the airport. I rattled in the corner of the great plastic sofa of a back seat. Monster cars sharked past, the cluster of Wall Street skyscrapers loomed; an elite of big names at a very mixed party

Freeway became mapled streets, buildings flattened into the four-storeyed Victorian Brownstones of Brooklyn. The cab driver dumped me outside my home for the next three months. I dragged a bloated suitcase into the basement flat. Fans were purring; it smelt of mouldering heat on city rain.

So, I was going to be living in a district with a Wholeperson's Clinic, and a Funeral Home up the street. Around the corner was a Hardware Store selling Croak-a-Roach and Roach Motels. Next door to that I could buy carrot cake ice-cream. Compliments took the form of,

'Hello Mommy, I've got hurting in my bollocks.' yelled from a passing Oldsmobile as I trod the sidewalk.

TV told me about the victim of child molestation who claimed, 'I owe my analyst my life'.

It showed sport in Super Slo-Mo, and got 'Close Up and Personal' with the stars. I was mesmerised by the prime-time show, *Lifestyles of the Rich and Famous*. One episode of this told the story of the bus boy from Ohio who bought an Italian baronetcy, owns three islands in the Canaries and is now the world underwater backgammon champion.

Equipped with such information, I decided it was time to hit the streets. First I went under. Dark, damp, noisy and stifling, the subway is an assault on each of the senses. It has an all-pervading stench of goat and rotting peaches. Even for the natives it is a point of pride to understand the system. Seeing me in a state of bewildered angst, they would come up and intone directions in a rhythmical and mysterious language.

> 'You take a D train down to De Kalb,
> Switch to a Double R, QB, or four . . .'

Surfacing from this Kafkaesque dungeon you can be sure only of confronting the unexpected. Nothing specific epitomises New York; its essence is extremity, and diversity, packed into the highest possible density.

My first shot of Manhattan was on emerging from the subway on to Fifth Avenue. I looked up at a sheer sheet of glass and steel, one of the 1930s Rockerfeller buildings. Indifferently magnificent, it sneered back at my eager camera lens, which could only fit in a pitiful few floors. The scale was intoxicating. Everything big. Fifth Avenue, sliced right down the centre of the island, felt liberatingly airy because of the gigantic proportions of every shape and space. Brash and confident as an arrogant all-American jowl. Looking down one of the Avenues is like looking at the inversion of a sunset. The outsized buildings march into infinity in shades of grey to mauve, blurred by a haze of fumes.

Pick a different subway stop. Washington Square; Greenwich Village, the part of New York which stays up all night and starts waking up around midday. A couple of middle-aged men with bluish legs were roller skating along the middle of the road. In the square a Quaker choir was performing, and old men in heavy overcoats were in uproar over a game of chess. Some man came up to me and asked,
'You wanna smoke?'

He proceeded to roll a joint, smoke it, produce juggling equipment and give a dazzling, impromptu performance.

I walked East to Astor Place, where the streets are paved with people sitting next to, and selling, their household rubbish. Perfectly safe, until I strayed a few blocks in the wrong direction and found myself, the only female, in a street lined with male prostitutes.

'Sexss lady?' hissed one through a gold tooth. The nearest subway entrance was blocked with trash. The place stank of violence.

Take an Uptown train to Columbus Circle; Central Park. I dodged herds of joggers, cyclists, people playing croquet, baseball, and walked into the theatrical bustle of an operatic cast preparing for an open air performance of Madam Butterfly.

Back Downtown, to Canal Street, where I found Chinatown, with the second largest Chinese community in the West, 30,000. I wandered into dusty, pungent shops selling live chickens, and dried snakes for rubbing into bruises. Pagoda-topped callboxes melted into the Mafioso restaurants of Little Italy, and the warehouses-turned-art-galleries of Soho.

Carry on down to the tip of the island; Wall Street. I bounced off fat people in double-breasted pinstriped suits, and strode beside young execs and briefcase-bearing, silked women, into the World Trade Centre. From floor 110, the highest point on the island, I gazed back at the midtown outbreak of skyscrapers, the Chrysler and the Empire State in their midst. With the edge of the island visible on either side, Manhattan sits in murky river, an absurd chunk of metropolis looking like a Gothic spaceship working up to an explosive departure from the planet.

New York is criss-crossed all over with fine dividing lines. As well as the grid system of streets, there is a territorial grid which is equally apparent. Starting exactly two blocks down from where I was living, there is a Hispanic neighbourhood, run down and emptying out. Ten years ago it was full of Italians, who, when the Hispanics moved in, drove through and shot from car windows. It was obvious when I missed my local subway stop. The line went on into a big Jamaican area, and I was the only white left in a full carriage. Feeling ridiculous, I took the next train straight back.

'This is a city full of alienated people,' my landlord told me. The blacks and Hispanics who live on the poverty line, in slum ghettos, feel alienated; so do the predominantly white middle classes in their 'good' districts, he explained. Not surprisingly, one common feature New Yorkers share is paranoia. I soon developed their reflexive habit of checking behind whenever someone walked towards me in a fairly empty street. Some people carry a ten dollar bill, to keep the potential mugger happy and stave off an angry attack.

Rent is high, accommodation scarce, and the chances of getting a knife in the stomach far from slim. The rats in this race bite back harder, and hungrier. Compensating for its disadvantages, New Yorkers live the city for all it's worth. The energy gets to you like a wire spring inside, being wound tighter and tighter the longer you're there. Once revved up to the standard, frenetic pitch of activity, one day becomes a limitless bank account with which you can do everything . . . and anything.

I met a boy in his mid-twenties, from Kentucky, who had come to New York to set up as a dentist. Down in Kentucky they call NY the nation's brain drain. He gave me two good reasons for moving to the city. He told me,

'I like to party.'

And then later, 'I like nice things.'

This is the reason why he chose to do dentistry rather than Art Restoration, despite the fact that,

'I lurv Russian icons.'

Doing it his way, he can make lots of money as a New York dentist, and buy a few nice icon things for himself. Such candid consumerism made a refreshing change after the squeamish English double stand over money. Money is the law of life there, which has to be lived by. No use in nobly pretending it doesn't happen. Rather than remarking on seasonal changes in the surrounding foliage, the majority of New Yorkers whom I met would relish a detailed discussion about the subtle fluctuations in Real Estate Value.

New York is a city of dreams. The dreams rely in part on the dreamer sustaining a faith in the American 'ethos' of freedom and liberty. Liberty, that is, to be like the bus boy from Ohio, liberty to realise any dream, be it at the expense of others, which, in this land-of-the-free, it inevitably has to be. Lack of adequate welfare services – health, housing, education – demonstrates the lack of sympathy for casualties. After all, they started out from the same nest of opportunities as the rats who are now fatter.

At the mouth of New York city harbour stands Liberty. She has welcomed the oppressed and disowned of the world to this paranoiac dreamscape for nearly a hundred years. This summer she was torchless, covered in scaffolding and swathed in white canvas. At night, lit from within, she looked like a stricken ghost, fleeing the city of glittering towers.

JOHN WILKINSON

# THE ROAD OUT OF PINJARRA

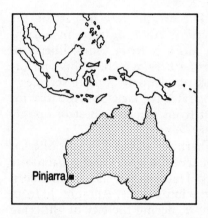

I am sitting in the shade of a gum tree, by the side of a dusty road in Pinjarra, Western Australia. It has taken me fifty lifts to reach Pinjarra; a name on the map you do not notice until fate holds you there.

After three months' travelling in Australia, hitch-hiking has become an addiction; the stimulation of a new acquaintance, a frank exchange of views, and then back on to the roadside – a self-contained experience without any repercussions.

I have been waiting for a lift for four hours. I seem to be a permanent figure in this small town, loitering under the shade of a eucalyptus, with my blue sunhat pulled over my eyes.

On the other side of the road, two old aboriginal women, one with a grey beard, stumble away from the local park after their afternoon drinking session. The road back towards the shops and bars melts into water, thanks to the oppressive dry heat. The beardless aboriginal, who is wearing a black polka-dot dress, collapses on the pavement. Her friend squats by her side, looking into the sun. I notice that she is squatting in the shade cast by a telegraph pole.

I have visited Sydney, Melbourne, Adelaide, Kalgoorlie and Perth thanks to the goodwill of timber-workers, fruit-pickers, farmers, sheep-shearers, pensioners, housewives, drunks, fishermen, truckies, a postman, a policeman, a ferryman and an inebriated, middle-aged Englishman who looked suspiciously like Ronnie Biggs. My duty was to supply conversation to break up the monotony of the heat-haze on the straight roads through the bush.

What will I discuss with my next host? How many snakes and kangaroos he has killed in his car, English as opposed to Australian beer, a possible Test successor to fast bowler Dennis Lillee, or Conservation. The latter can be a dangerous word for hitch-hikers in Australia, particularly with farmers and timber-workers. Most farmers I travelled with regarded National Parks as scrub full of snakes. One farmer was livid that he could not go into his local National Park and chop wood for his barbecue. Unless you like being marooned in out-of-the-way places with a half-empty water bottle, it is not a subject a hitch-hiker should get drawn into.

I fell into the conservation trap again with a Sydney chiropractor concerning native, and non-native, birds in Australia. After tea, if he was in the mood, the chiropractor would go out and shoot starlings in his garden, because they had been introduced from Europe. I suggested that starlings had probably been in Australia longer than his family, and if his argument was translated into human terms then an aboriginal would have a justifiable right in hoisting a spear into his chest.

'Do you mind being called a Pommie Bastard?' inquired the chiropractor. 'I hear that England is in a bad way. A lot of people out of work. Most of our trade union problems are caused by infiltrating Poms.' Only a foolish hitch-hiker makes this mistake twice.

It is not only individuals who get ravelled up in this native/non-native business. In Western Australia it is an offence to cultivate blackberries in your garden, and it is also your duty as a citizen to report to the authorities any sightings of sparrows or starlings. The information board outside the Freemantle Police Station displayed a poster which offered a reward for information leading to the conviction of a person who had murdered a High Court Judge. Next to it was a picture of a rogue starling with the caption, 'Have you seen this bird?'

Back in Pinjarra the old, semi-conscious aboriginal groans, and then lapses back into sleep; another fringe dweller out for the count. A white Australian boy appears, and proceeds to do 'wheelies' around the two old women on his racing bike. Could this scene be acted out every day at 4.45pm on the road out of Pinjarra?

Sweat pours from beneath my hat, and my shorts are going raggy at the hem. My peeling, sunburnt nose resembles a small bundle of rags. Australian flies must be the most persistent in the world. I wonder if the British introduced them? The heat is getting to me. I drink the last few drops of water from my flask.

'Want a tinny, son?' inquires a voice from behind me.

I turn around and see a small, fat man leaning on his garden fence. He is wearing white shorts, and laughter lines run in deep creases by the sides of his eyes.

'Oh, thanks very much.'

He delves into his portable coolbox and fishes out an ice cool can of lager. The beer slips down my throat. No sooner have I got excited about the cool sensation in my throat than the can is empty.

'Those two old abos look like they've had a skinful,' observed my benefactor. 'My son works for the housing dept around here. You know that when a black fella dies the whole family moves out of the house and goes walkabout. They'll not return for love nor money, because of the bad spirits. Now where's the logic in that?'

'I suppose it's tribal superstition,' I reply. 'They were more nomadic before the whites colonised the country, and their tribal huts would be more temporary structures than council housing. I wonder if they would sooner live in a tribal hut than the white man's three-bed-roomed house with fully-fitted kitchen?'

'I'd like to see them get the plans through the government housing regulations. Besides, what sort of life would that be?'

'What sort of life is hitch-hiking?'

'Your choice, son.'

'Exactly.'

'I see your angle. The whites repress the aborigines. Don't forget, son, that a lot of Australian people's ancestors did not ask to be deported from Jolly Old England! You know we were the Poms, not you lot. We were the Prisoners of Mother England.'

'Fair dinkum,' I replied.

'Honours about even, son.'

We both laughed.

At that moment the blue flash of an estate car passes my field of vision. The brakes are applied and the passenger door opens. I turn to say cheerio to the old man, but he is digging under a pair of stringy barks, with his back turned towards me.

Vince and Fred are part of an Italian rock band called Casablanca. They are going as far as Collie.

'Where are you from?' asked Vince.

'England,' I replied.

'Someday I would like to travel abroad. Travel broadens the mind,' confirmed Vince.

It certainly does when it is hot in Pinjarra and you cannot get a lift.

DAVID GREEN

# THE GULF OF FINLAND ON ICE

Perhaps they're penguins, I thought. But they were too far away for me to be certain, and the blinding light could have been playing tricks on the two of us. It doesn't help your orientation one bit when the land is indistinguishable from the sky, nor indeed when you're not quite sure whether you've left the land yet. Very soon we would not be able to see the line of tall evergreens that parted beach from cloud.

Our penguins remained elusively in the distance, though motionless. Underfoot the ice creaked and groaned dubiously: we were over the sea. An earlier wind had whipped up the surface snow into rivulets like tiny mountain ranges, and whirled spirals like ice cream from a machine. Beneath this the layer of ice was almost perfectly smooth, though occasionally an unseen force had pushed its plates together and upwards forming huge mountains amongst the hills and valleys. Every detail was spectacular, yet the whole formed a nothingness of intense light and cold (about twenty degrees below zero). We could only lock our vision onto those distant penguins and attempt to get that far.

In places the ice seemed to be frighteningly thin, and our boots turned it mushy as seeping salt water formed lakes in the snow-vales. The air, heavy with silent, still flakes, closed in behind us making our isolation almost absolute. The quietness seemed somehow to be incredibly loud, perhaps because wherever else I have been I could at the very least, listening hard, pick out some distant sounds of life, or even the wind in the trees. But here we were truly in a void; our footsteps had a booming, dull thud to them, and standing still with breath held left our ears desperately searching for something, anything, to catch hold of.

My senses were confused by this new experience, having previously associated sightseeing with sights to see, not to mention hear and smell. To keep my mind in check I decided to remember the journey here (a cavernous train with wooden seats) or the flight to Riga (alarmingly, the roof leaked), but I couldn't help falling into the mental free-form that this placed allowed. Here was somewhere in a meditative limbo between earthly chaos and spiritual ecstasy; we could have been on the crystal lake of the Apocalypse, half-way to paradise. . . If only it wasn't for the cold that nagged at us constantly. My feet had ceased diplomatic relations with the rest of me.

Our penguins held fishing rods and wore hats and coats of thick fur: they were humans – nay, Russians. I expect we were about three miles out to sea by now, though I could not smell any salt, hear any gulls or see any boats. The over-swaddled Russians had built curved walls of ice around themselves and drilled small holes through to the sea, over which they crouched with their fishing tackle, perfectly still. Some of them had faces: red-raw and wrinkled, with tiny eyes and pursed lips. Their breath hung about them indecisively. They looked – and there's no getting away from this – infinitely bored.

One of them gesticulated to us and, using harsh, staccato Russian (which neither of us understood) and rather violent stabs into the air, made it very clear that we had taken a dangerous route over the ice and that we were very stupid indeed. We noticed now a trail of well-trodden snow winding back towards the shore, obviously a route known to be safe by the experienced locals. We smiled feebly and re-frained from attempting any further communication with these intro-spective folk. They eyed us with vague curiosity and then returned to their (apparently fruitless) fishing. My friend and I settled ourselves onto the snow and uncorked a well-chilled bottle of wine in the hope of getting merry.

In a most oblique way this place was very exciting; the searing blanket whiteness was stunning and the sheer starkness ultimately beautiful. But it was not merry. We had to get up and gingerly stamp around to recirculate the blood. For an hour or two we trudged about trying to find something more (or something at *all*) to see, and even photograph. Finally, frozen stiff, we made our way back along the relative safety of the fisherman's path, with a cursory wave back to the huddled forms.

Ahead of us the tall pines that stretch out across the frozen plain of Estonia distinguished themselves from the snow-coated sky and earth. It seemed that the all-pervading light was weakening: it must have been late afternoon. This presented a thought that made me shudder with fright: this awesome, eerie world-apart in the dead of night, unbearably cold, no moon or stars, merely the moan of the mysterious gods beneath the ice . . . We hurried on.

What spirits lurked within the murkiness of the intertwined creepers of the forest? Such a dense blackness, and unreal noises . . . Oh, it wasn't like this at all, I'm sure, yet the shape silhouetted in the snow where the ice met the beach turned into our worst fears.

He was dead, there's no doubt about that. He was lying, clothed, on his back, legs apart, elbows resting in the snow with his arms inexplicably pointing straight upwards ending with contorted, blue fingers, like a pair of old, gnarled trees.

My heart gave me an unforgettable jolt when I thought him to be headless; yet there was no blood staining the fresh, even snow. Perhaps it was tucked under his collar. We were speechless, but we morbidly crept towards him when a sudden snap from the forest warned that someone was approaching and we ran along the beach then through the trees, hearts pounding, and gasping for breath. Never has fear gripped me so tightly, yet it was exhilarating, fantastic even. There was a schoolboy excitement about it, but weighed down by the heavy, weird atmosphere of the frozen Gulf. During the terrible siege of Leningrad in the last war supplies were eventually conveyed to the starving thousands on carts from Finland across the Baltic Sea and the Gulf of Finland (it was fortunately an exceptionally cold winter) – what must have been a fearsome journey. Now history is swathed in an inscrutable silence.

At the comparative safety of a deserted road we collected ourselves a little and then headed for the station, trying hard to chuckle about it all, though obviously we had both been deeply affected.

The final straw, as it were, came when we were back home: none of the photographs we had taken on that day came out.

# THE PHARAOH'S CURSE

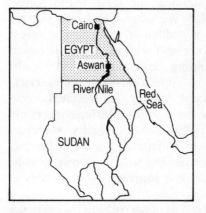

## MONDAY

The blastfurnace heat at Aswan jumps off the tarmac and hits us like a blow as I lead my group towards the terminal building. "Keeping the rest to clean your teeth?" nudges Doctor Whistler, pointing to my depleted bottle of mineral water.

"Aha, that's right!" I smile, through gritted teeth. My head's pounding like a sledgehammer, and my stomach feels frail. I touch my pocket for the reassuring packet of Diocalm. Tour Directors aren't allowed the luxury of being ill. Away from Cairo HQ I'm in sole charge of ninety physicians and their wives on a pre-congress beano – four days of cruising the Nile and doing the sites.

A trio of rickety buses takes us to our floating hotel, the *Hatshepsut*. Once settled in gracious colonial-style comfort, I relax a little. The air of excited anticipation builds as doctors dive into their Welcome glasses of Ribena-like Karkade and their Baedekers with equal enthusiasm, like kids out of school.

At sunset our dining-room view of the shadowy river is spellbinding. Less prepossessing are the three bluebottles on the table decoration poised to divebomb my fried chicken.

Doctor Rawlings from Bradford, having warned me long and loud on the flight about the perils of raw food, cold food and ice, passes beaming, with a mountainous plate from the buffet. "Iris is having terrible trouble remembering the name of this ship!"

"Tell her to try thinking of a hat and a cheap suit!" I suggest, pleased with my ingenuity, and blissfully ignorant of how much I shall shortly be needing it.

During the night I wake to dash the two yards from bunk to bathroom. Taking one of every sort of pill I've brought with me, I convince myself I'm just overtired.

## TUESDAY

Trouble strikes.

I'm sneaking a moment on deck before breakfast, feeling limp and

watching a heron gliding around like a poker with a crick in its neck, when there's a Northcountry whisper behind me.

"Iris is very poorly this morning. I'm afraid she won't manage the temple."

Why does my heart sink? After all, one case of the trots hardly spells disaster. But I have this nagging suspicion that my luck as a first-timer tour group leader cannot hold. Sure enough, there is only forty per cent attendance at breakfast. One after another physician approaches my table conspiratorially, to complain of feeling unwell, or tell hair-raising tales of a companion's sleepless night. As the boat's engines thrum into startling life, mild apprehension gives way to serious foreboding. Doctor McRae bounces up like Tigger, smiling fit to bust. "Well, at least if we're catching Egyptian bugs, we can all treat each other!"

Quite.

Aswan town front, reminiscent of Worthing in terms of Thirties-style decay, slides slowly from view behind us. An hour later we tie up, and a small party departs stoically up the bank for Kom Ombo temple.

I remain nervously aboard, to hear doctors exchanging advice on every deck: Doctor McRae recommends a diet of rice and yoghurt. (He has been addressing the problem rather more seriously since his wife succumbed after breakfast on her way down the gangplank.) Doctor Turner swears by a universal prophylactic of gin and guava juice, offering me a swig from his thermos. Imodium changes hands like cocaine on Eighth Avenue.

Reeling somewhat from the gin concoction, and making for the captain's office, I console myself with the thought that if I need anything from an apendectomy to open heart surgery, there is no shortage of equipment or expertise to hand.

But Something must be Done, and I collar our captain, who is not in his office but enjoying a cigar on the pool deck with the purser. A previously helpful fellow, he seems reluctant to discuss the matter, dismissing the whole thing with a wave of his bejewelled hand as just the usual English gippy tummy. Neither his English nor my Arabic is good enough to argue, and anyway, perhaps I'm over-dramatising. Later, sitting weakly on a disquietingly depopulated sun deck as we drift downriver towards Edfu, I put the worries of tropical viruses aside and watch the river banks roll lazily by, parallel fringes of lush greenery backed abruptly by the yellow hills of the desert.

Donkeys graze by fields of breezy sugar cane, and minarets rise phoenix-like from seas of palm trees, their fronds swaying together like a corps-de-ballet. The river, serene and still for long dreamy stretches, bursts with occasional scenes of activity where bunches of noisy children play in the shallows alongside gleaming water buffalo,

or groups of chattering women pound the weekly wash. A pair of feluccas drifts across our bows like lovebirds, their sails throwing long shadows across the tranquil water. Mesmerised by this biblical travelogue, and deliciously warmed by the late afternoon sun, I wonder if my lightheadedness is caused by the euphoric sensation of time-travelling or by imminent physical collapse.

Dinner is an even more depleted affair than breakfast.

### WEDNESDAY
Kom Ombo and Edfu, like the fitness of my charges, have been and gone, and now at Esna a few determined explorers rattle by horse-drawn carriage towards the town centre at 6am. Esna, a series of dusty streets and alleys, is still asleep, apart from the odd scavenging tat-eared dog.

The temple sits some fifty feet down in its own huge sandpit, buried for centuries until someone tripped over what turned out to be the top of a pillar. High above, in abrupt contrast, sit the comparatively recent buildings of the town, their roofs and turrets catching the early morning sun.

Back on board, the senior consultants, having had a council of war, open up with a full frontal attack of heavy verbal artillery, ending with a chilling final volley:

"Most of us will be taking samples home for analysis."

And sending each other massive consultancy bills, I think to myself, while my well practised straight face almost lets me down with both this thought and that of the possible scenario in the Heathrow customs hall.

I assure the grim-faced surgeons in front of me that representations will be made to the shipping line on our return to Cairo, and that, meanwhile, the captain and I will, after appropriate consultation, revamp the menus.

"Revamp to rice and yoghurt!" trills Doctor McRae, *en passant.* "I'm still fine!"

I give him what I hope is a suitably withering look. Late that afternoon Plague Ship *Hatshepsut* reaches her final mooring in ancient Thebes, and there is a chorus of clicking camera shutters as we pass the unexpected splendour of a silhouetted Luxor temple.

Doctor Turner takes me aside to acquaint me in funereal tones with the details of a colleague's latest symptoms. I wish he hadn't.

### THURSDAY
The decks are a little more lively, with the genuinely and partially re-covered sitting about in little groups, eyeing me accusingly whenever I pass. (I'm sure the Ancient Mariner had an easier time.) At least the numbers on the shore excursions are slowly swelling, although the

collective preoccupation is not so much with details of what site we are about to visit, but how many "comfort stops" there will be.

Magnificent Karnak, with its corridors of stone rams, sky-embracing pillars and gigantic inscrutable statues, stretching apparently as far as the eye can see, is breathtaking. Ozymandias, whose famous admonishment has been haunting me from Day One, seems to lurk round every corner, laughing up his sleeve.

The captain, possibly in an effort to make some amends for our problems, offered today's trippers airline paper bags, just in case. Several who declined this gesture now regret it, and I'm thankful for the sandy ground which provides the perfect means literally to kick over the traces.

Back on board, the hoped-for but unexpected sight of a *deus-ex-machina* in the form of our travel agency chief is immensely reassuring. Gratefully, I enlist his help; he confers with the various spokesmen with charm, patience and a magic defusing device called being The Boss.

Relieved, I turn my exhausted attention to the details of tomorrow's expedition to the Valley of the Kings, and our return flight to Cairo.

*FRIDAY*

Finally back at base, it's amazing what a five-star hotel can do to revive the spirits.

The difficulties of the cruise are all but forgotten by most. "We've had a marvellous time," they beam, "really marvellous." Before I retire to bed, one small item appears for the stop press. Doctor McRae, the only one to have survived the cruise unscathed, has tripped on a kerbstone and broken his foot.

STEPHEN LAWSON

# ABOARD THE TRANS-SIBERIAN EXPRESS

She started sobbing three hours before the border. The conductress tried to console her with a glass of sweet, strong tea but without much success. She remained in the long druggeted corridor, a crumpled figure in a pink dressing gown watching the forests spinning madly by. The tankard holding the glass depicted a Slavic swordsman defending a child and she held it tight as a keepsake.

It certainly was a crying matter. The birch forests of Siberia, so upright, so elegant in autumn, had been broken by this winter campaign. Brought into perfect arcs by wind and snow, the younger birches littered the track-side like ribs and tusks while the old and brittle, unable to bow before the onslaught, rose into the air like splintered spines. Even the express was beginning to show signs of vulnerability to the elements. The sinks and toilets were blocked with ice and the narrow cubicles connecting the carriages were thick with snow, their door handles stinging. Each cubicle was a treacherous no man's land, now braved by only a few passengers seeking out the dozing heat of the restaurant car which, nearing the end of its journey, had little to offer. She was, of course, crying for none of these reasons.

Her daughter loved the stations. She was usually dressed and waiting half-an-hour before the express pulled in. Arm-in-arm with the day-conductress, she would walk the length of the train, watching the ice being tapped off the water inlets and the track-hoppers getting a warning from the new MCK engine elbowing its way backwards. When the conductress and the girl turned and began their precarious stiff-armed run along the platform back to the wrought-iron steps of carriage No 3, it was the signal for a dozen others to do likewise. Feet were wiped, the steps were brought in, the samovar was stoked and nostrils which had stuck together like prickly gauze snuffled back to life.

At one station they had cut short their promenade and dived back to get a thermometer. A huddle of passengers gathered round the steps of the carriage to get a look at the reading and, lest their breathing distort

the figure, Nadia held it aloft like a fish between finger and thumb. Thirty below. Several minutes before the express was due to pull out, the platform was empty. The station master was in retreat and only the ever-watchful V.I. Lenin peered down the track in the direction of the heroes who had to work on. They stood up from their points-cleaning to watch the express pass when, to the delight of her comrades, one of them bellowed "Mishka!" to the train driver through a rolled-up magazine. A brief and warming thigh-slapping routine ensued before headscarves bound tight as bandages were again bowed before the task in hand.

It was around Lake Baikal that the woman in pink had been able to share in her daughter's delight with the journey. She explained to us that she had spent her childhood in a village near Irkutsk. She pointed beyond a wooden pier to the place where she used to sit on a crate beside her father as he fished through the ice. At the age of ten, her talents had taken her away to Moscow where she had studied, married and made her home. As we watched the train's shadows turn and fold on the snowy shore, it became clear that she had not forgotten the stories which made this much more than a stark inland sea stretching as far as the eye can follow. Once, before she was born, her father had found a curious bloated and boggle-eyed fish on the shore. He had made a meticulous drawing of his find and had insisted that she take his handiwork with her to Moscow where it adorned, in turn, dormitory, flat and office. She was now taking it to Peking. She could imagine what was going on in the lugubrious depths of Baikal. These strange survivals from pre-history the *golomianka,* were no doubt nosing around the wreck of Old Prince Khilkov's locomotive which had plunged through the ice eighty years ago.

"Don't worry," she reassured us. "That was in the days when they were laying tracks on the ice; in the days, too, when you could get married out there." She swept her hand towards the endless expanse of ice and water. "And on a boat made in England." Her face became as bright as an icon as if she had momentarily glimpsed the old customs of Irkutsk: a bridal party bearing skates of bone and bodices of the finest needle-point standing on the southern shore and looking across Baikal; a sallow-faced groom from Chita smoothing his first moustache and pacing the deck of an ice-locked paddle-steamer.

By the time the express clattered into Zabajjkal'sk, on the Russian side of the border, the attentions of the conductress coupled with her own resolve had prepared the woman for the formalities. All that remained was paperwork and a passage to Peking. She had taken her last look at this obscure outpost of the Soviet Union and now stood with her back to the low sun.

"We will be here for some time. The wheels need to be changed for China and the officials . . ." – she indicated a rank of grey-coated

youths further up the platform – "they will expect you to stand in the corridor while they search your room. So please," she started off towards her own compartment, "no reds under the bed."

It is indeed the room which interests them – the room, the space, into which a Trans-Siberian stowaway may be fitted. There is room for a couple: one here behind the luggage (hunched like a cosmonaut hurtling into the unknown) and another there beneath the bottom bunk (blankets burying a crouched figure waiting for rebirth). All the lights are up and cold air has come in with the officials. Young men with pale, waxy skins, they are straight out of some Moscow academy. Old hands wear leather gloves, old heads wear fur hats, as if they are badges of office: we hunt, we trap, we tame. These are reluctant hunters, ill at ease and inexperienced, wary lest a nervous glance could give flesh to fear – the fear of coming face to face with a cowering countryman, the fear of finding the loaded chamber in a game of Russian roulette. In this compartment, in this carriage, on this train, it does not happen and they move on to check the papers of the woman and her daughter.

Even as the guards are ushering them into the corridor, the carriage rolls into an immense echoing workshop. A tankard on the compartment table sits as a reminder of the glories of Soviet technology – sputniks and rockets spin out of a world inhabited by the Spassky Tower and an olive branch – and, as if to demonstrate that the mundane is as attainable as the sublime, not a spoon rattles, not a single drop of sweet Georgian tea is spilt, as the carriage is smoothly elevated and the task of fitting a Chinese-gauge undercarriage is taken in hand. The mechanics wink and whistle and smoke aromatic cigars. They look as though they should be on horseback flying towards the sun. Now they swing beneath the iron horse, a race apart from the officials pacing the corridor. Ruddy mortals, crouching and crawling around the undercarriage, they can look up for inspiration to the immaculate lives portrayed high on the walls of the workshop, to those models of determination and robust heroism familiar to all Soviet citizens: Riveters and Liberators, Welders and Flag-bearers, beaming Foundrywomen with goggles thrown back on their brows like aviators from the Great Patriotic War.

"We all have to do something for the good of our country." She had returned to the window and was watching me photograph the posters. "I will be spending three years in Peking, at our Embassy, so perhaps we will meet again when you collect your return visa."

One month later I did visit the Embassy, a little Russia behind a wrought-iron gate and walls once used to confine Cossack prisoners. There, in a small panelled office, was the drawing of a queer fish waiting like a fabulous train with headlamps ablaze in a Siberian night.

## David Shanahan

# Dolmens and Blarney

It was a bright, clear spring morning when the boat docked in Rosslare and I disembarked in Eire.

Finding the roads almost traffic free, I decided to push on as quickly as possible towards the harsh and romantic west coast.

I was making good time when my eye was caught by a small, wooden sign, on which was written, "Harristown Dolmen". I pulled up opposite, wound down the window and stared. At this point I might as well confess to being what is called in the trade a "megalithomaniac". Any stone, no matter how small, if it has the tag "megalithic", then I'm hooked.

The sign pointed down a small lane running off the main road. Had I got time? It was still early, so why not?

Turning into the lane, I was overwhelmed by a feeling of plunging underwater. Dense masses of vivid green vegetation swayed and lapped in slow motion. The shifting surfaces scattered and diffused the light, so that it fell down, dappling the already dappled cattle browsing under the trees like schools of fish. The road became narrower and ran ahead of me like a twisting silver elver. I saw no signs and had gone a few miles before I saw my first human being.

A tall, thin man stood staring at a stone wall, as if waiting for an answer to a question he had put to it. I wound down the window and asked him if he knew where the dolmen was.

"The dolmen? Sure, of course I know where the dolmen is. Isn't it just over dere, behind dem hills?"

He gave me an armful of left and rights, and off I went.

Half an hour later I stopped the car, got out, sat down on a bank in an empty green world and admitted to myself that I was lost. After a while, the feeling that I was completely alone in the world became less frightening. I sat watching with passive pleasure an unending variety of greens weave and dance in the breeze. Above the shuddering tree-tops, swallows darted like pond skaters across a thin, blue film of sky.

The approach of an old woman disturbed my nature watch. As she came level, I got to my feet and said hello.

She gave me a great, gummy grin which almost split her face in two. She was small with coarse, wire-wool hair and bright bird's eyes that missed nothing. Her hands, resting on the pram she was pushing, were those of a giant. The pram was full of what appeared to be nettles. In the middle of these, nestling like an egg, was a bottle of milk.

Nervously, I asked her if she knew of Barney's Dolmen. As I heard the words I knew they were wrong, but couldn't for the life of me remember the dolmen's proper name.

She gave me another cavernous smile and said: "Barry's Dolmen? Sure, of course I know it. Follow me an' I'll lead yeh right to it."

The thought of creeping along in a car behind an old woman pushing a pram full of nettles didn't appeal so, mentioning a pressing engagement, I got a garbled set of directions and bade her good day.

I must have passed in and out of several counties that morning, looking for that dolmen. People cheerfully pointed me in the direction of Barry's, Harry's, Carry's and, in one case, even the Black Dolmen. Sometimes, if they didn't know the one I was after, they sent me off in search of one or two they had of their own.

So, when at last I came to a small village with a large church, I decided that perhaps the priest might be the best person to tell me where these prehistoric pagans buried their dead. A woman arranging flowers around an anaemic statue told me that Father Burne was, "even now, in the sacristy".

I passed an old man cutting back the undergrowth with a rusty scythe. He said hello, so I thought I'd give him a try first. He was the first person I'd met that day who didn't know what a dolmen was. When in the course of my explanation I mentioned the word pagan, he jerked as if he were on the end of a wire.

Looking nervously over his shoulder in case the priest should hear, he scratched his head and rolled his eyes, all the time muttering that terrible word. Then suddenly he clicked his fingers and spat the word out.

"Pagans! Dere's an old Protestant graveyard, overgrown now, you understand, up dere, by de old crossroads, as used to be dere."

I waited patiently while he told me forty different ways to get there. Then, thanking him, I beat a hasty retreat to the sacristy door and knocked.

The door was opened by a tall, bulky man in his late sixties. His stern, bloated red face overflowed the shining white barricade of his dog collar. Profuse amounts of grey and ginger hair sprouted from nose and ears. Above his eyes a thick, prickly hedgerow jutted at right-angles to the bone. He listened with a terrible look of disdain on his face. Then he thundered:

"What in God's name do ye wantta be looking at tings like that for? Are ye a Catholic?"

I shifted uncomfortably and confessed that I was.

"A lapsed one, I suppose." He sniffed, and oceans of hair swayed in his nose. Ignoring my mumbled apologies, he turned and conversed with a shadowy figure which had spread like a silent stain over the carpet as we talked.

The shadow appeared to have an extensive knowledge of dolmens and their whereabouts. It passed this information on in a terrible hushed whine that seemed to creep in and fill the head.

The priest relayed the directions, spitting out the words as if they were poison. I thanked him and his shadow, and hurried back to the car. The shadow's information proved to be correct; fifteen minutes later, I found my dolmen.

It stood in the corner of a small field, larger and more impressive than any I'd yet seen. The great, grey stones seemed to be heaving themselves up out of the earth like pieces of ancient bone, to squat in the alien flesh of the present.

These majestic stones, flecked with orange and white lichen, are the last of thousands that once littered the prehistoric landscape. Most have long disappeared; many of those left have been pressed into service as gateposts on farms, or blacken slowly as lintels over fireplaces.

Late bluebells grew in profusion on the tumbled remains of the great mound. In a stream nearby, two stones from the cairn circles still stood upright. Over a hedge I could see a large stone sitting in the middle of the field, basking in the sun like a great toad.

I took some photographs; then, tired and happy, lay on the mound and watched some large, white clouds with grey bellies drift like giant manta rays through the swirling air. High above them, thin wispy cloud lay like plankton on the endless surface of the sky. The search had taken it out of me and I must have dozed off. I was woken by voices and saw two elderly ladies seated at a nearby bench, which had almost disappeared in the undergrowth. Feeling curious, I went over to say hello.

They were an odd couple; dressed in old-fashioned summer frocks, blue with white spots, their hair cut level with their chins, pudding-bowl style. Odd hairs straggled out of various warts, and the brown freckles of age gave them a strange resemblance to the stones.

"We're sisters and spinsters," they told me with a laugh; but, more importantly, members of The Waterford and District Friends of Ancient Monuments Society. This august body had been responsible for placing the bench we were now sitting on. It was there in order that people might have a picnic by a monument, on just such a day as this.

We talked of dolmens and stone circles. They shared their tea and sandwiches with me as the day slid away behind us. They laughed like a couple of schoolgirls, hands fluttering to their mouths like butterflies when I told them of my encounter with the priest.

"We're Quakers, you know," one told me, and, "Oh, we do find the antics of the natives so terribly funny!"

This statement, from two ladies as eccentric and charmingly Irish as anyone I'd met that day, just about summed up my own feelings. Towards evening I went in search of bed and breakfast; the mad rush to the west could wait.

# THE SKY BURIAL

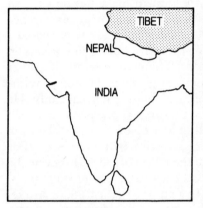

Six AM. I wake before the alarm, filled with apprehension. I had resisted attending the sky burial. However, I know that experiencing such a unique, ancient ritual is the essence of travelling. If I avoid it, I might as well be on a tourist bus, shielded from Tibet and from myself.

Pascal, Doune and I begin the hour-long walk out of L'hassa. We pick our way through a rubbish dump and climb to the burial site, a stubbly patch on top of a rocky hill, surrounded by desolate bare mountains, looking like wrinkled old elephants' hide. Five Tibetan men and a boy of about ten, dressed in worn jackets and trousers, are seated around a fire, drinking tea, talking and laughing. They smile welcome. Nearby is the altar rock where the burial is to take place, a large flat rock with bowl-like depressions, separated by a gully which is strewn with discarded clothing and hanks of hair. We sit by the edge of the gully facing the altar rock. Pascal gestures toward the mountains. I look up. Rows of large silent birds are perched on the mountain ledges – vultures. Their colours blend with the mountains. Ravens swoop in the gully and gather nervously in black clumps on the altar rock. A white square bundle, tied with rope, sits among the ravens. A small dog struggles up the rock and chases them. The rising sun slowly turns the drab greys and dull browns of the mountains to patches of pale gold and dusty pinks. It becomes warmer. About fifteen Westerners trickle in. No Chinese. In the past some have jeered at the burial procedure. Now Tibetans stone them. Westerners still seem welcome, though they too have created "incidents". Several days ago an Australian, desperate to capture the sky burial on film, although Tibetans forbid photographing, hid behind some rocks. He was discovered and chased. Next day Westerners were stoned. Yesterday several filtered back. Today we are greeted with smiles. Tibetans are wonderfully tolerant and forgiving. Still, I feel certain our days at the burial site are numbered.

A little after eight o'clock the sun touches the altar rock, the signal for the burial to begin. One of the men dons a grubby white coat and a surgical-type cap. He says something in Tibetan. Someone translates:

"While we work, no pictures." The man in white, two other men and the boy, climb onto the rock. The remaining two Tibetans, relatives of the deceased, sit by the fire. The man in white is thin and wiry with flashing black eyes and black hair sticking out from under the cap, wild looking. He unties the bundle. A woman, naked except for an unbuttoned faded red blouse, tumbles out. She looks pregnant, young-ish, with long black hair. (Later we learn that her body was carried a long distance on someone's back, for there are only a few places in Tibet where sky burials are performed.) The man in white drags her body over the rock and lays it face down in the centre. He begins with-out ceremony by pulling off the blouse and flinging it in the gully. He pulls a large knife from his belt, and with surgical precision cuts a slit down her spine. Starting from the shoulder blade he strips the flesh down the left side of her back, using swastika-patterned cuts. (For Tibetans the swastika is the symbol of the wheel of life.) This done, he neatly hacks off her left arm and tosses it to the young boy, who, squatting on his haunches, pounds it to a pulp with the back of an axe. He grunts and groans with the effort. The man in white continues to hack the left side of the body, panting loudly like someone chopping wood. The two men, also squatting, are thrown flesh and bones which they pound in the bowl-like depressions. The sounds of panting and puffing combine with those of flesh being pulverised and bones being smashed. *Tzampa,* a mixture of barley flour, tea and yak butter, is added to the flesh and bones to make a paste. Everything happens quickly. The men work with practised skill, pausing only to sharpen their axes or for a short cigarette break.

The woman's right side is begun, the flesh sliced expertly from the ribs. The man's white coat becomes splattered with blood. By now the rock looks like a butcher's shop, bloody with tattered flesh and strewn limbs, and the woman like a butchered carcass. I turn away many times, unable to watch, then am drawn back, unable not to watch. The butcher flips over what remains of the body, a torso with no back or limbs. He chops hard through the chest cavity and reaches inside to pull out the heart. Holding it up, he shouts something to the two Tibetans by the fire. They nod. He chops the heart to bits. Then the stomach is slit open and the organs removed. These are cut up and kept separately. The work is easier now. While they work, the men talk and joke. The Westerners are silent. Lastly, the head is separated from the neck with one precise blow. The butcher holds the head by the hair and deftly scalps it, then, tying the long black hair into a knot, he tosses it into the gully. Next he picks up a large flat stone and, hold-ing it overhead, mutters a prayer and smashes the skull, twice. One of the seated men brings tea to the rock. An old man dressed in traditional clothes appears and, facing the rock, says a prayer and prostrates him-self.

At this point the butcher, turning to the vultures, calls: "*Shoo* . . .
*Tzshoo* . . ." At the signal about a dozen vultures, the vanguard, leave
the mountains and swoop onto the rock. The butcher throws them
bits of flesh as they gather around him. They are huge beautiful birds
with white necks and legs, and speckled tan and white bodies. Their
wings flutter and spread to reveal white undersides and dark brown
tips. Some are so close that we can see their bright blue eyes. The boy
bundles the chopped organs into a cloth. Several vultures try to steal
bits of flesh from the boy. The butcher chases them off the rock with
kicks and abusive shouts, as though punishing them for bad behaviour. The boy carries the bundle off the rock, the two men accompany him. Then the butcher, facing the mountains, addresses the vultures in a shrill sing-song voice, calling, "*Tria* . . . *soya* . . . *tria* . . ."
Suddenly hundreds of birds fill the sky, hover in a quivering cloud
above our heads, their wings beating a nervous fluttering sound, and
descend on the rock, completely covering it. As the vultures vie for
space, the ravens cling to the edges. The butcher serves the preparation
of flesh, bones and *tzampa*. The *tzampa* has been added to make the
mixture more palatable, for it is a bad omen if anything is left uneaten.
The vultures eat greedily, fighting over scraps, slipping off the rock
in their haste to consume. The ravens, uninvited guests, must be content to scramble at the outer edges, snapping up any morsels the vultures accidentally drop.

At this point several Westerners attempt to photograph the vultures. The butcher becomes incensed. Leaping off the rock, he rushes
at two German girls, brandishing his knife and shouting. He points the
knife at the heart of one of the girls. Livid with rage, he grabs their
cameras and rips the film from them, tearing it to shreds and throwing
it in the fire. The other cameras are quickly hidden.

The birds finish eating but do not leave the rock. They flutter about
nervously in staccato hops. I wonder why they linger. The answer
comes quickly. The bundle of organs is returned to the rock. They
have been waiting for these choice morsels – dessert. They voraciously
consume every last bit. Finally the feast is over. The vultures take to
the sky bearing the deceased with them, upwards to the heavens. The
rock is empty. An hour ago there was a body on the rock; now there is
nothing. The butcher sits with the other Tibetans around the fire in
animated discussion. There is no sign of mourning, no tears, no wailing, no prayers. Except for the two men, there are no family or friends
present. Attending a sky burial for a Tibetan must be the equivalent of
going to the morgue for a Westerner.

Two men climb the rock to check that all has been eaten and to clean
it for the next burial. I sit too stunned to move. This has been the
strangest, the most bizarre thing I have ever witnessed. Powerful images rage through my brain. What amazes me is that, in spite of the

horrific nature of what I have seen, I feel neither repulsion nor revulsion. One reason must be the inevitable distancing of oneself from the intensity and nearness of the experience. But more important is a feeling that the sky burial fits in with the isolation and strangeness of the setting. In that alien environment, somehow it all makes sense. I am the last one to leave.

Thailand: Climbing the ladder
of knives in Phang Nga

Limestone islands in Phang Nga
Bay
(*A Day in Narnia, A Night in Phang Nga*)

Dominica: Once the childhood
home of the writer Jean Rhys,
now a 'sleazy guesthouse'

A very public convenience
beside Freshwater Lake
(*A Visit to Dominica*)

Matata mending his nets (*Big Game in the Okavango Swamps*)

The monastery at Petra in Jordan, cut into the rose-coloured sandstone cliffs
(*A Second Shufti at Jordan*)

(*left*) Hi-tech confectionery: a chocolate calculator
(*right*) Sacred smoke: a sniff a day ensures long life and happiness

A typical breakfast includes pickled plums, mussel soup and seaweed
(*Women and Socks*)

The railway at Raxaul, North Bihar (*In North Bihar*)

Mongolia: Yurts to let in the village of Terelj

Inside a yurt: the accommodation is basic but comfortable
(*To the Middle of Nowhere*)

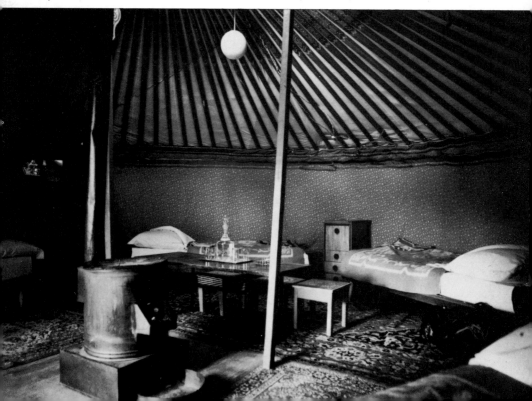

The gigantic carved pillars of the great temple of Karnak. (*The Pharaoh's Curse*)

Dug-out canoes being towed upstream by the barges, while their owners barter goods on board. (*River Journey up the Zaire*)

The men set out their second-hand clothes stalls while the women do the washing-up. (*River Journey up the Zaire*)

Camp at the foot of Lapporten. (*Kebnekaise Mountain Station*)

Alexis, Boo and Ben growing up fast in the jungle. (*Boys' Own Expedition*)

The spectacular 300ft drop of the Victoria Falls. (*Shooting the Zambesi*)

The 'J and K' Palace houseboat at Srinigar and its proprietors – Ali, Gulum and Abdul – waiting for the British to return. (*Not Memsahib*)

Mountain architecture in fortress Hajjah. (*Getting High in the Yemen*)

Refilling the radiator before fording the stream. *(Five Days in Guinea)*

Camp life at the Ballinasloe fair. *(A Fair Show)*

Part of the main procession at the Kumbh Mela, the largest gathering in the world. (*The Crazy Kumbh*)

Upwards and onwards. (*Midnight on Mt Blanc*)

Local fiesta in Peru, with accompanying band. (*Triple Alliance*)

A. H. COOPER

# PLEASE TO MAKE A RESERVATION

"Excuse me, do you speak English?"

"Oh yes, certainly."

"I want to reserve three seats on a train from Calcutta to Patna."

"Please?"

"I want to reserve . . ."

"Where are you wanting to go?"

"Patna."

"Have you a reservation?"

"No. That is what I want."

"Please you wait over there."

"I want to go during the day so that we can all see the countryside."

"Certainly. Over there."

A long queue shaped like a cobra waits "over there". Everybody pushes in front. The clerk behind the screen works with only half a mind functioning. From time to time he wanders off and chats to someone. At every transaction he writes copiously and painstakingly slowly in a book. The lazy punkas overhead do little to ease the discomfort of the temperature and humidity. I count fifteen frustrating moments before I reach the counter.

"I want three tickets for the train to Patna – on Friday – the day train."

"Where do you want to go?"

"Patna." I speak as if to a child, and add, "On Friday."

"No train Friday."

"Is there a train on Thursday?"

"Of course."

"At what time?"

"It leaves Howrah station at seven o'clock."

"Good. Can I reserve three tickets?"

"Where is your reservation form?"

"I was sent here to get it."

"Oh no. You must get it at the end counter."

I can feel the perspiration trickling down my back. I must keep my temper under control, Remember you are in India. Don't get impatient.

I wait yet again. A white form is handed to me.

"Please fill it in and come back here."

"Can't I do it here and now?"

"No, sir. Please to come back."

The form seems as complicated as a tax return. Date, time, destination all seem obvious. Age?

Here we go again. Yet again I have to write down passport numbers, visa numbers, when and where issued. Just my luck to have left the passports in the hotel.

Back to the hotel, fill in the details, another fifteen more minutes (seems like an hour) in the queue.

"Ah but you are British tourist."

"So?"

"There is special allocation of places for tourists."

"Splendid."

"You must take this form to the office round the corner."

"Not here?"

"Not here. Round the corner."

My knees are sagging. This wretched heat and humidity. Out into the sun yet again, into the noise, the crowd. Two beggars hold out their hands. I am too hot to bother with them. Round the corner. In here? A dingy doorway. No, try the next one. Yes, this must be it. Eastern Railway. I queue.

"Not here. Round the corner."

"Round the corner?"

"Yes, sir. This for second class only."

"But I want second-class tickets."

"Tourists in first-class office."

The logic of all this is beyond me. Temper is beyond me. I stumble out again. Another entrance to Eastern Railway. Another queue.

"Can I buy my tickets here?" I plead. I produce my reservation form.

"Where are you wanting to go?"

"Patna." I point to the form, then add, "What time does the day train go on Thursday?"

"Ten to nine."

"But the man in the other office said seven o'clock."

"No, sir. Ten to nine."

I wonder if anyone knows what is going on. I get my money out ready to pay. The reservation form comes back across the counter.

"Please to take this upstairs."

I look through the crowd at the steep stairs to the upper office. Will I get these tickets in time for Thursday?

Up and into a small office. At least it is quiet here. Four clerks sit at a long desk, chatting. Another lies peacefully asleep in the corner. I approach. I am directed to the man at the end. He is a polite little man with a worried expression. He collects the reservation form, writes something on it, the third person to do so. Words and figures seem to cover it.

"Please to sit down."

After ten minutes, I get up.

"Please. Just one moment."

Patience. Just remember. The other clerks chat. The sleeper sleeps. I am beckoned.

"You must take this down to desk number twenty-three. They will give you your tickets."

I am beyond thought. My shirt is soaked through, my head is spinning. I am back in the hubbub, back in the queue.

At last I am holding six beautiful tickets, three for reservations, all meticulously written on. I turn to walk out.

"Please take this with the tickets upstairs."

I thought I'd got rid of that wretched reservation form.

The stairs seem like the north face of the Eiger, the temperature sheer hell. I sit while the worried little man examines the tickets. He writes in a book. He talks over a telephone.

With a broad smile he comes over.

"Here are your tickets."

"Good." I refrain from sarcasm.

"The train leaves Howrah station at nine-thirty . . ." he pauses. I hold out my hand. ". . . PM."

"Night, but . . ."

"Certainly. Very good train. Sleeper reserved too. You like it."

JANIE HAMPTON

# RIVER JOURNEY UP THE ZAIRE

*"Into the eighth day and I really feel I've had enough. I'd like to be transported to a bathroom in the Ritz and then to a dry Martini in the bar."* Graham Green, *Congo Journal, 1959.*

Eighth day, Zaire River, 1985. We often lost each other on the seven barges being pushed a thousand miles up the Zaire River, once Conrad's Congo.

I found my son Joseph, aged seven, in one of the five bars with Sammy, a young soldier. Sammy was concentrating on Joseph's dot-to-dot puzzle.

"He's very good at them," said Joseph. "He never misses a dot."

"Where's Daddy?"

"Gone for a pee at the back."

It was all right for men, they could go over the side. Women had to cope with the dark, smelly "cabinets" and first invite the rats to leave through the crumbling rusty holes. These were the boats left at the Belgian Congo's independence in 1960.

The bar is a scattering of upturned beer crates around a fridge with music pounding out of an oil drum. Only two feet above the glassy water a dozen dug-out canoes are lashed to the side and more join us all the time.

A man leaps from his canoe as it hurtles towards us. His chest reads, "My Mom and Dad went to Canada and all they brought me was this lousy T-shirt". He hangs onto the bark rope as his wives clamber out carrying flat baskets of headless smoked monkeys. Their faces are split by blue scars down the forehead and nose.

The man has come to barter hippo ivory earrings for cigarettes and a Chinese fishing net. In the flat bottom of his canoe a fire smoulders under a clay pot full of red palm oil.

Orlando appears on the next barge and leaps the gap, plugged with water hyacinth, refuse and a dead pig.

"What's the joke, Joe?"

"Smiling keeps me cool," says Joseph nonchalantly, sweat dripping from his chin.

"I've given Oscar a nice wash and mended his tail with Elastoplast." Oscar was Orlando's tenth birthday present, a crocodile bought for £3. He died the next day and became stew.

"As it's Orlando's birthday, I need another beer," exclaims André, the resident nurse. Any excuse to cadge a drink. The barman tosses the notes into a pile in his fridge. Inflation has made them worth as little as ½p.

André has just delivered the third baby this week. He says he loves me. Well, not just me: he loves all white women. If I won't divorce Charlie, can he marry Daisy?

"But she is only eleven years old."

"Never mind. How much is she?"

To emphasise her beauty and intelligence, I quote a ridiculous price.

"O, she is expensive, but I will pay in instalments."

"She won't be ready for ten years."

"I can wait. But she must be a virgin. Is she?"

Charlie rejoins the shouted conversation in pidgin French and Lingala.

We glide past islands with huts on stilts and waving people. Each island bears a white arrow to show the way, but the riverbed changes continuously and new channels have to be navigated each trip.

Talk turns to the night before when we were woken as the convoy hit a sandbank with such force that the steel cables holding it together were torn loose. The leading barge was tilted at right angles and the rest floated gently apart. Bollards, decks and railings were ripped up. By morning we were on our way again.

"C'mon, let's get food," says Orlando.

In single file we push past traders ranged along the narrow decks. They sell everything from expired penicillin injections, pirated cassettes and old clothes to skin lightening creams – "As Used by Top American Society". It had taken three days for the anarchy of two thousand Zaïrois to transform themselves into an organised travelling market.

Eliki, a disabled dwarf, sells old copies of *Jane's Defense Weekly* and *Merseyside Trade Annual*. His wide chest tapers to a minuscule waist and spindly useless legs. Every morning he runs along the deck upside down on his hands.

We climb the slippery metal stairs to our cabin on the upper deck. On the roof of the next barge is a group huddled round a radio, cheering a football match in Kinshasa, five hundred miles downstream. It reminds us that today is a Sunday.

Daisy is having her long golden hair plaited by giggling young women. They are fascinated by it and she is picking up French fast, compensating for five months out of school.

I step over tiny children drawing with their fingers in spit on the rusty floor outside our cabin. They are not allowed out of this dark passage, in case they fall overboard.

No light and little ventilation penetrate our tiny cabin. The aroma of drying fish hangs heavily and it is stifling. Cockroaches scuttle under the narrow bunks. I grope for the saucepans and our meal tickets. The £40 fare includes one meal a day for fourteen days, regardless of when we arrive at Kisangani. The last trip took forty days, by which time a dozen people had died of hunger.

Across the passage Titi is cooking sliced green lizard with chillies. It tastes like chicken. Her fine features recall the Arab slave trade, long before the Belgians came. President Mobutu's face nods on her behind as she pounds plantain in an ebony mortar and then slices the yellow dough with cotton thread.

Kofi, her husband, has done well in four years of selling plastic shoes on the river. Their cabin is a shining example of conspicuous consumption – fridge, light, fans and two ghetto-blasters. Beautiful Titi is his prize possession. In the next candlelit cabin four men sit round a trunk of loose pills, carefully arranging coloured antibiotics in tubes of cellophane. One has a withered leg from polio.

The meal queue winds its way around the upper deck between trunks, sacks of salt and dozing traders. Many people have succumbed to torpor after a week's heavy drinking. They sit staring at the sunlight reflected off the monotonous river.

Pinching our children gives rise to brief entertainment, especially when the children yell abuse in retaliation.

An enormous old woman spills over a fold-up chair. Her watermelon breasts rest heavily on her lap and her cleavage starts where other women have a navel.

"Do you think the crane lifted her on at Kinshasa?" whispers Joseph. She returns his toothless smile and waves as graciously as the Queen.

Four boys pose for a polaroid wearing eye-shades advertising Mercedes-Benz. One enhances his image with the photographer's watch. A fisherman passes, dragging a child-sized fish. Its blue eyes swivel sadly and its red gills flap in terminal gasps. Rust, mud and bottle-tops cling to its gleaming grey scales. It, too, is hauled into the picture while the fisherman is bargaining with the *"chef du barge"*. The camera flashes and everyone applauds. A price is settled and the fish is pushed back down the stairs, flumpity, flump, bump. The photo appears, the boys standing drunkenly at an angle, inert and bleached, the fish in darkness. ·

I hand our saucepans and tickets through a hatch and shout *"Cinq!"* into the cavernous kitchen, manned by ten Brueghel-fat women. The giant pots rest on wheel-rims glowing with charcoal.

At another hatch an arm appears holding up bright enamel bowls and someone dashes forward to claim the grey cassava and fishheads. We can afford to supplement our diet with pineapples and crunchy caterpillar kebabs from the fishermen, tinned milk and plenty of beer–cheap and cold. The bread on sale is hard and green, though the same price as a week ago.

Tied to the railings are crocodiles of all lengths, turtles craning their long necks towards the water and two thieves – their heads shaved in asymmetrical patterns. They will be handed over at the next town in two days.

We eat our meal watching a hundred canoes drift downstream into a blue and gold sunset, to their villages five miles across the river. Young men leap past us from the roof above, splashing into the water to catch up with their canoes, beer bottles held aloft. Standing to paddle, the fishermen are extended by their reflections and appear to be walking on the water on wavering stilts, their long paddles a second leg.

Strings of paraffin lamps gleam along the upper decks and dance in the inky water. Ahead of us lightning flashes in the navy clouds.

Yes, you were right, Mr Greene, and there are another eight days until we reach the "Bend in the River" and the centre of the African equatorial rain forest.

PAUL HARVEY

# SPRINGTIME FOR CZECHOSLOVAKIA

Irena lived in a late-Seventies block of flats on the edge of town, half a mile from the Russian barracks, part of an ugly outer-urban sprawl. After buying me lunch in a new concrete hotel called, romantically, The Interflora, she drove me back at high Skoda speed through the centre of town – choke full out, engine howling in second gear as we skidded across wet cobblestones, clipping kerbs and narrowly avoiding the numerous potholes and dug-up sections where slow attempts were being made to repair the water mains, shattered by the minus-twenty-five February temperatures. The only vehicles Irena took any notice of were the thin double trams, locked inscrutably into their own system, clanging their way up and down the narrow streets making unmistakable tram noises. Saturday afternoon shoppers shared the pavements with soldiers in iron-grey overcoats wandering about in twos and threes.

"You can tell the difference by their boots," Irena told me before I'd had a chance to ask the question. Some of the Russian soldiers (pull-on boots, no laces) looked Mongolian and very young.

"We hate them," she remarked casually.

Olomouc, former capital of Moravia and reputed to be Czechoslovakia's second most interesting city, doesn't look its best in mid-March. The botanical gardens are bare and there are few signs of the famous flower festival exhibitions in the cold grey wet transition between winter and spring: on the four days I was there it rained every day, finally removing the last traces of soot-encrusted snow from the pavements but leaving everything streaked with a post-winter dampness. Even the drainpipes, clinging half-heartedly to cracked walls and rusty gutters, looked as if they'd had enough.

The Gothic and Baroque buildings in the centre of town seemed somehow to reflect the gloom with their peeling plaster and crumbling façades: a once-proud city of towers and spires, balconies, alleys and doorways, with the university – a jumbled collection of yellow buildings and small courtyards – standing on a rock above the River Morava gazing severely down on a gold-domed Russian Orthodox church, now boarded up, its green roof tiles slipped and broken. Everyone I met kept apologising for the shabby state of the buildings and I had the feeling that if I went back in ten years' time it would look like the set for some grand-scale horror film, all broken banging shutters and cobwebbed windows. I tried to explain to Irena that I didn't mind, that this was how I felt it *should* be – the real Central Europe – and anyway I preferred that kind of place to ordered museums and shining monuments. She gazed at me with ice-blue eyes and murmured, "I see."

Olomouc is full of churches, huge and chillingly ornate, freezing inside and – as far as I could see – deserted during the week. Our Lady of the Snows was full of gilded pouting angels, but despite the heavy rain I was the only visitor, devout or otherwise. St Michael's Church – "a gem of Baroque Moravian architecture" – was firmly shut and St Wenceslas Cathedral, founded in 1109 and rebuilt at the end of the last century on a vast neo-Gothic scale, was dark, impressive and so cold inside it made your head ache. In front of the church of St Maurice I met Lenka, a music student who had promised to show me what she described as "the biggest organ in Central Europe", all 2,311 pipes of it, the largest more than thirty feet tall, the smallest eight millimetres of solid silver. Built in the 1740s and housed in the only remaining Gothic interior in the city, it's now electronically operated and can imitate anything from bagpipes to a brass band. Lenka adjusted her fur coat, blew on her hands, opened it up and let rip: the noise nearly blew me off the balcony, a stupendous megalomaniac combination of centuries of Bach fugues and the Incredible Dr Phibes. She said it had taken her seven years to learn to play it, and the only problem was when there was a power cut. That and the temperature during the winter.

Irena took an unofficial day off work and we wandered through the damp streets while she told me about being a student at Palacky University in 1968 (and what happened afterwards: "It is strange how the history books of a country can change, isn't it?"). Two soldiers (lace-up boots) were taking photos of their girlfriends in Peace Square, also known – at various times in its turbulent career – as Lenin Square and Hitler Square. Hiding from the rain in a smoky bar we missed the twelve o'clock chiming of the Town Hall clock. The original sixteenth-century clock was badly damaged in 1945 and has been restored, somewhat incongruously, with mosaic figures of model socialist workers.

"I am glad we are late," Irena growled. "Look at them, they are ridiculous."

Opposite the clock, angels and bishops stare moodily down from the Holy Trinity Column in what is now the middle of Red Army Square.

As a change from wet feet and sightseeing I was smuggled into an

English-language class where we drank home-made slivovitz and one
of the students, a lugubrious-looking individual called Miroslav who
played the bassoon in the Moravia Philharmonic Orchestra, invited
me to a concert the following evening. Irena produced a suit from
somewhere – I had nothing appropriate to wear and the Czechs dress
up to go out – and on a cold wet evening Miroslav, who once behind
his bassoon couldn't stop smiling, dragged me in off Red Army
Square where I'd been waiting under an umbrella watching a group of
Czech soldiers trying to stand up, and escorted me up to the balcony of
the Fucik Hall to watch the performance. He was wearing immaculate
white tie and tails and the cloakroom lady kept shaking my hand and
shouting "Welcome!". Irena arrived looking stunning, and the entire
audience spent the interval walking about studying each others'
clothes.

Olomouc has a population of about a hundred thousand but it's a
small town: I kept bumping into people I'd already met, and Irena
appeared to know everybody.

"It is necessary to have connections, you do not understand," she
told me when I remarked on the fact, though even the normally impassive Czechs leapt to their feet and gallantly opened doors for her at
every available opportunity. In the Post Office while I was trying to
phone Prague, Irena was getting free phone calls in exchange for cor-
recting a German text for the manager, and when we went to a book-
shop she had a friend who sold her books at half price.

The morning I was due to leave – the day Chernenko died – I woke
up to the sound of Russian troops singing marching songs from the
nearby barracks. On the radio the Voice of Moscow was retelling their
fifty per cent of the story of the Vietnam war, and every half-hour or
so large green helicopters flew overhead as they did every day.
Nobody I saw in the streets ever looked up.

Irena drove me to the station, past the monastery that is now a
military hospital, along the main road north where tanks rumble
across at night. We flew round corners and bounced over cobbled
junctions, ignoring traffic lights and scattering innocent pedestrians,
speeding through puddles and swerving to avoid the steaming man-
hole covers. As we parked outside the station Irena reversed into a
1964 Mark One Cortina, crushing a wing.

"Never mind," she purred, "it is not important. I know the director
of the insurance company. They are all bastards."

She kissed me and wouldn't let me pay for the ticket. It was still
raining.

The train going west to Prague was empty and unheated, and
arrived two hours late at a different station; but the weather in
Bohemia was a few days ahead of Olomouc and the capital was clear
and bright. Springtime for Czechoslovakia . . .

DAVID GODOLPHIN

# In Pursuit of the American Dream

"Kis mah grits," said the waitress, conversing with a regular customer as she served me up a 99-cent breakfast in the diner at Orlando Airport.

I was frequently to hear Americans exhorted to kiss each other's fried porridge, in a parody that seems to be the last legacy of the Southerner who occupied the White House in the dark days before Ronald Reagan. Kissing grits has supplanted the fashion for kissing ass, which is surprising in an upwardly mobile society.

An hour later I was drinking (what else?) Florida orange-juice beside a motel swimming pool while the early-morning sun gently warmed away jet-lag. The lady on a nearby lounger ordered the waiter to put a slug in her juice.

"I always have screwdrivers for breakfast," she confided to me by way of introduction. A strawberry blonde, she wore a two-tone lilac bikini over tanned cellulite. She was close to seventy years old. "Join me," she invited, or possibly commanded. I joined her.

She was from San Bernardino, I learned, visiting her son in Orlando. She stayed at the motel because "my daughter-in-law is a twenny-fower-carat bitch who makes Joan Collins look like Miss Ellie".

We talked travel. She loved Paris. The Pompidou Centre has more class than the "Louver". The metro is so quaint, and the shops around the Shamps Ulysses are almost as good as those in Palm Beach or Beverly Hills.

She had done "Iddaly" but did not share my passion. Rome is badly in need of renovating. They should widen the streets of Florence and landfill some of Venice's canals to put in a subway sytstem.

Conversation turned to politics. Jimmy Carter had been pathetic but she couldn't support Reagan because of his policies on social security. She described herself as a "liberal conservative" and plainly warmed to my reminiscences of the Edward Heath administration.

Lunch in the motel's coffee shop – fresh melon, lobster salad, ice cream – cost a little over five dollars. My single room, with a bed designed for Bob and Carol and Ted and Alice, was twenty-eight dollars a night. Notwithstanding a pernicious exchange rate, Florida is cheap.

Superficially, Orlando resembles Crawley or Milton Keynes, except that there are palm trees and no hills. The climate has plainly been modelled on the Garden of Eden. Florida is beautiful.

The people are bronzed, fit, not young but still active, and candid. My neighbour at the luncheon counter boasted equally of his golf handicap, a part-time job as superintendent of a condominium to supplement his pension, and three full-time girlfriends. He was sixty-four; the youngest of his girlfriends was fifty-seven.

Florida is bracing.

The epitome of the American Dream, in pursuit of which I had, after all, braved the airways over the Atlantic, can be experienced at Walt Disney World, an exercise in total fantasy expertly stage-managed with scarcely an ugly glimpse of how anything works.

As well as all the souped-up funfair attractions designed to impose new limits of endurance on your stomach, there are mechanised pageants which glorify the past, present and future achievements of the land God gave to Mammon.

A cinema with a 360-degree screen affords an enveloping thirty-minute tour of the US, climaxed by a swoop across the Hudson River at twilight. Before you rise the towers of Manhattan, behind you Liberty bears her torch in the gathering darkness. A choir, in the style of the Ray Conniff chorus, sings *God Bless America*, and in the breathtaking splendour of the moment you are sure that He does.

On my last evening in Florida, after six gruelling days pursuing the American Dream from Disney World to Sea World, Epcot, Cape Canaveral, two waxwork museums and an alligator farm, I chanced to dine in my first Stateside McDonald's. A couple from Texas shared my table. Inevitably, we ended up talking politics.

The husband, a grizzled caricature of LBJ, was a staunch supporter of the latest elderly cowboy on Pennsylvania Avenue. He had a favourite word with which I hesitate to soil the pages of *The Sunday Times*, but in his opinion Jimmy Carter had it between the ears and Ronnie Reagan is gonna drop it in large amounts on the Eye-ranians and the Commie Dagoes and anybody else who tries to put one over the US of A.

"Am I right?" he asked his wife in conclusion, "or am I right?" His wife nodded unenthusiastically.

I ventured to express nostalgia for the Kennedy era, the "New Camelot", when I, like many Britons, believed we were at the dawn of a second Renaissance.

The Texan heard me out. Then:

"Crap on the Kennedys," he said vehemently. "And crap on the Pope," he added, for good measure.

In my taxi next morning, en route to the airport, the driver's girlfriend, a big, black, breezy hooker from Carter country, suggested from the front seat:

"Honey, whah don't Ah clahmb over an' sit theyuh in back with you-all?"

"My dear," I told her, "you can kiss my grits."

DAVID HAY JONES

# KEBNEKAISE MOUNTAIN STATION

Three of us got off the train at Abisko in the mountains of Swedish Lapland: two men and a dog. I sat on my rucksack while the dog and his friend strolled over to the station building. When they were out of sight I stood up, glanced at my map and took a compass reading. It's difficult to look confident in the mountains, so I always check map readings when there's no-one to question my judgment.

I was going to walk south through Lapporten to Kebnekaise – Sweden's highest mountain, 7,000 feet above sea level – and on to Nikkaluotka, a Lapp settlement by a beautiful ribbon lake. If the weather was good, it would take about a week. If not, I told myself that ten days would do.

Abisko is 200 miles north of the Arctic Circle on the line to Narvik in Norway. It sees plenty of trains, carrying iron from Kiruna and Gallivare, but not many people – just a handful of Lapps and mountaineers, and a dog or two.

In early summer Abisko's lake, Abiskojaure, is still frozen and the high ground is covered in snow. The sky is a crisp, clear blue. The mountains are darker. This far north the snowline is low at 3,500 feet.

I was travelling in the second week of June to take advantage of the midnight sun. If you walk at night, the snow is harder, enabling you to cover five extra miles each day. In June it's best to avoid the valleys because the thaw is well under way. Rivers burst their banks, carrying snow and ice until it melts. Walking in the valleys means days spent wading through water and melting snow. I choose to climb up to the mountain sides and beat a path with my ice axe, only coming down to the valleys to sleep. At this time of year you can walk for a week without meeting anyone. I like that, and rarely use the marked tracks that scar some valleys in Lapland.

When you walk south from Abisko, the obvious landmark to aim for is Lapporten, gateway to the Lapps. It's haunted by trolls and must be treated with respect. Lapporten's bleak mountain walls and lifeless valley floor don't encourage you to stay. A nod of respect, head down and keep walking, that's how Lapporten should be treated.

The climb up is simple but hard work. First there's a slog through a jungle of birch and willow trees. Look out for a walking stick here – a sturdy birch branch that will help you on loose rocks or in deep snow.

It's important to talk to yourself, coax yourself. Talk aloud about the sort of walking stick you want to cut, or what you're going to eat later in the day. Pick on an easy song and chant it over and over again in time with your walking. It numbs the pain of aching legs. When you lose sight of the railway line and the station, the loneliness hits you. Keep your mind busy. Never sit around for too long doing nothing. When you stop walking, pitch the tent immediately, take some photographs, collect firewood – if there is any.

Ritual in the mountains can save your life. The tent is put up in the same way each day. This has a practical value, too. If it's dark, or you are cold and wet, you can get inside the tent quickly and forget about the mountains. The thin sheet of canvas makes loneliness easier to bear. It breaks the silence. I love the hiss of the gas fire and the orange glow inside the tent. For a while you can forget the nagging feeling of uncertainty that follows you on each solo trip.

Mountaineers make poor philosophers. They romanticise danger and like to be afraid because it makes them cautious. Only a stupid few are prepared to forget commitments to their team members and friends and family at home. When you are in control you can sleep well. I dream about fresh food. I can taste the meat. I can feel its texture. The fruit juice is sliding down my throat.

From Lapporten to Kebnekaise the snow was deeper than I expected. One night, fighting hard to get out of the valley, I waded for three hours up to my waist in snow. One leg forward – rest – push – second leg forward – rest – push. I could feel the cold water inside my boots, which was fine as long as I kept moving. Anger follows tiredness – lashing out with my ice axe at snow that's too soft; cursing rocks that trip me up in mid-stream. All sorts of daft ideas seem sensible: throwing away my rucksack to lighten the load; eating all the food or feeding half of it to the lemmings; making snow shoes out of my walking stick and climbing rope.

I fell down a hole up to my ears in snow and just wanted to sleep. Only five minutes, I thought, then I'd be strong enough to carry on. Talk to yourself: "Yes, you can sleep, but only when you get out of this mess. Today it's soup . . . no, mashed potatoes and a tin of sardines . . . drinking chocolate and porridge . . . something special, but first get out of the snow."

The map said there was a Lapp hut about four miles away. If I walked without rest I could be there in two hours. I'd only stop for water and a chunk of chocolate every half-hour. Then I could sleep, make a fire, dry my clothes. If the hut was closed, I'd break in with my ice axe.

I could see the hut after I had walked for three hours. I fixed my sight on it, packed away the map and compass and pushed harder. There was smoke coming from the chimney. If it was another climber he'd let me sleep. A Lapp would probably tell me to sleep outside – and charge me the next morning. Perhaps I should offer him some food. What did I have to give him? Soya meat, packet soup, Oxo cubes, porridge – nothing worth having. I could pretend to be ill. I could try limping, say that I needed to rest for a while. Whatever he said, I was going to sit by his fire.

A man came running out of the hut to meet me. He was Danish and wasn't making a lot of sense. He looked tired and out of place. "Have you got any food?" he asked.

"Yes, why?"

"I've got nothing at all. I've eaten everything. Two days stuck here. The weather's been real shit."

"Is that a fire?" I asked, wanting to get inside.

"Sure. Come on in. I need someone to talk to."

It was soon clear that the man had no idea what he was doing. He shouldn't have been in the mountains. I asked him where his gear was. "Over there," he said, pointing to the corner of the room. There was a tiny rucksack, a summer sleeping bag and a pair of Wellington boots. "Is that all?" I asked.

"Shit man, I didn't expect this. I came straight down the path from Abisko. It was beautiful the first two days. Which way did you come?"

"Over the mountains through Lapporten."

"What was it like up there?"

"Cold and too much snow."

"Where are you going?"

"Kebnekaise."

"Can I join you?"

"I'm climbing. You haven't got the right stuff. You wouldn't like it."

"But I haven't got any food. You can't leave me here. I won't give you shit, man. Let me come."

I wasn't keen. I didn't trust him, so I offered some advice instead.

"Look, there's another hut thirty kilometres down the valley. If you keep high you should be able to make it in a day. Keep away from the rivers. Two days' walk from the hut there's Kebnekaise mountain station. You can buy some food there. I'll give you enough to eat for three days. I'll catch you at the hut. If you leave before I get there, write a note."

It was five in the morning. If he left at six, he'd probably reach the hut after twelve hours – six in the evening. That would give him time to cook, sleep and leave by six the following morning. I'd take about nine hours to reach the hut and planned to start walking at five in the evening. We should meet up.

He left as I was dozing off. I kept an eye open to check that he didn't steal my boots or food. Silly bugger, he should have stayed at home. I fell asleep.

The heat from the fire woke me at four. The air was so dry it tickled my throat. I got up and opened the window. It seemed fine outside: no sun, but no sign of a storm. The Dane wouldn't have far to walk now, and I doubted whether there would be much snow between him and the mountain station at the foot of Kebnekaise. I hoped the man had learnt his lesson.

An old reindeer trotted towards the hut. I watched as he nosed around near the rubbish bins and firewood, but I couldn't stay still enough and he was soon gone.

My clothes were dry and stank of burnt wood and sweat. I'd put them on later. It was warm enough to wander around in my underpants while I packed my rucksack and prepared a bowl of porridge. I'd be away by five. It promised to be a good evening's walk. I was strong and my shoulders had stopped aching from the fifty-pound rucksack.

Before leaving the hut I left a few packets of food behind. Someone might need them. For the first three hours I couldn't get into my stride. I was trying too hard to avoid getting my socks wet, and I hadn't put enough clothes on. Not wanting to stop and pull on an extra sweater I decided to walk faster. I couldn't think of a song to sing, though.

I can't remember the shape of the mountains, nor how the river flowed on the way to the second hut. There was a lot of snow and I thought of my advice to the Dane about keeping away from the river. All I cared about was to reach Kebnekaise quickly so that I could buy at least ten bars of chocolate. Only one brand would do: Marabou milk chocolate made in Sweden. I thought about the many kinds of chocolate bar I would be able to buy: fruit and nut; hazelnut; almond; nut chip; white chocolate. I ranked them so that I would know what to buy in case the shop had no milk chocolate. I wondered whether they sold fresh fruit. I fancied an orange. It was too much to expect them to have pineapples or mangoes, but they might have pineapple juice. By the time I saw the hut I had decided to buy a packet of blueberry soup, a carton of pineapple juice and a bar of almond chocolate. This hut was much bigger than the first one and could easily house five or six people. Perhaps the Dane had met some other climbers. That would have cheered him up.

The door was locked so I used my ice axe to prise open the window on the roof. There was no sign that anyone had been there recently: no ashes in the fire; no smell of cooking or sweaty clothes. There was plenty of chopped firewood in the corner of the room. The hut might have been empty for weeks or even months. I made some soup and went to bed.

As I predicted, the walk had taken me nine hours. I can't remember it as hard work but it must have been. The Dane had probably camped halfway, thinking me stupid to recommend a twelve-hour walk in one day. Many climbers say that five or six hours is enough. But the Dane was desperate to get out. He would arrive, I thought, while I was sleeping.

Because I didn't think there would be much snow between the hut and Kebnekaise (for the next day or two I wouldn't climb above 2,000 feet) I thought it would be no problem to walk during the day and enjoy some warm weather. I was prepared to wait until noon to see whether the Dane turned up. If he didn't, I'd tell the rescue services at Kebnekaise. He'd no longer be my responsibility then. I didn't fancy sending the rescuers out for nothing, and the Dane was quite likely to be wrapped snugly in his sleeping bag dreaming of roast beef, bottles of beer, or whatever he liked. Anyway, it was his own fault.

I must have been exhausted because I woke at three in the afternoon and just didn't feel like moving. I had a good excuse to stay in bed, and read the labels of my food packets. Up at five and away by six, I thought. The Dane didn't turn up.

I hate unreliable people. If the Dane showed his face I'd tell him to stop pissing people about. If you have an arrangement you stick to it, snow or no snow.

I was ready to leave at seven. Everything was packed and stacked against the wall of the hut. I was scribbling the man a note: "It looks like I got here first. I will tell the rescue people that I arranged to meet you but you didn't turn up. When you get to Kebnekaise tell them you're the missing man." I dated and timed the note and pinned it to the door.

I'd have to try to reach Kebnekaise in a day. It was thirty-eight kilometres away: fifteen hours' walk if I pushed hard. If I only stopped twice I might be able to do it in thirteen hours. The Dane could be dead by then. What was the alternative? I wasn't going to leave my rucksack behind and run to the mountain station. What if it started to rain or snow on me? No, the Dane would have to put up with it.

The walk was easy and I would have liked to have taken my time. I was right, there was very little snow on the ground and it made a huge difference to my mood to see some greenery and a river without ice. It made me want to finish the walk in twelve hours. I wanted to know how fast and for how long I could keep walking without rest. There's enormous pleasure to be had in stretching yourself despite fatigue and lack of food. I imagined that I was a reindeer covering the ground in graceful, bounding strides. Kebnekaise, no sweat. I'd show that bloody Dane. He'd had a head start and still he couldn't keep up. I was master of the mountains and couldn't be beaten. All I needed was Lapland water, a few cubes of chocolate and a tin of sardines. Kebnekaise mountain station, easy, easy.

Ten hours later I was leaning against the wall of one of the huts at Kebnekaise. My right leg had seized up and I couldn't bend it, nor could I sit down or walk about. The toes of my left foot felt like they were bleeding. The toenails had dug into the flesh. When I threw my rucksack off I was lifted a few feet into the air. I felt so light. I didn't want to eat, just rest and maybe sleep.

I didn't make myself very clear to the woman at the desk inside the hut. She thought I'd had an argument with my Danish friend and left him in the mountains. I tried again. This time she understood. Missing person near Kebnekaise. "It happens too often," she said. "Never travel alone. This isn't Switzerland, you know. You might have an accident and not see someone for two or three weeks." People were difficult to find in the snow, she said. I'd done my job and went away to pitch my tent.

Next day I'd walk the final leg to Nikkaluotka and catch the bus to Kiruna. I'd be back in Copenhagen in a couple of days. I wanted to get out.

The loneliness eats you. Only yesterday I'd sat reading the labels on my food. Why? Because it was the only contact I had with the world outside the mountains. Another week and I might well have gone loopy.

While I was having a wash outside the bus station in Nikkaluotka I heard a helicopter overhead. It landed a hundred yards away from me near the road. There was a body attached to the side – covered completely in a green blanket. I didn't want to look, but I needed to make sure it wasn't the Dane. The pilot was smoking a cigarette and tapping the road with the toe of his boot.

"Is someone ill?" I asked.

"Dead."

"Who is he?"

"Some Danish guy we found up near Kebnekaise. Poor bloke was stuck at the top of one of the mountains. I don't know what he was doing so high, but you can't tell these people."

I nodded. I was back in Copenhagen in two days. I have no plans to return to Lapland.

NICK KIRKE

# Boys' Own Expedition

The night is pitch black, the jungle floor sparkles with fireflies. Monkeys screech and monsoon rain thunders on tightly stretched groundsheets. I lie uncomfortable, anxious, within a mosquito net on a hammock. Slung in similar positions between other trees are Alexis (fourteen), Boo (ten) and Ben (ten). Though it's 2am, I know they will be awake and won't hear reassuring words, even if shouted. Eventually, to our relief, daylight emerges hazily through the jungle canopy. Date: August 15, 1985. Location: deep in primary jungle, Kota Tinggi, Malaya. Event: the climax of a 1,400-mile expedition in the Far East.

Having been in Singapore twenty years ago with the army, I had thought what a marvellous adventure playground Malaya would make for my two sons, Alexis and Nicholas (Boo). This Peter Pan and the Lost Boys fantasy became reality in 1985. Ben, a school chum, came to keep Boo company. The plan: fly to Singapore, buy food, hire a car, travel up the eastern Malayan coast to Thailand camping on beaches and in jungle, and return via the west coast arriving in Singapore eighteen days later. Kit to be supplemented by friend at 22 SAS and to include machetes, web belts, water bottles, hammocks, maps, paludrin, purification tablets, medical kit etc.

## August 1

Departure photograph and champagne send-off, Plymouth. Surrounded by piles of baggage which made nonsense of the 22-kilo allowance. Dressed in assortment of civilian/military clothing. Suddenly I feel nervous. Margaret (my wife) and Jane (Ben's mother) look at their children more lovingly than usual. A brave hoot and we're away!

A thirteen-hour flight, dumping of kit at our hotel and into the heart of bustling Singapore: Bugis Street. The only part that remains smelly, alive, exciting and Chinese.

Where are the transvestites? The children ogle at the street traders.

"Look at their black teeth," says Boo. No transvestites, but pirate tapes at 50p each tempt us all. From this point we become the subject of constant, often amazed curiosity.

Difficulty hiring a car with a Malaya permit at such short notice. Purchased four bolted bars to make roof rack and some perished bungees. Canned food and cereals, burner fuel, bought locally, fit into boot leaving the four-man tent, two water jerry-cans and four back packs to put on the roof rack. Decided to keep a diary, writing a day in turn.

*August 4, Nick*
Johor Baharo customs, Singapore/Malaya.
"Which hotel will you be staying at, sir?"
"We're camping." Look of disbelief.
"Sir, people don't camp in Malaya. It's dangerous." A suspicious glance into the boot and at the enormous hump on the car roof and we are through. Mersing: palm-fringed bay. Erected tent for first time: went up a dream! Boys went swimming at dusk. Lost a beach ball and a flipper. Boo badly cut foot, Mustn't get irritated. Hot, humid; all being bitten by mosquitoes and giant red ants. Tent unbearably hot. Horrendous night for us all. Ben cries for his mother. They'll have to get used to dressing before going for a pee, closing the mozzy net, and undressing on return. I think the boys, especially Ben, will mature tremendously this trip.

*August 5, Alexis*
Woken by the wailings of a mosque through a mega-wattage microphone. Sat on a log and read *Pet Sematary* by Stephen King. Ben appeared naked, to be confronted by a car of inquisitive Malays. Embarrassed, he tried acting naturally, covering his bottom with one hand and his personals with another whilst beating a hasty retreat. Snorkelled, then breakfast when the new primus expired. Travelled on to find new camp site further north. Fabulous fishing cove. Supper beef stew. Started making raft with driftwood/bamboo. At dusk lit camp fire.

*August 6, Boo*
5am. Alexis and I re-kindled the fire. Large group of locals helped launch the raft which had a sail and was held together by paracord. Christened her Physicotic Hernia. After a swim we went exploring past lots of swamps searching for anaconda snakes and crocodiles. Discussed the army and jungle.

*August 7, Ben*
Went to buy eggs. On my return a Mongol boy was kicking coconut shells barefooted and throwing them at lizards. We gave him a mug and a tin of burnt spagehetti. Drove into Nensi. In 'Café' had ten Cokes,

six portions of chicken and four of bean sprouts. Wrote cards. Went on to Kuantan. Discovered we'd lost diaries and a camera. Had a better night's sleep on new airbeds. Talked about how far we were from England.

### August 8, Nick
In 1966 Kuantan was a small village. It's now a modern city. Camped within sight of five-star Hyatt Hotel. It's too tempting. We booked in the following night. Entered the foyer like a bunch of Kampuchian refugees. Dirty, unkempt, with not a case between us, but with me holding aloft my gold Amex card. The kids are soon cleaning themselves in the swimming pool, sipping iced orange from semi-submerged stools set in the water. Reminded Alexis it was his birthday two days earlier.

### August 9, Alexis
Woke in a cool, clean, comfortable bed. Nick complaining that I'd left a window open and a squadron of mozzies had attacked him. Loaded up, refilled jerry-cans and drove north towards Kuala Terenggau. Whilst pitching tent got caught in an incredible monsoon. Dark sky, violent winds, and the rain stung. Boo and I played with the locals in the sea. Long walk that evening into the town and drinks at the "Musik Bar". Dimly lit booths and full of Malayan ladies. We realised too late that this was a brothel. Boo and Ben very interested. Returned to the beach and collapsed.

### August 10, Boo
After forty miles, stopped to cook breakfast in bus shelter. Beef and scrambled eggs. Roof rack broken and lilos burst. On asking a man where to put our rubbish he pointed to the ground! At Kota Barharu Nick got car stuck in sand and Ben and I put up tent. Cracked coconuts with machetes and drank milk. Watched Everton beat Manchester United on television at roadside bar!

### August 11, Ben
Reached Thailand border where Nick had to put on long trousers before the officials would let us through. Travelled half around the world looking for Yala. Camped. Nick was watched by at least thirty grinning Thais as he burnt rice. A couple invited us into their house. What we call a shack they called a palace. The man played guitar and gave us tea and nasty cakes. Returning to the tent we fussed a bit, then went to sleep.

### August 12, Nick
Tent surrounded by Thais. Boo and Ben showing off like mad.

Prepared muesli, shaved. Alexis packed while Boo and Ben dismantled the tent. What a help they've become! Back into Malaya via Betong. Annoyingly, border guards charge us sixty baht each because it's the Thai Queen's birthday. Then an epic journey through Pinang and Ipoh to Kuala Lumpur in the rain, with large logging lorries overtaking our overladen vehicle. Too late to camp so we find a hotel. Though exhausted, boys are in great spirits.

*August 13, Alexis*
Continued south for our Jungle Adventure. During journey played many games: speaking for a minute without repetition, hesitation, etc. Boo and Ben made list of numbers of wheels on lorries. Camped by roadside near Gemas. Nick, Boo and Ben were invited to someone's house. I went off with a boy on his motorbike! He told me about Malaya and how lucky we were not to have been attacked by drug-crazed robbers, which is now a commonplace occurrence. He gave me biscuits and a leaflet.

*August 14, Boo*
Left early for Jungle Warfare School, Kota Tinggi. A Malayan sergeant called Nick "Sir"! Made him sign for a map. We went into the jungle and had to cross rivers over logs. I practically died of heat. Nick rationed water. Ben wanted to go back. Found a place to "basha up" (make camp), only just in time, because it monsooned. A monsoon is rain four times English rain. After supper of tinned Chinese duck on mostly bone, lay in the hammocks. Ben nearly put his hand on a snake. God what an uncomfortable, cold night.

*August 15, Ben*
Terrible night's sleep. Headed back to the waterfalls. Took ages to get through heavy undergrowth and up Lombong Hill. Lots of obstacles like fallen trees and "wait-a minute" creepers, a sort of bramble with fish-hooks. Nick got splinters in his hand hacking a path. When we got back we jumped into the water fully clothed, then we laid everything out to dry. That night we made an enormous fire. What a brilliant day!

*August 16, Nick*
Over the next four days we travelled back to Singapore where we visited Tiger Balm Gardens and the magnificent national zoo. Had a day's water-skiing and finished with a final fling in Bugis Street tape buying.

Most certainly a holiday we'll never forget, a daring adventure that paid off. The boys *did* mature, and so did I.

# TONY CROFTS

# Matanza

Six-thirty am. I'm already dressed and out of the couchette as the train slows to a halt in the darkness. Outside, nothing but gravel and a road on one side: on the other, the small halt with its sign *L'Hospitalet* and the bus waiting to bear us on the long winding climb, leaving behind an ever-lengthening panorama pierced with points of light. The snow stands in cliffs on the uphill side of the road, cut by snowploughs only hours before.

In Old Andorra, Peter is waiting with his Santana Land-Rover, and greets me heartily. Has there been a *matanza* yet? I ask. "There was one at Margarita's on Monday. I think there's another tomorrow at Mestre's," he answers.

Our goal is fourteen dizzying kilometres up into the Spanish Pyrenees. A community still living in an almost cashless economy, to a pattern already set in the fourteenth century. One of the last outposts of a peasant culture which is rapidly passing from the world, governed entirely by the seasons and depending little on manufactured inputs.

Their days, months and years move to the pace, and are sustained by, the products of their pigs, cattle, sheep, chickens and rabbits – which are, in a sense we have long forgotten, domestic animals.

It is those pigs which are the engine of the domestic economy. Bought as weaners in early spring, they are fed on kitchen scraps together with some bought-in meal; and in their pen below the kitchen are a living larder, evidence that the household will be able to feed itself in the following year. The climax of the year, and the time when next year's meat supply is laid down, comes in a hectic fortnight from Christmas Eve through into January, when the Festival of the Pig takes place. Or as the people themselves call it more plainly, *La Matanza*. The Killing.

Next morning, the appointed day, I find myself with the whole village, thirty-six people plus two generations of children and grandchildren who have come out from town for the occasion, gathered at the home of the mayor, whose *matanza* it is. Everyone has coffee, anisette, brandy, toasted bread and aioli for breakfast at 8 am. And then the work starts.

In the little square where three alleys meet, one man takes a spade and lifts away a few slabs of frozen snow, and makes sure the killing bench sits steady on its four short legs. It is a kind of long U split from the fork of two parallel branches, with legs drilled into their backs.

Up the steep alley beside the house, from the pens in the downhill basement, saunter the three pigs, with a neighbour, Cisco, shushing them from behind with a switch of scrumpled-up feed bags. They take their time, sniffing the stones and the muddy corners as if he wasn't there. Everyone stands round in a ring, closing the exits from the square between the houses. No-one hurries.

Andres, the slaughterman, has a long butcher's hook in his hand, about two feet long and sharpened at one end. The other end curves round the heel of his hand. He walks up to the first pig, hooks it through the jaw and drags it to the bench. The others all gather round to push it from behind, and then, once there, grab it by the legs and hump it up onto its side. The other two pigs continue their wayside investigations, taking no notice of the first one's screaming. Screaming like the brakes of a train. *Eeeee, eeeee.*

It doesn't stop as Andres put the broad-bladed knife into its neck and cuts the carotid artery. Margarita, the lady with the village telephone and the warm, kindly brown eyes, crouches with her bucket to catch the blood, whisking it to stop clots from forming. Andres opens the wound a little further so that it runs in a free jet. The pig carries on screaming, but its voice grows lower and softer. The men hold its jerking legs. The screaming is going to sleep.

In half a minute the bad dream is over, and it lies peaceful. Four sets of hands lift it across and lay it on a bed of arm-thick branches. Cisco brings half a bale of straw and covers the carcass reverently, as if tucking it up in bed, before putting his cigarette lighter to it. While it burns, filling the air with the smell of singeing hair, Margarita carries her bucket across to the steps by the front door of the house, where the owner's wife has placed a tin bath full of stale bread for black puddings. She pours in the blood and stirs with a big wooden spoon until all the bread is soaked. Andres hooks the second pig, and she follows back over with the bucket. The ash on the cigarette between the slaughterman's lips is barely a quarter-inch longer than before the first pig was taken.

Soon all three carcasses are lying on their stick pyres. Someone brings a long-spouted tin oil-jug full of alcohol, pouring a thin stream all over, drawing squiggly patterns of fire along the pig's side. The flames lick and join up, glimmering like brandy on a Christmas pudding. After that, water, and a scrape with an opened sardine can until all is smooth and clean.

Now Andres takes complete charge: he is the master butcher as well as the killer. The others merely wait on him like assistants in an operating theatre. As he works, others come to carry away each part as he frees it. A big bowl, large enough to bath a baby in, receives the entire coiled heap of intestines; the lungs and heart are bestowed like the Three Kings' gifts of gold, frankincense and myrrh, borne on open palms.

Men's and women's work is rigidly separated. The women take away and work the material, preparing the laborious transformation, while the men cut up and supply them. The ham is freed from the hip joint, lifted high and taken away; as much as a man can carry, ready for salting. Then the shoulder blade is freed and lifted out, cut away from the shoulder, the whole foreleg borne away likewise.

Twelve hams in a day, a year's meat supply. When cured, they will be hung in pillowcases in the airy upper rooms of the house; not cooked, but eaten raw. Fine Parma ham, the strong, resilient red meat beloved of peasants all over Europe.

Andres is working so fast that he is taking out slabs of meat more quickly than his workers can fetch them away. It is impossible to over-praise the skill and precision of his dissection. None of the crude chop-ping and sawing that our butchers do. Finally, all that is left is the pig's white waistcoat of backfat. Later in the week, this will be boiled up, together with any waste olive oil from the kitchen and some caustic soda from the pharmacy in town, to make soap.

Inside the house, the women have a long table set out. The town cousins are set there inexpertly to trim the meat off the bones, hand-ling their knives clumsily, hacking and scraping, piling up the trim-mings. Nothing will be wasted. To the left, at the sink, Pepita, one of the older women, is washing innards, dunking them in a big can of water. When she has finished she lays them aside and carries her can along past the toiling apprentices at the bone table, and empties it over the rail into the alley below. Beyond, the mountains can be seen, al-ways brooding, always protecting. The winter sunlight dazzles in, and as the stream of scarlet liquid falls, it glows like molten rubies. On the table, a complete spine is almost clean. Guisepp, the son of the house, picks it up and puts it over his shoulder like a small pet dinosaur to bear it up to the bedroom for storage. All the bones are kept and dried for soup stock.

There must be thirty-five people in the house now, all working in a scene of incredible industry: purposeful, concentrated, happy – yes, happy above all. It is, after all, a harvest time; and by tonight the whole harvest of a year's meat will have been gathered and stored. Now all the men sit at the table; the women wait, or eat standing out on the bal-cony. We start with thin soup, meat balls and elbow noodles; then plates of white beans followed by boiled mixed meats, with thin slices of liver and chops after that.

Salad – sliced tomato, red pepper and olive in oil and vinegar – comes before plates piled with biscuits, puffy and sugar-sprinkled. Then the meal is cleared, the table scrubbed, and two big mincers set up at opposite ends. This is the women's empire, and they range themselves all along each side. The task of mincing three whole pigs – all but their legs – and blending in onion, salt, herbs and spices to fill the carefully-washed guts, will stretch out into the evening.

Some sausages are boiled; others simply hung in the upper rooms to dry in the winter air. Treated that way, they will keep fresh and tasty, redolent of mountain herbs, until July or August. Giusepp carries a trayful of them upstairs to lay on a sheet on the floorboards for a while. Probably to the room that was his sister's before she married and moved to town. Today they seem to have no. bedrooms for sleeping in: only sausage-rooms and bone-rooms.

In between filling the gut casings with mince, little Miguel reaches up a hand and lets the moist trails of meat hanging out of the mincer rest in his palm, feeling it like a breast, squeezing it between his fingers, playing with it. No-one wants to stop him: he is experiencing food, the goodness of the land and its animals.

Drinks are brought round in a big pot, warm spiced wine ladled into glasses, so that all can quaff and refresh themselves. It is half past three, and everyone knows the work will not be finished until midnight. The numbers of people thin out, some come, some go, but several have gone off to feed or milk their animals. They will return later for the next phase, to relieve those toiling at the table. Everyone is tired, but all know the job must be finished before they can stop. Then we shall eat and drink together again.

And indeed, at midnight, we are all still sitting round the table, the mincers stripped for cleaning, the empty plates from a meal lying in front of us, the coffee cups being filled for the second time and the brandy bottle passed around. Little Miguel is prancing around in his grandfather's beret. He has picked up one of the mincer nozzles and holds it in his teeth like a trumpet. *"Pa para pa para,"* he goes. Time to celebrate.

## RICHARD POOLEY

# SHOOTING THE ZAMBESI

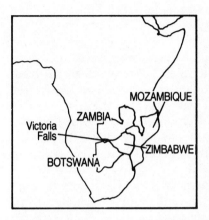

A white line still bisected the bridge, but its meaning had gone and the menace with it. Now the only sentry was a baboon sitting on a fence barking at a warthog on the other side of the road.

Early morning, sun up but cool, just two of us on the bridge at Victoria Falls, between Zimbabwe and Zambia. We looked down at the pale green Zambesi 300 feet below. Cecil Rhodes had wanted the bridge built close enough to the Falls to catch the spray. Usually it does. However, this was September and the "Falls" in front of us were just a curtain of rock. The rains had been good; not good enough, though, to make up for years of drought. Only on the Zimbabwean side did the river reach over and plunge in. Its noise was like distant motorway traffic.

We were about to go down the river on a rubber raft. We were to start at the bottom of the Falls and travel six miles down the Zambesi through zigzagging gorges . . . and over nine rapids. Why on earth had we agreed to it? Sarah didn't even like putting her head under water in the bath. As for me, the wake of a passing launch under a scull on the Thames was the nearest I'd ever got to white water.

"Triple A," the caricature Californian told our subdued party of eighteen outside the Zambian hotel. "A for scenery, A for excitement, and A for ease of access." Better than Omo. It took a little time before I realised he was talking about a river in Ethiopia. Through his organisation, Sobek, he seemed to have shot most of the world's rapids. "I'm Jib." His chin did indeed have a confident look about it. "Now let me tell you." The 'you' appeared to be a tiny seventy-year-old American woman. "The real danger is getting down on in there. That's where the legs get broken. The rapids is easy. And then there's the climb right on out at the other end. Five hundred feet straight right on up to the top." The lady was unimpressed by the string of prepositions.

"Ah did the Choler-ado end Ahm dooin this one."

So we clambered down to the whirlpool – the Boiling Pot – past the grinning curio sellers. "Hey! Buy now, madamsir. You are being too, too tired after Sobek, isn't it?"

A steep path through spray forest and then we were on to mossy boulders. Only one of us slipped. Me, twice. Collapse of the agile mountain man pose.

Our three rafts dangled over the water, small against the black cliffs. The river, a mile wide up there, squeezed into 150 yards down here. It objected to the constraint. We were all trying not to look at the first rapid, delicately yet furiously turning in on itself. I tightened my lifejacket for the fifth time.

"Okay!" Jib bellowed at us a couple of feet away. "No-one has to flip if they just remember a few basic rules." A twist of his flat hand showed what flipping meant. "All you gotta do is hold on hard to the rope around the side. And go where the wave is. If there's a wave hanging over you on the right side, then you throw yourself on that side. That's the *high* side. You gotta go for the *high* side! Okay?"

The high side. He'd shouted it as if it held the key to the meaning of life. I glanced at the rapid. Maybe it did.

In our raft were a middle-aged dentist from a Namibian diamond mine, his silent, teeth-baring wife, a thin and earnest German ("What is bail please?"), two perfectly mannered teenage sons of a senior Zambian official whose mountainous wife we had left behind at the hotel ("I'd sink it"), us and Jib.

We were last to cast away, but first through the rapid. Whatever happened to queuing? Why us? . . . Dentist and I threw ourselves half out of the bows to become a bouncing, double-headed figurehead. The waves swept over us; we came up, twisted, went under again, rammed the gorge side and finally got flicked out into the calm.

"Bail!"

The German was picking up English fast.

The water, very cold, sent up streams of bubbles. We shivered in the gorge's shadow. Above us was the bridge. Little figures lined the railings. As we waited for the others to come through, I thought of the first time I had crossed here, nineteen years before. Two armed soldiers had stood either side of that white line, three feet apart, both black, silent and avoiding each other's eyes. The next time, in 1971, the soldiers had moved back out of sight. The young white Rhodesian I'd passed on the bridge had told me not to bother trying to get into Zambia. "Bleddy munts, man . . . told me I was illegal!"

I was luckier. An immigration officer in Botswana had given me a full-page visa with "VSO" stamped all the way across it. It didn't mean anything but it opened every border. I had made sure, too, that no Rhodesian stamp sullied my passport; instead I got one on the back of a piece of cornflakes packet. Now there was still tedious form-filling. But the hostile line had moved on, "down south", to the Limpopo. The mighty Zambesi had become a tourist's plaything.

The next two rapids were similar to the first. We were all joining in the atavistic yell: "Hit the high side!"

Jib soon cut us down.

"Okay, guys. Now, the Real Thing. *Yoohaa* . . . Number Four!"

We could hear it. It was round the bend. Dentist's wife's rictus smile showed that we all were.

"Second Gorge," Dentist said. "That's where that Canadian girl got shot . . . by the Terrs." He glanced nervously at the half-caste Zambians. But they were staring hard at Number Four.

Sucked in and spat out, I still don't know how we avoided being liquidised. But the terror wasn't enough for Dentist. He had to tell his tale of murder. I nodded. Why bring up yesterday's war? Wasn't this exciting enough for him?

Number Five had us falling into a very deep hole, riding vertically along a wave called the Rooster Tail and bending so far that bow almost touched stern. At least, that's what Jib told us we had done.

Dentist decided to look around for rare falcons instead of guerrilla ghosts. Sarah began to feel that the bath-dipping had not really been adequate preparation. The German appeared to have been reduced to a fearful mute. Dentist wife kept on grinning. The half-castes sat on the raft side as if waiting for cucumber sandwiches to be served. And Jib rolled his words around the gorge and gave us a geology lesson.

A klipspringer buck leapt up an invisible path on the cliff face. Most of the others weren't interested: they wanted their lunch. I remembered the comments book in the self-catering lodge where we had stayed the previous two nights in Zimbabwe. A narrow strip of chopped grass and scrub leading down to the Zambesi had been the subject of a long-running dispute. Forget the bushbuck, baboons, vervet monkeys and warthogs that could be seen there. Instead:

"Why no lawn?" (a Brit.)

"Go back to the UK for your bloody lawns." (an Aussie)

"A *lawn* equals *civilisation*." (another Brit.)

Lunch came out of sealed containers together with the cameras. Some were eager to cut carrots and avocados. Others stared at the next rapid. The American lady sat down very gingerly on her patch of rock ledge and said little. A group of English students – "Coal not Dole" on their T-shirts – talked politics. "British politics are a sham by comparison with South Africa. They mean something down there."

Dentist looked disapproving.

Nobody flipped. We were all disappointed (provided it had been somebody else's raft, of course). The end was the slow toil up Jib's 500 feet – "straight up". Local carriers climbed steadily past us with oars, rafts and boxes. No hesitation, no pauses for breath, sweat runnelling down their backs. From the top we watched the progress of aged America. An hour to push and pull her up like some truculent donkey. But at the end: "Ah tol' you'all Ah cud do it. Just gimme time. Okay . . . why don' we'all do that agin?"

## SHEILA FOX

# NOT MEMSAHIB

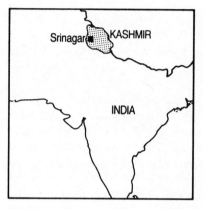

Every time I heard the word memsahib I wanted to take an ice-pick to the user. I'd gone on the Hindu trail clutching my libertarianism to my bosom, a cosy cocoon from which I could rationalise and contain the shrieks from the inferno – not that Dante, I'm sure, ever went to Calcutta. Very right-on. Very arm's-length. But keep your liberal sensibilities Gandhi-pure? Emerge unscathed? Forget it.

Sympathy, empathy, had long since given way to simmering hysteria, cringing shame and a seething, at times uncontrollable rage which was generalised in its target but oh so localised in its pain. It wasn't even a consolingly righteous anger at the pulverising poverty, the callousness of caste or the stalinisation of women – more a deep-seated disgust and hatred welling up from deep down and spewing out over all humanity, most of all myself... Well, OK, you try and make sense of the matchstick people of Madhya Pradesh, the execrable excrement of Bombay and Dehli, the obscene opulence of Jaipur jewellers, the blinding, vivid hues of Rajasthani women's skirts – and all of it sinking in one great ubiquitous quicksand of suffocating, strangulating bureaucracy.

I arrived in Srinagar, Kashmir's tourist paradise, demented and not exactly in holiday mood.

"J and K Palace" houseboat was where my companion and I were headed – on the bizarre recommendation of an English couple encountered on a camel in the Great Thar Desert. I asked one of the shikara boys to paddle us over – much to the incredulity and amusement of the whole Lake Dal Wild Bunch. Ten minutes later I could see their point. A forlorn and faded chicken shack that floated is what it looked like. Our arrival caused something of a tidal wave – hysterical joy and wild terror chasing hard on the heels of utter bewilderment. It took a good fifteen minutes of hard talking to convince Gulam, the youngest of three brothers and self-appointed front man, that he actually had paying guests on his hands. When the wonder of it had finally penetrated, he clasped us tearfully to his bosom and cucumber sandwiches appeared as if by magic. It was at this point that we entered the fantastical world of Rajarama through the looking-glass.

Coughing and spluttering as, with a flourish, he majestically whip-ped off the dust covers from forty years of unrequited Anglophilia, he ushered us into a faded English drawing-room, circa 1930, choked up with the solid, silent self-satisfied paraphernalia of the past. Here was one patch of water where the memsahib, evidently, still ruled the waves. And I was expected to fill the daunting doyenne's snug smug slippers. Terrific. Funnily enough, though, Gulam was never in danger of an ice-pick. Unlike the deeply distressing, scraping obsequi-ousness encountered along the road, his kow-towing to the Brits had been refined to an art form.

He was a chancer of the first order; a half-deaf alcoholic with the backside hanging off his trousers and the swagger of a screen idol. He had a languorous air about him, heavily tinged with the melodrama of the star-crossed. And, indeed, the gods did seem to have had it in for him. He was slowly drinking himself into a coma, an apparently ir-reversible process of disintegration triggered by the drowning of his beloved only son. Now he was the talk of the lake because he insisted on dressing up his little daughter as a boy. They could be seen everywhere together, he shooting his mouth off, she looking pained and wounded about the eyes – tattered, fractured Laurel and Hardy reflections shim-mering in the shikara-splintered waters of the lake . . . But he had charisma – and he loved the camera. There but for the grace of God walked Valentino. I quickly learned to make my financial transactions with Ali, the long-suffering middle brother, arch-pragmatist and solitary beacon of reason, moderation and the good old Moghul work ethic.

Ali was desperately trying to make a little money. Not an exorbitant ambition, surely. But as hard as he would bale out water in futile but ever-giggling attempts to keep the operation afloat, either Gulam or Abdul, the eldest brother, would lurch towards a mirage (alcoholic or metaphysical) and up-end the lot. The Marx Brothers, it seemed, were alive, well, drinking and kicking in Kashmir.

Except that Abdul didn't drink. He didn't eat much either. And he wasn't exactly a wow at social intercourse. He spent most of his time crouching gloomily behind three big black cooking pots whence came, every night, a magnificent feast, deep-frozen since Indepen-dence. It was absolutely pointless – more, it was a downright insult – to ask him to cook anything Indian. "Rubbish," as Gulam would say when, with flattened ears and shifting feet, we tentatively suggested that a curry might be nice for a change. "What you like? Roast duck? Roast chicken? Apple pie?" And so it would inexorably come, course after course, vegetable after vegetable, jam roly-poly after spotted dick. A miracle.

Ali normally waited on us with his usual no-nonsense aplomb during the (duck) soup, whereupon, on a good night, Gulam, fresh from his fourth bottle of gut-rot would lurch in, sweeping mediocrity in front of him like Dorothy Lamour's skirts scattered men, and brandishing a dirty napkin over one arm and an expression of pained patronising subservience. We had no choice but to comply. They expected us to play the Raj duet and, after all, it was the least we could do. And so it was that we'd sit like relics in that creaking, lugubrious dining-room, under the extravagant gaze of the gaudy plastic flowers, primly playing culinary cricket with Lady Bracknell – while outside . . . the mighty, barbaric Himalayas as a backdrop and the primeval shrieks of a suspected child molester, burned to death and then thrown in the lake, echoing in our ears. It was unhinging, to say the least. But I wouldn't have offended Abdul for the world – and the world, for him, was his English cooking.

He was the nearest I reckon I'll ever get to one of Gurdjieff's remarkable men. A fine tortured soul. The nights were often fractured by his wailing. He was a failed Sufi mystic, a marked man – one fatal Shakespearian character flaw, the gossips on the lake would have it, having led to a lifetime of spiritual flagellation. His nocturnal crying was a fearsome, heart-rending lament which still haunts me . . .

It was usually thrown into grotesque relief, however, by the pantomime which preceded it – to wit, normally a ding-dong of cataclysmic proportions if Gulam had drunk one bottle too many. Indeed, the cook first impaled himself on my memory during one of these fraternal fracas. Gulam was running amok with a burning log that night, stopping frequently to plead for my approbation regarding fratricide or, at the very least, boat-burning – when a supercilious, black, sooty face peered round the doorway and, with plummy BBC vowels, invited him to desist as he was "disturbing" the guests. And all the while Ali sobbed, drowning the sofa in his tears . . .

But things began to look up for "J and K Palace" – as I noticed on my return from a trip to stern and seductive Ladakh. Rowing out from the jetty long after dusk, it felt like I was coming home. But what was this? I saw the lightbulbs first, beckoning promiscuously where before there'd only been dark, deep, time-pocked sockets. Then the ebb and flow of contented murmurings. I boarded the boat to find, to my horror, that the plastic flowers had been replaced by real ones. And there were current copies of the *Times of India* on the coffee table. I felt cheated, abandoned and, yes, usurped by the new guests. I couldn't help it. I'd taken the brothers to my heart and, like a lover, I was sensitive to the smallest slight, the smallest indication that my moon was on the wane.

But, oh God, maybe this was just the memsahib bug sitting up and biting me at last. Maybe I'd simply grown to like being top dog – a Brit in a country which, maddeningly, still looks up to its one-time overload, however mediocre s/he was back home. From Simla to Bangalore the miracle of the nobodies into somebodies.

At any rate, I needn't have worried. I was greeted like a prodigal daughter. They're hanging on to the runaway rickshaw until the Return of the Memsahibs, you see. Abdul, in particular, is riding shotgun, in the firm conviction that the "London Government" is poised to regain the handlebars any moment now. And then we'll be back to the grand old days of bear-bagging in the mountains, gin slings on the veranda and telegrams across the lake. That's why he's keeping his English cooking on the boil and his white turban in the trunk. You never quite know when the call for crême caramel might come again.

Until then he'll have to make do with stragglers like me. I'm not exactly *Jewel in the Crown* material, he knows – but we can all pretend. There's no harm in that . . . Is there?

## FRANCIS R. GARDNER

# GETTING HIGH IN THE YEMEN

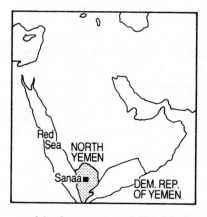

Question: how can you see London, Paris and New York simultaneously while sitting in a remote corner of the Arabian Peninsula? Answer: adopt the national pastime of North Yemen and devote the entire afternoon to chewing the narcotic *qat* leaf. Our host, his eyes dreamy and his cheeks bulging with the drug, rocks with laughter at his own joke.

We had landed that morning to find ourselves catapulted into a medieval Manhatten, a confusing world of centuries-old mud skyscrapers and lavish exteriors that make a mockery of the Middle Eastern practice of living behind blank façades. Resting in a secluded courtyard we watch a veiled face peer out from behind a half-opened shutter high up on a crumbling wall. A basket lowers itself to the ground from a distant rooftop. A train of three camels, loaded down with bundles of *qat*, squeezes through a tiny alleyway and lurches past the massive studded door of a mosque.

This atmosphere of the unreal is compounded by the costumes: a shaft of sunlight catches the billowing crimson robes of two completely veiled women as they emerge from a garden; a turbaned old man pauses in a doorway, his gnarled hands fingering the hilt of his dagger. This, we tell ourselves, is the Old Arabia, the Arabia that has already vanished from most Arab cities, to be replaced by tenement blocks, glass-fronted banks and supermarkets.

Round the corner roars a motorcycle driven by a seven-year-old with his two brothers on the back. In true Yemeni style every inch of surface on the machine has been decorated: there are panels of assorted mirrors, arrays of lights, swaying ostrich feathers, a horn that plays *Silent Night* and a radio that competes with the horn for sheer volume and distortion. This, we realise, is part of the New Arabia that has swept through Yemen since the mid-1970s, bringing television, motorcycles and bottled water to every village.

Sanaa, the capital, is full of surprises. From out of a mosque springs an eager young man, his eyes flashing beneath his pure white turban. "Does God exist?" he demands, pointing up into the sky. "Of course." "And did Muhammad exist?" "Beyond question." "And is

Muhammad the Prophet of God?" "Yes." He looks disappointed and retreats back inside the mosque. Later, the sight of a Yemen Air Force MiG–17 jet in a backstreet does not seem out of place. Complete with camouflage markings and undercarriage intact, it is neatly sandwiched between two buildings, partially blocking the entrance to a busy café.

The road from Sanaa to the Red Sea coast is an adventure in itself. With consummate skill the driver spins the bus round hairpin bends as we career through some of the wildest landscapes in Arabia. Plunging valleys bracket the road, sometimes disrupted by the vivid green of terraced crops, sometimes bordered by sheer drops of hundreds of feet. Spiralling down towards the coast, faces break out in perspiration as the temperature soars. Papaya groves and banana trees appear where before the road was lined with granite.

At sea level the heat becomes intense. The local architecture has shifted from flat roofs to conical thatch huts that would look more at home in Africa across the water. Within the space of an afternoon the change in scenery has been so dramatic that when we pass a road sign bearing simply an exclamation mark we feel that this applies to the whole of Yemen and not just to the bend in the road.

Heading south towards the coastal village of Khokha, we stop to eat at a wayside stall. A dark-skinned boy kneels down to put his arm into a clay oven in the ground and pulls out a smoking bundle wrapped in banana leaves. It is knuckle of goat, baking in hot ashes, and surprisingly good.

As in most countries, you change down a gear when on the coast. Here pelicans float between palm groves like obsolete airships, men sit cross-legged as they caulk their boats, and little stirs save for the flurry of elbows and lines as the day's catch of shark is brought in.

The town of Harad comes as an unpleasant shock. Being only a stone's throw from the Saudi border, the prices are exorbitant and we find ourselves forced into the cheapest hotel at twenty pounds a room. A thick layer of dust covers the soiled mattresses, the remains of discarded food fester behind the beds and the nearby lavatory is in a perpetual state of flood. We eat poorly that night and return to a shower room that is alive with cockroaches and a fan that ceases to function as the electricity is cut off. Bathed in sweat and troubled by scuttlings in the night, we sleep fitfully.

The following morning I try to convince the taxi drivers that a road which is marked on the official "tourist" map must exist. As the temperature tops a hundred degrees a dozen voices chant advice at me while oil-blackened fingers tug at my sleeve. "No, my friend, you must go back to Sanaa!" "You must go back to Hodeida." "Come this way and I will show you." "May God help you!"

We reach the mountaintop town of Hajjah in the cool of the evening after passing the burned-out hulk of an armoured car, a souvenir from the Civil War of the 1960s. Our first impression is that the inhabitants are pleasantly insane. Two venerable old men wander into the café, draw their daggers and execute a quaint little dance around our table. We applaud and one comes over to show us a coin in his hand; he then passes his other hand over it and the coin disappears completely. We look on perplexed as, feigning great solemnity, he blows his nose into his hand and out pops the coin from his nostril.

It is *qat*, of course, that sends the Yemenis slightly off the rails. Looking and tasting like a privet hedge, it is cultivated legally, sold in sprigs costing about five pounds each and chewed all afternoon by the vast majority of adult Yemenis. Only the tenderest leaves are plucked, and then they are crushed into a ball inside the cheek where they are sucked continually, producing a long and imaginative "high". "It makes me think I am driving an aeroplane," taxi drivers are fond of telling you as they hurtle past the wreckage of other vehicles that never made it.

At Saada, in the wild and barren north, we are awoken one morning by the crackle of gunfire. During the civil war it was from here that the Royalist rebels marched on the capital and, although ultimately defeated by the Republicans from the south, they were never wiped out. Almost every male, from ten-year-old to wizened shepherd, totes a machine-gun, loaded and cocked. Today it is the Eed Al Adha – an Islamic festival – and the gunfire is peaceful.

We drive north with Yemeni friends to indulge in a little weekend sport. A Yemeni shooting range has to be seen to be believed. Just off the road, in a natural bowl in the mountains, tribesmen cluster together on prominent boulders and blaze off in all directions while their children swim naked in a nearby stream, the bullets whining over their heads. Our friends open fire at a small crag and an irate farmer comes charging towards us, screaming insults. The bullets, he says, are ricocheting all around his farm.

Returning from Marib on our final excursion, we are stuck with a maniac driver who does not know the way. He plucks at his leaves of *qat*, he takes a swig of water, he selects a cigarette, a match, a cassette, he adjusts the wing mirror, combs his hair and spits out of the window – he will do anything, in fact, rather than look at the road while he is driving. At last we pull up at the military checkpoint outside the capital. The soldiers are searching the vehicles. "What for?" I ask. "Weapons," replies our driver with his pistol resting pertly on the dashboard.

The following morning we are on the way to the airport when it occurs to me that, like our taxi driver, Yemen seems uncertain of which course to follow. On the tarmac, glistening in the monsoon rain of August, Soviet-built troop helicopters are parked side by side with American-built jet fighters. In the departure lounge heavily-veiled wives queue behind their men, clutching jewel boxes; forty minutes later, as we swing out over the Red Sea coast, these paragons of modesty emerge from the toilets dressed for a night on the town. Skintight lurex trousers, fluorescent T-shirts and cascades of flashing jewellery. I look for smiles on the faces of their husbands but I find instead that familiar glazed look and a trace of foliage around the lips. For them, London has begun thirty thousand feet up in the air.

FENELLA BILLINGTON

# A MOST AUSPICIOUS STAR

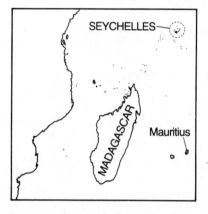

The double doors were stiff with salt from the sea, but I managed to pull them apart and, stepping out on to the beach, gazed at the familiar scene. It was not as I remembered it. The lagoon was oily calm, there was no breeze rustling through the palm trees, the sun had vanished and heavy clouds could be seen gathering on the horizon. There was no-one on the beach.

I felt tired, homesick and dispirited. The journey had been long, but I had been buoyed up with my eagerness to arrive, with excitement at the chance of fulfilling a dream. All I would need during this particular week of March was a clear sky. Now, thanks to the threatening approach of a cyclone named Honoraria, I had to face the sickening disappointment that my dream might not materialise.

From the air the island had seemed like a tiny emerald, nestling in the unfathomable blue of the Indian Ocean. It was all that remained of an extinct volcano and, because of its remoteness from the rest of the world, had housed, and still does, some unique species of animals, plants and birds. The large, slow, flightless dodo had lived here in peace for centuries, for there were no predators on the island. That is, until the advent of Man. Then the story changed for ever . . .

It had been my driver, beaming with pleasure at my arrival, who had first broken the news of the impending cyclone as we drove away from the teeming airport of Plaisance, along the rutted, winding, crowded road that led eventually to the hotel. My heart had given a little lurch. I had known the risk but had thought it was worth taking, for March it had to be. I tried to concentrate on the road, to put dismay out of my mind. It was not difficult. Everywhere one looked there was colour, brilliant in the hot, tropical sun. The Indian women, like butterflies in their dazzling saris, walking with languid grace along the road, waved and smiled as the car passed. So did the children, their deep, dark eyes lighting up with pleasure when I waved back. Luxuriant vegetation abounded, exotic flowers bloomed profusely and the air was hot and scented. It was so beautiful and, at that time, I was so happy to be back.

Later, as I stood alone on the beach outside my room, it was different. The weather had deteriorated alarmingly. Within an hour of my arrival the wind had steadily increased in strength, the palms were lashing their fronds and the rain had begun. Lightly at first, but gradually, through that first evening, the downpour became a liquid wall of water, relentless and torrential as only tropical rain can be.

It was soon impossible to venture into the corridor to walk to the main part of the hotel. I began to feel afraid. Wished I was back home in grey, dull, boring, safe England, instead of seven thousand miles away at the mercy of a force of nature over which there was no control, whose whims were unpredictable and whose reputation was awesome.

Notices were pushed under the doors announcing that Warning Two had been issued and that Warning Three was imminent. This last indicated that the cyclone would hit the island full square in all its fury.

To help pass that endless night, and the long, long day that followed it, I carefully recalled my two previous visits to Mauritius. Then there had been long, lazy days in the hot sunshine, and fun-filled evenings when I had not been alone. Laughter, friends and parties. Happiness and security. Different now. I remembered vividly the places we had visited: the sugar estates, with their romantic names such as Mon Tresor, Belle Vue and Beau Regard; the Pamplemousse Botanical Gardens where there are eighty-seven species of palm, including one specimen unique in the world; the mountainous, jungly Black River region; the bird sanctuary where the fabled pink pigeon is being so carefully nurtured for survival; Ile aux Cerfs, not far away – an idyllic little offshore islet surrounded by limpid turquoise water where one could laze all day in the sunshine . . .

There was a pounding on my door. It was two in the morning. I shot up, heart thumping thickly. A voice called urgently from the corridor, above the din of the storm.

"Missy, Boss say you come quick. Sea coming this way."

Feeling sick with fright, I left. Quickly. I followed the Indian to another room on the opposite side of the hotel on the upper floor. We had to fight our way there, bent double by the force of the wind. There I stayed for a further day, racked with fright and despairing that my once-in-a-lifetime opportunity was disappearing. For I had only one more day and, more to the point, one more night in which to achieve my ambition. After that, the chance would be lost for ever.

There was a book on the table describing the history of Mauritius and tracing its story up to Independence in 1968. It well illustrated the unusual aspects of this small volcanic rock, forty miles long by twenty miles wide, which teems with one-and-a-half million inhabitants. Ninety per cent of them are Indian, but important parts of the mix are the English and French influences that grew up through the historical seesaw as the island changed hands between the two warring nations. It was finally ceded to England after the defeat of Napoleon but was allowed to keep the French language, many place names and the French cuisine. Hence its present day charm, resulting from the successful marriage of three cultures.

As I read on, my desolation threatened to engulf me. My ebb was at its lowest.

As dawn should have been breaking, I suddenly became aware that the buffeting of the wind against the windows seemed to have lessened slightly, that the fury of the palm trees crashing around was abating. I waited and waited, scarcely daring to hope. By seven in the morning I was sure.

Suddenly I heard footsteps running along the passage. They stopped outside my room. Someone banged on the door, calling my name. When I wrenched it open, mind numb with the anticipation of horrors to come, it was the young manager of the hotel who stood there, panting, soaked through, and white-faced with the exhaustion of three nights without sleep.

To my amazement, he hugged me hard.

"Have you heard?" His shout was exultant. "Have you heard? It's changing direction. It's veering right off to the west and going flat out. It's going to miss us completely! It's all over!"

The relief was staggering, weakening. When I could speak, I managed to croak out the question that was uppermost in my mind.

"Is there any chance that the clouds will be gone by tonight? That the sky might be clear? What do you think? Oh, what do you think?"

He considered carefully, knowing only too well how much his answer would mean to me.

"Well, it's possible I suppose. Hard to say. I rather doubt it, I must admit. Cross your fingers."

I did.

During the day that followed I returned to my original room, people began emerging from their hiding places and life slowly came back to the hotel. Late that night, my last before I was due to fly home, I set my alarm for 4am. When it shrilled in my ear I was in a dead sleep and it took me a few seconds to recall why I had woken myself up at such an hour. I remembered.

I tugged open the stiff double doors and stepped cautiously out on to the beach, into total, inky blackness. The night was full of eerie noises. Palm trees crashed all around me, for the wind was still strong, and the sea thundered constantly out on the reef. I stood stock still for a long time, adjusting my eyes to the darkness. I hardly dared look at the sky for fear of what I might see. When I did, my heart pounding, I saw that the cloud had, for the most part, disappeared and that the stars were shining. I strained my eyes hungrily upwards for a glimpse of what I had come so far to see. I looked and looked.

Suddenly, the last thin wisps of cloud parted, and there it was – incredible, unmistakable, unforgettable; the ancient harbinger of doom, a portent, an augur; the cause of wonder and speculation through countless centuries of human observation; the sight that I would one day describe to my grandchildren, as yet unborn, who might, in their lifetime, witness the same. It seemed fuzzy when compared with the sparkling brilliant stars that surrounded it, but its huge tail, streaming away below it, was as spectacular as I had imagined . . .

Halley's Comet . . .

As I gazed and gazed, I wondered how the Earth would be on its next visit, and the next. It seemed benevolent, an object of wonder not fear. Was this the star that Prospero looked upon, as he too stood on a similar island, after a tempest had passed over? Could it have been this same apparition that moved him to say

> *I find my zenith doth depend upon*
> *A most auspicious star, whose influence*
> *If now I court not but omit, my fortunes*
> *Will ever after droop.*

A most auspicious star . . .

I gazed in wonder until the light from the rising sun robbed me of the sight.

Later that same day I flew home to England.

## ANDREW DINWOODIE

# FIVE DAYS IN GUINEA

DAY 1

During the night the rats stole my soap. A garrison of them lived beneath the floorboards and above the sagging, mildewed ceiling of my room. They swaggered about the place as though they owned it – which I suppose they did really: few people must have stayed in the old barrack-house since Nova Lamego ·was a beleaguered outpost of the Portuguese empire in Africa, surrounded by guerrilla-held bush, as the long war of liberation surged back and forth across the frontier with its neurotic Marxist neighbour, the People's Republic of Guinea.

I rubbed the sleep of history from my eyes and stepped outside into the present: nowadays Nova Lamego is the peaceful market town of Gabu, in the east of independent Guinea-Bissau, and a couple of battered old civilian vehicles wheeze across that frontier each week.

Blinking in the unwashed light of dawn, I located the formidable old Russian lorry that came close to my idea of the archetypal truck. It had one headlight missing and was blind in the other; sported a complete set of bald tyres, and was incontinent on all counts: punctured exhaust, cracked radiator, and oozing a fuse of oil and petrol whenever it moved – which wasn't for some time, as it took all morning to attract a full cargo of thirty passengers and their belongings.

I passed the torrid morning chatting with Hamidou Baldé, an elegantly-robed Guinean who had been working as an "agricultural agent" in Senegal. His ambition was to study at a school he'd heard of for private detectives in Brussels – apparently the best in the world. Hercule Poirot crossed my mind, but Hamidou wasn't looking for a new career: rather, he thought it was essential "to be aware of their methods in this modern world". There were many shadows still in Guinea, which until the revolution two years ago had supported a whole social class of professional informers.

Hamidou's wife sat apart from him throughout the long journey to come, and on the shady verandah of the shop where we waited in the market place. They rarely spoke, but shared the care of their small daughter and occasionally shy, warm smiles. We drank *kankolibá,* a local infusion of stewed whole leaves, which they referred to as "coffee" for my convenience.

I discovered I was at some geo-economic nodal point where the blackmarket values of three currencies coincided:

1 Guinea-Bisau Peso = 1Guinean Syli = 1 CFA Franc (= 0.2p).

The CFA Franc is one of the sanest things about travelling in West Africa. It's used in a dozen or more states throughout the continent, is convertible as it's tied to the French franc, and is a blessed relief from the perpetual casino of *marché noir* that prevails in most other countries. The ride to somewhere off the bottom of my map cost 1,500 of whatever I chose to pay in.

As I had arrived first I could claim a place in the cab, which can often be worth a five-hour wait: finally, at high noon, the laden truck lumbered out of Gabu. It managed a majestic 25kph in top gear. After an hour of rapid progress we turned off the tarmac and things got slower.

In the midday sun at the empty town of Pitché the mean men of the Guinea-Bissau customs went to work: *"Descendez tous les bagages!"* A lone cyclist and his kitbag were scrupulously searched ahead of us. They took twenty minutes over him alone, but detective Hamidou had deduced his real game, and we imagined him riding away sniggering, pedalling a smuggled cycle across the border and returning by truck each week.

Then the half-dozen officers, most of them wearing sinister Samuel Kanyon Doe-style sunglasses, turned their attentions to the rest of us, and waded through our scattered belongings like bargain-hunters at a jumble sale. They confiscated a few items of interest or value from unprotesting passengers, and collected the customary service charge from the driver.

Everything reloaded, we followed an inconspicuous track south. The lorry's engine laboured heartily. It felt like you could depend on that engine, however much the rest of the vehicle might leak and let you down, though all the gears except fourth seemed to grind their teeth sadistically against mine.

When secluded by a clump of trees, we heaved to a halt in a cloud of our own dust, whereupon most of the men leapt out and thrust bundles of CFA banknotes at the *chauffeur*. Trial and expensive error seemed to have shown this to be the safest strategy for entering Guinea with hard currency, as the Customs search very thoroughly and confiscate all *dévises:* the driver is the only person by custom never searched, since he has to carry assorted currencies to ply his trade, and anyway gives the *douaniers* good *argent de passage*.

The *chauffeur* collected the fistfuls of cash and issued carefully-worded duplicate receipts on scraps of paper, an elaborate transaction as most of the men seemed to be called Mamadou, Diallo, or in several cases both – the driver himself, for one. I reluctantly handed over a sealed envelope of French and CFA francs, sterling and dollars, and kept the pesos, dalasis and traveller's cheques to fend for themselves. I wondered whether it might have been a better bet to conceal it all somewhere in the truck, until I saw later how assiduously that was searched. The Mamadou Diallo we were entrusting our collective fortune to was a shrewd, stringly fellow in a thin safari suit: all his buttoned pockets now bulged extravagantly.

During this flurry of financial fervour the women sat calmly in the back of the truck and chatted over their sleeping and suckling babies, having concealed their money with the minimum of fuss.

At the border river a final fastidious Guinea-Bissauen official inscribed comprehensive details of identity cards and passports in a huge, historic, hidebound Portuguese ledger.

I sat in the shade of a Koliba tree until the rubber-stamping was finished. Then the broken cable-raft – which had once possessed the useful facility of a working winch – had to be tugged back from the Guinea bank 200 metres away across the tree-lined Kolibar River. The *bac* arrived bearing an irate, almost-naked old woman and three half-washed great-grandchildren she had lately been lathering in another country. They all leapt soapy and shrieking from the raft as the truck growled up the ramp. Most of the men gallantly hauled on the hawser to propel us across, while the Women's Institute assessed our efforts amongst themselves.

Up the steep bank on the Guinean side there was a cosy collection of wood, cane and thatched huts, warm and welcoming in the afternoon sunlight. The gendarmes harassed the other passengers while the commandant and his wife invited me to share their bowl of rice, vegetables and meat. When we'd finished I asked what we'd eaten, and he thoughtfully fetched the cute little bush-antelope's head in case I'd like a souvenir.

He demonstrated his juggling skill with four green oranges while he told me how much freer Guinea now was under the Second Republic: since his death, the tyrant Sekou Touré is seldom mentioned by name, but referred to obliquely as *"l'ancien régime"* or *"la République Populaire"* (with heavy sarcasm).

There were rigorous baggage, body and vehicle searches going on all around, but the commandant waved his men past my pack. He detailed one of the soldiers to take his prized Italian hunting-rifle – which had recently dispatched Bambi – and ride shotgun with us to the next village to fetch him his blue suit, a razor and any edible wildlife he came across on the way.

"Hey, *chauffeur!*" he called, "Did we remember to search you too?" Mamadou grinned conspiratorially and went on attending to his engine. His apprentice emerged from under the chassis – where he had been variously drenched while failing to staunch the flows from the broken radiator, oil leak and ruptured fuel pipe – and lit an heroic cigarette.

The track was rougher on this side of the river, and it was almost dark when we stopped for the night at the village of Foula Mori. There were more immigration formalities by the light of a kerosene wick in a beer bottle, which gleamed on the gendarme's cap badge and buttons as he stamped documents and entered particulars on sheets of graph paper torn from a child's exercise-book covered with Disney cartoon characters.

Beside a log fire, beneath a tree as tall as a cathedral, some of the village woman brought me a mat, blankets and pillows, and *kankolibá* in an old oil–can – probably a relic of one of Mamadou Diallo's previous transits.

As I fell asleep, someone strummed a *kora*, a transistor radio was announcing an astronomical devaluation of the Syli, and Orion straddled the heavens.

AIDEEN MOONEY

# A FAIR SHOW

Through Leinster and Munster, along Connaught lanes and highways there's a movement. Brazenly on verges, tucked behind hedges, parked in laybys there are caravans. Not tourists but the homes of the Irish Travellers, the Tinkers. Herds of their horses hold up the traffic. Greys, chestnuts, roans, bays and the especial pride, the batty mares: great coloured, patched horses, piebald and skewbald, hooves swathed in shaggy hair. They're all heading along roads which lead to the nub, the October fair, Ballinasloe. A convergence for horses and horsemanship, dealing and drinking, exchanging news and the "crack". "You'll never see as many horses together as you will at Ballinasloe. Once Seamus McGinty rode down the high street at the head of sixty, his sons as outriders flanking their wealth."

Beating hooves on the smooth tarmac. Sealed in our motor car we've drawn up behind a berserk cacophony of colour – buttercup, marigold, poppy, cornflower, peagreen and fuchsia burst out of the drear drizzle. A barrel top, horse-drawn waggon. Polished brasswork and picture panels of horses and dogs lurch and sway on their way. The grey-haired wife expertly handles the flat cart at a sharp trot.

"Charlie Donovan! I remember when I first met him. A wagon hurtling down the hill towards me. Out of control. Driverless? But when it was almost on top of me I saw a pair of boots on the footboard and then the rest of Charlie, flat on his back, reins in one hand, whip in the other, shouting the horse on. Dead drunk, laughing and roaring, off on a bender. Two miles behind was his wife, sedately on the flat cart piled high with their breakables, smiling, letting him have his fling."

Motoring down to the pub that evening, and there, in the gentle rain, beside the road, is his camp. The old man with his pipe squats by the fire. A blackened kettle hangs over the flames from an angled rod stuck into the ground. A chicken is tethered to a wheel of the cart by a piece of string knotted around its leg. A litter of terrier pups in a cardboard box. There is nothing modern, nothing plastic here. He sees no point in change, everything as it was, always has been. His wife's inside the waggon on the high back bunk. I get a glimpse when I greet her, the roof's lined with a patterned cotton fabric and a small wood-burning Queenie stove gives off a good heat. I'm catching the last moments of an era, sharing their fire, listening to the stories of an old-time traveller. "There was wance upon a time, and a very good time it was. Neither my time nor your time but somebody's time . . . " Embers fall, gold-vermillion. We accept a cup of heavily sugared tea. "Yes we'll be at the fair."

It was on the next day that we stood on the hill looking down on the crush. Sleek flanks, arched necks, powerful hindquarters, glossy and firm flesh. Whinnying and snorting; stamping hooves. I want to bury my head in a mane and remember childhood adventures of riding lessons. Horse and candyfloss in the breeze.

On the fairground there is a sharp division. One half is farmers and county. Fine-boned hunters with fine-boned riders in tight, white jodhpurs and long, black boots. Arrogant and upright on their proud animals; tight, white control. On the other side are the Traveller horses. "You'll never see a saddle at a Traveller fair." The young lads are equally as proud of their horsemanship. A slap on the arse, shouts of encouragement and the horse plunges through the crowd, a wave of people backing off before it. It's a matter of balance. They sit well back, tipped on the base of the spine, reins held high, legs loose. It's so easy, flowing with the horse in a mad hurtle, this is the way Travellers ride. Up down, up down, this is the way the Gentlemen ride.

The Travellers give a spirited display. That horse has good brakes! It stops short in a controlled skid, heads again into the crowd and pulls up two feet before a wall. Some pull light sulky traps, merely a tubular steel frame, and there are some alacritous and alarming turns in small spaces. The horse rears. There are people under the flailing legs. Hooves hit the ground and it races back. In the crowd, watching the show, keen eyes detect almost imperceptible faults. Heavy, dark tweed suits and intent, rough-hewn faces. They sweep you out of the way before a torrent of horse but you sense they'd get a thrill from any catastrophe. You creep behind the lines of tethered animals. Is that hoof cocked to kick?

A deal is being done over a dog. It hinges on the middleman. He's brought buyer and seller together and now steps into the spotlight nudging the punter up a few pounds, drawing the asking price down. The audience clusters closer, watching one intransigent face and then the other. Voluble, cajoling, seducing, the moving force of the negoti-ation, this middleman will persist until the deal is done. The asking price was a hundred pounds. Now there is stalemate at fifty and eighty. Notes emerge. Cash is pushed into the owner's hand. "Now that's all he has except for five pounds for petrol home." The lure of a handful of paper. Will he? There's a nod and a smile and the dog is passed over with one pound for change "for luck"; in accepting money you must always return some. A spit into the palm and a thwack of hands and the deal is ratified. The middleman relinquishes his role and relaxed, happy murmurs discuss the dog's heritage and abilities. The crowd smiles with genuine delight that a deal has been done.

Lips dip into foaming white and take deep draughts of black:

"You remember that mare I bought in the spring? She'll fetch a good price now. I knew she had the makings. For sure, that meadow she was in, she hadn't room to change her mind."

And, "I'm telling ye, brush the animal with sump oil and that'll keep the flies away".

By late afternoon, seeping from overflowing pubs, the men are at the height of inebriation. Growls of aggression rumble in corners. Every man has a stick. Trying to herd animals into a horsebox a dozen Travellers have created a frenzy of disorder. The creatures are taking a thrashing from the ash plants, hazel wands and lengths of plastic tubing. Then in a flash the herd have dashed free of the cordon of men. Fuel for mercurial rage. Explosion. Each man has turned upon his neighbour. Bash, thrash, wallop. Comic strip figures. Little dancing men from *Beano's* pages. An old character, watching, catches one of the animals by the head, steadies it, whispers in its ear, strokes its nose and the horse is calm. That's a fellow with a genuine understanding and communication with horses. He'd know all the old cures.

The cures, the stories, the old nomadic way of life. How soon until it's all lost? There are some people who are fanning the embers of this dying fire. They came over to Ireland as hippies in the sixties, seeking waggons to live out gypsy dreams. The Tinkers thought they were of one travelling family. On Irish roads there were the tribes each with their chief, the Danahas, McGinleys, Donovans, Connors, Clarkes . . . and now the Hippies. Many of the Irish Travellers adopted their long hairstyle, and hippies were respected for their dealing abilities and that they bred fine hunting dogs. Traveller girls lived with hippy men, and Tinker men lived in greedy expectation that they might share some of the hippy women who moved so easily from partner to partner.

Now the hippy waggons ring the campfire. Their shafts point inwards and become the spokes of a giant wheel with the fire as the hub. The hub of camp life. There's always a kettle on the boil, someone chopping vegetables for the pot. Take a place beside the fire and become part of the circle, the chat, the stories. In a circle we are strong. But this camp is only a pretty, antique button lost in a plethora of plastic and aluminium Traveller caravans. Some are lived in and some seem to be only for show. Strips of glittering chrome on the outside and lines of shining cooking pots and china inside. Pots and china reflected a thousand times, bedazzling in an interior panelled with mirrors.

A glowing fire is the only gleam amongst the muddy and soot-encrusted hippy utensils. Last night there was some unpleasant communication between the women of the two camps. An English girl, just over, some said she'd just been flirting, some a gang-bang with the Traveller men. Whatever, she'd broken a living code amongst the women, and to be fair, they came to warn her friends "get her out of here or she'll find a knife in her back". She went.

We went. It was raining and our windscreen wipers had been stolen.

# PAT PHOENIX DIED TODAY

"At Wimereux in August there is a Mussels Festival with flowered float parade and seafood tasting."

All the way over to Boulogne my son regaled me with snippets from the handouts they gave us at Folkstone. I scanned the coastline for Wimereux but all I saw for miles were topless sunbathers. I'll never have the nerve. Who wants burnt nipples anyway?

An Eastender with a ghetto-blaster swung the news at us as he patrolled the deck.

"Pat Phoenix, who is suffering from lung cancer, had a comfortable night."

People paid little attention to this as our ferry, *Hengist,* was negotiating the entrance to the harbour.

"Who was Hengist?" I asked my son.

"First King of Kent, invited by Vortigern to defend Britain," replied Matthew.

He packed his handouts away and put forward our watches.

Boulogne-sur-Mer! A 2CV buzzed by like a liver and cream wasp. A *boulanger* van honked dementedly after it. On the Quai Gambetta a courier in a red and white blazer waved a clipboard, gathering his flock for a coach trip, perhaps along the coast or for *shopportunités* at the Auchan hypermarket. His rosy cheeks, hooked nose and striped jacket lent him an air of Punch in a rare convivial mood.

The Orient Express was waiting too, a bit standoffishly, to receive its customers from England. Such ornate livery! Black and crimson and gold, it was very regal, rather like a packet of luxury Russian cigarettes laid out end to end.

"Like a cardboard model of itself," said Matthew.

Though very inviting, the restaurants were too dear for us so we looked for Place Dalton and its open market. Here we got baguettes, two slabs of runny Brie and mammoth Marmande tomatoes. Orange cans of Fanta and misty green bottles of beer *sans alcool* completed our feast. A man who sold nothing but biscuits pressed two broken custard-creams into our hands. They had layers of yellow and pink filling and left a sickly taste, a bit like dolly-mixtures.

We lugged our provisions up to the *haute ville,* which is the old medieval area of Boulogne. Virtually all the ships that lie within the ramparts here line the rue de Lille. At Nicholas and at Vins de France there were remarkable bargains, but we didn't avail ourselves. We stood in silence at Confiserie Bethouart where there was a ravishing window full of marzipan fruits and fish. It might have been a set for Hansel and Gretel – pineapples, pears, lush snails, herrings, seafoods, shells, even tins crammed with silvery marzipan sardines.

Though it was sunny, the streets around here were all but deserted. At the corner of rue de Lille we saw an old woman in a calico nightie, feeding pigeons at a ledge. She stood at an oriel window, crumbling yesterday's bread. Her expression was something to see as the birds came to rest on her gnarled hands. She started when she saw us and her birds vanished. I thought of Flaubert's *Félicité* and her *perroquet gigantesque.*

The medieval ramparts form a rectangle which encloses the *haute ville.* By the shallow steps here, well shaded by a horse-chestnut, sat a young mother. In one hand she held her magazine, *Marie-Claire,* and with the other she rocked her baby's pram lightly over the first fallen conkers on the gravel. Bent so attentively over what she was reading, she had the concentration and the stillness of a genre painting. The baby, far too plump for its pram, was smooth and shiny as a new croissant. On the bib of its rompers was its name – Hervé.

The ramparts contain seventeen towers and four gates. We lunched at *tour verte.* It was after twelve, a mild warm late summer day. On the lawn a few yards away a circle of nuns sat mending linen. One of them was reading to the others. Shrubs, sheltered by the sunny ramparts, blazed with blossoms – purple, violet, lavender blue. We rubbed bits in our hands to get the scent. It was peculiar, a lemony smell. Below us the town, the harbour and the vast calm channel stretched out peacefully.

"Julius Caesar used this area as a base for his invasion of Britain," Matthew informed me, swigging his beer *sans alcool.*

The ghetto-blaster fiend came puffing up to the *tour verte,* laden with iron saucepans, sets of crystal glasses and carrier-bags of duty-free, clearly tuned in still to the BBC.

"Children in Manchester are saying prayers today for Pat Phoenix. Her husband maintains a constant vigil at her bedside."

Evidently the news meant nothing to the nuns, though their eyes followed the noise reprovingly.

"Let's go and look at the Cathedral, Matt." The Cathédrale Notre-

Dame has a marble altar and a fine italianate dome. It was too cool for us inside but the spicy incense and the candles were seductive. We never got to see the recommended Norman Crypt, as they were about to start mass.

"Any idea where the toilets are?"

"Place Dalton and rue Nationale."

I went in some nettles behind the Cathedral as somebody went whistling by on the ramparts. I prayed he wouldn't look down.

The modern area of Boulogne, the *basse ville,* has largely been rebuilt after damage from Allied bombs. At Fromagerie Philippe Olivier we goggled at two hundred cheeses before coming away with a crusty triangle of Camembert, succulently steeped in local *calvados.* I ached in Nouvelles Galeries after two fine mannered figurines, evocative of *Les Enfants du Paradis.* One was a soubrette, pert and engaging as Garance, and the other a harlequin, naif and mournful as Baptiste. Though we lacked the nerve to enter Parfumerie Gilliocq, my son fixed me for ever in Polaroid there, before its glitzy pink façade.

"You said we could go to the mini-golf."

"You're the guide."

Beyond the harbour lay the little park where *les chiens doivent être tenus en laisse.* Sure enough, on the whole, they were. The mini-golf course was a model of the *haute ville* – castles, turrets, gables, lodges, a medieval landscape in miniature. Cedars and scented pines fringed this sandy area of the park. It was fresh and pleasant. Playing behind us on the course were an elderly French couple, reticent and watchful, like figurines in the shadowy corner of a Monet garden.

Once I hit the ball right over a turret and into the park. A terrier, not *en laisse,* ran up and chewed it.

"*C'est difficile n'est-ce-pas?*" said the old lady.

"You wally," said my son.

Refreshed by *citron pressé* we lingered in the park, at a café table, looking out to sea. In the late afternoon the harbour was smellier – stagnant water, fish, drains, diesel. A crane and a grain-elevator, angular and neat as Meccano, clanked away on the quai, while *la Liane,* a rusty grab-dredger, lunged tenaciously at the silty mud in the harbour.

Our ferry appeared far off, like a bath toy becalmed on the horizon. We made out the Union Jack, and later HORSA, LONDON.

"Horsa, brother of Hengist was eventually killed in battle."

The blue and yellow funnel was a squashed liquorice allsort, stamped into the deck by some giant.

"I am the salt of the earth," said Horsa, throbbing importantly towards Boulogne.

Longer shadows darkened our road back. On the side of a grain warehouse we passed a poster of a cat of Cyclopean proportions. It had elongated droopy whiskers and sad, sad eyes, round and green as gooseberries.

"*Ce soir y'a pas de Kit-e-kat,*" it complained hungrily.

A necklace of *frites* vans graced the Quai Gambetta now, anticipating the homeward-bound. We took away two newspaper cones full, splashing them with fruity brown sauce.

The final van sold peasanty soup bowls painted with yachts and sea-gulls. Names encircled the rims. I found *Cathérine* at once, but we had to dig deep for *Matthieu*.

"Why did you call me Matthew?"

"When you were inside me I followed *Roads to Freedom*. On BBC 2. I was nuts about Matthieu."

The bowls, meticulously wrapped for us in layers of flower-patterned tissue paper, saw the last of our francs.

The cliffs between Folkestone and Dover held on to the late sun. One by one watches were put back and last glasses of draught Stella balanced on the rails as people congregated for the arrival. As he swung the ghetto-blaster near us one last time, I saw how the French sun had reddened the back of his neck.

"Pat Phoenix, star for many years of the serial *Coronation Street,* died today in a Manchester hospital. The end came peacefully. Her husband was at her side."

"She was a real scorcher," he said.

"A belter," agreed Mr. Punch, blowing his hooked nose.

# THE CRAZY KUMBH

It is the largest gathering of people in the world, it happens every twelve years and it could happen only in India. They come by train, they come by bus, they come on foot. But they come. They come to bathe in the Holy Mother Ganga. This year four million come to be in one place at one time. The place is Hardwar, the time is eight minutes past two on the morning of April 14th, 1986. It is unbelievable. It is unique. It is the great Kumbh Mela.

The Hindus love a good legend and the mythological beginnings of this unparalleled religious spectacle are no exception. Many moons ago, the son of Indra, king of the Gods, managed to retrieve (not unlike some sort of celestial "Repo Man") a *kumbh* (pitcher) filled with the elixir of immortality that some demons had stolen from the bottom of the ocean. During the twelve-year chase that followed, one of the places in which he and his ambrosia happened to take refuge was Hardwar. Meanwhile . . . back on earth it seems the Mela started as a vehicle for the propagation of Hinduism; a forum where the Sadhus, the Holy Men, could wax enthusiastic about its many virtues to all who cared to listen. That wasn't very many, so, in order to attract more people, it was decided that anyone who bathed in the Ganga at a Kumbh Mela would be absolved of all their sins. No questions asked. This, of course, had the desired effect, and since the thirteenth century it has become part of Hindu culture.

This year there had been a call for the Mela, once again, to be the platform for a serious Hindu revival, but the millions flooding into Hardwar didn't care. They were coming because of their unquestioned belief that bathing in the Ganges on April 14th would cleanse their souls; the Holy River washing away those stubborn sins and taking them, and any other flotsam that might happen to be in the water, somewhere off in the direction of the Bay of Bengal.

To wash my own sins away, even at such an auspicious occasion, would have taken far too long, so, leaving my swimming trunks in downtown Delhi, I found myself sitting on the top of a crowded pilgrim bus heading for Hardwar in the foothills of the Himalayas. Jupiter was in conjunction with Aquarius and, as any astrologer worth his star charts should know, it could mean only one thing. After two months of frenzied build-up, the next day would be the climax of the Kumbh Mela. Four million sinful Indians all trying to bathe in the same place at the same time? There was only one place to be in India and, excited and nervous, it was exactly where I was going. Nothing could have prepared me for the next twenty-four hours.

From several kilometres outside the town a seething mass of humanity was inching its way towards the banks of the Ganga. It was on a biblical scale. Only Charlton Heston was missing as this swarm of people was sucked inexorably towards the water's edge; the river of Life and Salvation. Gradually, as the streets narrowed, the multitudes became locked together into a solid lump and I was no longer able to stop or go back. It was too late, and as night fell I was pulled deep inside the Kumbh Mela and deep into India.

Lost in a swirling mass of people, colour and energy. Wet, cold, shivering bodies pushing their way through the crowds; people silhouetted in the clouds of dust thrown up into the air; small babies being held up and unceremoniously plunged headlong into the water; old couples desperately clinging to each other and to their precious vials full of "Holy water"; the very old being carried down to the river for their last act of purification; and everywhere people bathing in touching individual displays of faith.

Inevitably Melas such as this also drag the weird, wonderful and absolutely berserk out of the Indian woodwork, and that night they all seemed to have appeared in Hardwar (apart from the infamous and lusty Bhagwan Rajneesh, holed up somewhere in Uruguay). There were the magicians; the Yogis; the jugglers; the preachers; the Hari Krishna devotees (looking more at home if no less limp than they do wandering down Oxford Street); and, perhaps the craziest of all, the Sadhus. Many of these supposed spiritual pioneers of Hinduism were sitting in large groups smoking their *chillums* (pipes) filled with marijuana, which they held high above their heads, and which were no doubt taking these holy men even higher. The Mahatma condemned this sort of hollow spirituality saying, "These men were born only to enjoy the good things in life". However, this couldn't be said about some of the "Naga" Sadhus who, standing near the river, painfully demonstrated their rejection of desire by piercing their penises and hanging rocks from their genitals. This extraordinary self-mutilation didn't even merit a free radio. Maybe they should have kept their lingams in their lunghis?

These colourful characters were a minor distraction compared to the frantic scenes at the water's edge, where people were pouring down the steps into the river and whole families, young and old, were splashing each other in a joyous celebration of their faith. Small fires were burning among the blanket of people that stretched back from the Ganges, and while some slept others were chanting or singing. Occasionally the loud moan of a conch shell summoning the spirits soared above everything. There was nowhere to rest as the crowds moved on and the bathing ghats, stretching up and down both banks, were covered in a solid wave of pilgrims forcing their shaved heads down to the water. It was a humbling experience.

In the middle of the night the crowd thickened, winding its way through the bamboo barricades and over the thin wooden bridges to Hari-Ki-Puri (the holiest site in Hinduism, where the waters supposedly wash away seven generations of sins). The piercing whistles of the police, trying to control the crowd, shrieked above the hum of chanting and prayers, and a sudden surge forward lifted me off my feet. Considering the painfully short time and small space the gods have given the Hindus to attain salvation, the crush was quite understandable.

Among this unimaginable human chaos, pilgrims pushed their way through until they found what space they could; undressed and, impervious to everything and everyone else, lowered themselves privately into the Ganga, offering the Holy water skywards in cupped hands.

For some this was the most important moment of their lives and, as these people immersed themselves in the water and their belief, it was impossible not to feel the power of their faith. This was the heart of the Kumbh Mela. Garlands of yellow marigolds were swallowed up by the water as it rushed past, and flickering spots of light from hundreds of small candles danced all over the human mosaic that dissolved into the river. It was indeed a spectacle for the gods, and wedged into this crucible of believers you could feel the magic in the air.

The splashing, the bathing, this awesome demonstration of faith carried on all night, and it was only as the sun rose that the frenetic activity at the ghats seemed to slow down. The crowds began to line up behind the fences, in the trees, packing the embankments and covering the ground like an enormous, colourful jigsaw. They were waiting for the climactic six-hour procession of the different *akharas* (holy sects), on their way to Hari-Ki-Pari.

News had spread of a stampede early that morning in which fifty people had been crushed to death, but this was India and it had happened before. So, apparently indifferent to the tragedy, thousands of completely naked Sadhus brandishing maces and spears swaggered past with their matted hair, smeared in cow dung, trailing behind them in the dust. Other *babas* waving their huge banners lapped up the adoration of the crowd. It would have been quite easy to seat a family of four on the buttocks of some of the larger gentlemen arrogantly wobbling out in front. After them came their "Spiritual leaders" sit-

ting regally in their brightly decorated chariots, distributing consider-
able largesse while their emaciated acolytes struggled manfully to stop
these "men of God" toppling earthwards. Had these *sanyassis* really
rejected the pomp and vanity of this world?

As the crowds cheered and bowed to this impressive, imperious
cavalcade, J looked back towards the Ganga at the unending stream of
pilgrims still bathing in their own private rituals of purification, and I
thought of the old couple huddled together struggling along by the
river with nothing but each other and their faith. What *was* all this?
This was India and India at its best. Crazy, magical, and always
unforgettable.

# JULIA BUTT

# LES MALHEUREUSES

Napoeleon greeted us when we arrived in the palm-fringed port of Ajaccio and disembarked onto the jetty. Corsica's capital exhibits boulevards, bars and boats in honour of its most famous son. The white-glossed vessels glide out slowly with their cargoes of rich French and Italian mariners, perhaps south to Sardinia or Sicily before venturing upon Poseidon's homeland in the depths of the Aegean.

We wound up into the mountains for three hours at the back of a stifling minibus, rucksacks on knees, to arrive at Petreto-Bicchisano to au-pair and keep shop for two months. The villages of bleached stone are perched on crags, almost indistinguishable in the dense green forests. Grey stones on distant, wispy mountaintops become crosses and tombstones as one ascends. Every village has its protective saint and little dark chapel. Children play in the street with its one-thousand-foot drop to the bronze river below. The old women in black do not shout warnings. It seems that one is born to Corsica with an instinct of its precariousness.

The Bungelmi family are politicians, part of the recently-formed Corsican Assembly, which gave devolution to this tiny French *département*. They are like God to the villagers; we, as their servants and the only *"anglaises"* (actually *"écossaises"* and therefore even more rarified) to have visited this mountain ledge are held in high esteem. Once it is established that our guttural French accents are not of German origin they are our friends. Old wars die hard.

The Wild Man of the Woods stops us as we climb the steep mountains, pushing Denis in his baby buggy (imported from le Continent or mainland France) to see his cousins in the next village five hundred feet due north.

"You are the English girls," he says. "What is it like now?"

When asked if he has visited our country, he smiles sadly and says in English with a touch of Geordie, "I was in the British Navy in the Second World War. It was too much. I deserted ship at Marseilles and came here to hide. This is the first time I've spoken English in forty years."

He continues down the mountain to his wooden shack and his bees.

Our Corsican charges are bandits born to shriek and howl all day in the white heat. Their parents are on the point of divorce. The primordial sense of God so strong in these ancient villages has no pull on the young Corsicans who escape to the sophistication of Paris to marry in register offices. After all, why worry about Heaven when Paradise has been experienced first hand on this Ile de Beauté? We are caught in the middle of theatrical scenes beginning with Roland's selfishness in bed and ending with Marie-Laure throwing a runny round of ewe's cheese against the wall. Drama being the simplest form of communication, we quickly pick up the Corsican dialect! The atmosphere explodes every hot evening and echoes round the valley so we run away in the middle of the night. There are no street lights so we walk in the middle of the road to avoid hidden scorpions on the grassy banks. In the distance the the mountains glow like coal embers to light our way. The forest fires have begun – shall we escape before they reach our ridge?

Having hitched to the capital we make camp on the beach in the early morning. We have another job by lunchtime – waitresses in a nightclub. This solves the accommodation problem. We can work by night and sleep by day on the beach, leaving Mathieu, the old man who sleeps in his beach café, to guard our rucksacks. Our pretty floral sundresses and espadrilles look out of place in the red-lit club beside the glittering harbour where the waitresses wear black rubber and gold chains. There is only male clientèle. As foreign blonds we are greatly in demand – we stay behind the bar nervously washing the same glasses whilst the black rubber girls mingle, dance and suction on to the customers, giggling at our behaviour. Madame Catya pokes us crossly and tells us to circulate but the conversation is disjointed:

"The mountains, the sun and the beaches are so beautiful here," I attempt to a hotel tycoon.

"Your tits are like great big melons," he replies, smiling.

I wonder if I have misunderstood, but when his counterpart signs a cheque for £150 for a glass of Perrier and Caroline, I know it's time to make another escape, the second in twenty-four hours.

My twentieth birthday present from Caroline is a secondhand 1963 military blanket on which to sleep on the beach. On our first night under the stars we awake to blinding torches and Inspector Clouseau, who moves us on. We sit in the eerie square at 3am with Napoleon looking down menacingly for half an hour and then return to the beach to sleep until morning.

Fabienne wakes us. She is pretty in a New York Jewish sort of way – cracked nose, olive skin, beautiful drooping eyes with lots of kohl, smoker's teeth and bitten nails. Wrapped in a peasant blanket she talks of *"le business"* in Soho and Piccadilly – prostitution to pay for her drug addiction. Her arms are scars, dead veins with hanging skin which will take no more abuse, and so her ankles have become the focal point of her masochism. Corsica is vacation after hospitalisation in Amsterdam and, more importantly from her point of view, stamping ground of many Moroccans who come from the hash crops of North Africa to supply France from this paradise isle.

Mathieu now lets us sleep under the tables in his café and feeds us coffee and croissants. In return we fetch his one hundred baguettes steaming from the bakery in the silver dawn in one huge basket which feeds the beach at lunchtime. Then we jog behind the French Legion whose Mediterranean base is in the hills at Cap Corse. The annoyed P.T. instructor quickens the pace and we soon fall behind in the 8am heat. Bottled water for lunch. Jasmine tea from flasks with the learned Chinese Parisians from the Sorbonne as an afternoon ritual. Then more bottled water (by this time boiling) until the beach is empty and we light our gas burner to boil eggs for supper.

"Look at what happens to the bad boys and girls," a man warns his little son as they stare at us over the beach wall.

The ferry arrives with new beach bums and we play guitar and sing *American Pie* into the night, although none of us wants to look any further for the Promised Land. Richard arrives from trekking in the Sahara with another burner so we feast on pasta and ratatouille.

The next day we decide that haircuts are in order. Someone produces nail scissors and a Swiss Army knife and the Ajaccio set look on in horror as we create Sassoon's on Sea. A German under the next parasol who works for *Der Spiegel* takes photographs while the New Assymmetric is being created. We hear Mathieu tell the old town codgers that he feels duty bound to help us, *"les jeunes malheureuses"*.

We live on fifteen francs a day but still lend our precious coins to an English family for their taxi fare back to the next resort when we meet them arguing noisily in the main square under the fountains. They return to our home on the beach the next day with the money and two bottles of wine. Everything is shared in this communal society we have founded – food, advice, confidences, waterlogged newspapers and our bible, *Hitch-hiker's Guide to Europe*. We shower under the cold hosepipe on the beach yet become accustomed to our permanent sandy skins. We swim all day to keep cool and only when our faces blister do we long for a tiled villa with dark recesses instead of our parasols. We have lost our Aberdeen granite looks and are now sinewy, lean, mahogany animals used to twenty-four hours a day in the open air and terrified of enclosure.

We travel to Bonifacio, the southernmost tip of Corsica. Huge sedimentary rocks rise as high as cliffs out of the sea, having fallen from the mainland centuries ago. The town juts out of the cliffs and seems in danger of tumbling into the blue-green *algue* below. We watch the flat, barren coast of Sardinia twelve kilometres across the strait enviously. Another land to discover but the fifteen franc ferry crossing is a whole day's survival.

And so the summer draws to a close as the money runs out. We pack up our temporary home and leave the Island to face another year of law school. *Malheureuses?* Perhaps now, yes.

# MIDNIGHT ON MONT BLANC

Depression lurked over me like a Lakeland storm-sky: oppressive, inevitable and apparently unending. "What you need," said Bernie over the top of his beer, "is to take your mind off it; get out onto the hill. Let's go and climb Mont Blanc. We can drive down on your bike."

The suggestion seemed suitably absurd – neither of us had done any serious climbing for a decade and I had never done any work on snow and ice. So we went. Friends took the heavy gear in a car. (I had failed to accommodate two full sets of climbing equipment, a tent, books and spare clothes in the panniers of my new BMW and felt slightly cheated.) On the open roads, the apparently deserted French *péages,* I relished the lack of baggage and flew south.

We stopped at service stations for coffee and short rests in the sun, parking among the admiring summer super-bikers. I quickly fell into old habits as the cameraderie of the motorcycle fraternity reasserted itself – a quick flash of the headlamp as you pass at high speed, a full wave to the rider of another BMW, the critically admiring glances over the ranks of other machines, the knowledgeable chatter of performance figures, and the bullshit of personal near misses and friends lost.

Chamonix, when we arrived, was hot, expensive and distractingly full of beautiful women. We drank beer and listened to tales of the good old days when our boys fought the French climbers in the streets, and won. Beside the bar, Maurice counted the takings, his blind eyes having seen it all. We took to the hills.

"I know an easy route to do as an introduction," said Mick, "the Traverse de Dômes des Miage." We conferred and studied maps. To my untutored eye the route looked long but straightforward, and I nonchalantly agreed. After a sleepless night in the dormitory of an alpine hut we set out at 3am. The fresh pre-dawn air was a luxury in comparison with the foetid heat of the bunks, and the stars were brilliant in the black, black sky. As we walked up to the glacier I felt, for the first time in months, glad to be alive.

I felt worse, later. The route took fourteen hours and wrecked my fect. For most of the way it was a long plod up the glacier, an interminable slope of ice and snow. My borrowed crampons fell to pieces and my new boots were too large. The clear night sky gave way to a perfect day and Bernie, who had forgotten a hat, nearly died of sunstroke. At the highest point we rested and ate a snack. I looked around at the peaks and across at the bulk of Mont Blanc, looming above us. "It'll be easy," said Mick, following my gaze. "We'll do the standard route; get the train out of the valley and walk up to the Gautier hut for a sleep, then get up at midnight and be on the summit for dawn. Mind you," he added as he effortlessly set off down the slope, "it may be crowded. This year is the two-hundredth anniversary of its first ascent."

I finished my chocolate and followed him, my crampons, blisters and fear making me hesitant. Below me the snow slope steepened, a long seductive white arc ending abruptly in . . . My mind wandered. I imagined a slip and the gathering speed, the futile inexperienced attempts to stop myself with the axe, a moment's despair and then capitulation to fate as I hurtled over the edge into an unbroken, terminally exhilarating, one-way flight to the glacier 4,000 feet below.

Bernie pulled on the rope and cursed me for stopping; I plodded on. My feet hurt.

Four days later, the train heaved its way out of the valley towards the end of the Bionnassay Glacier. Through the glass I stared at the pine trees and the brilliant meadow flowers. The carriage filled with the perfume of tourists, up for the day, and the sweat of climbers, rucksacks balanced on their knees, all heading for the Blanc. When the track wound alongside a cliff the small girl sitting opposite looked out in disbelief as the trees gave way to nothing. She pulled her eyes away in fear and looked around the train – the view there was worse, rucksacks, hairy knees, ice-axes, unshaven climbers lost in contemplation of the weather.

We arrived at the top station and the train disgorged. Tourists wandered slowly across to the café or to the viewing platform from which they could look up at the great bleak sweep of the mountain opposite. Down the valley the world became more sane, as the stone desert below the glacier gave way to meadows and woodland.

The climbers had no time for niceties. A hundred packs were shouldered and a long queue of people marched purposefully up the track which, like a motorway, led uphill from the station. I looked in horror – was this the beautiful isolation of the mountains about which I had been told for years? Heavy boots crushed the life out of any remaining plants and sent small showers of stones down onto the people below. Walkers jockeyed for position on the network of tracks which zig-zagged up the first slope. The hillside crumbled visibly under the onslaught, and I couldn't help but think of the devastation which has been wrought on British mountains by a similar recreational assaults.

Beside the path was a small hut, a shelter for hunters, and standing around it was a group of chamoix waiting, like the sheep on Helvellyn, for the tourists who would photograph and feed them. The climbers pressed on oblivious. Bernie stopped me and pointed forwards. Ahead, a long long way ahead, and at the top of a seemingly vertical rock face, was a silver blob. "The Gautier," he panted, "about four and a half thousand feet above us. Three and a half thousand vertically from there to the summit." I nodded and we walked on in the heat as the sun grew higher in the sky. "Mad dogs and Englishmen," I thought, but I couldn't see the dogs.

The hut appeared to get no closer. We walked and scrambled, gradually passing most of the others who had come up with us on the train. Our chances of getting a sleeping space seemed remote even without the crowds who were following us, and I had no wish to sleep outside on the ground. In the early afternoon we came to the foot of the final climb to the hut. Below us to the right, across the glacier, was another hut, the Tête Sauvage. Someone there was playing a flute and the sound blended beautifully with the superb landscape. Some of the walkers began to go that way, not lured by the Pied Piper, but to spend the night at a lower altitude and to use the Tête Sauvage as the springboard for their attempt on the summit the following morning.

As we climbed upward, the cloud began to close in and I wondered if the following day would be too bad for the attempt – the summit can be swept by winds of 100mph. Bernie had tried this route twice before and each time the weather had forced him back. We passed a rusty iron cross, a memorial to a dead climber, and finally reached the hut, a metal-skinned structure perched on the cliff edge. Already people were staking claims to places on the ground, and when I opened the door I knew why. A waft of hot sweaty air hit me and a pile of rucksacks threatened to follow. I edged my way inside.

Tony and Mick were perched on a bench at the back of the room surveying a sea of humanity. "There are no bunks and no food," said Mick with a smile. "I've booked places on the floor; same price." The hut was mayhem. I wondered how the staff retained their sanity, let alone their obvious good humour. We ate sardines and I scrounged a bowl of coffee. At nine, the floor was swept and people bedded down on tables, on benches, even in the sink. I tried to sleep but only dozed. The room was full of mumbles and curses, scratching, and a restless anticipation of the morning.

At midnight we got up and weaved our way out between the bodies. In one place hands were held up for me to walk on – there was no floor space. Bernie had to go back to get Mike, who had failed to wake up, and his passage was marked by a sequence of incredulous French swearing. We fixed crampons, turned on torches and set off. The path was obvious, a yard deep trench in the snow behind the hut.

But soon we were spread out on the huge slope of the Dôme de Gautier.

I plodded up, pausing for a rest at each turn. Snow glittered beneath my feet in the torchlight. Down in the valley the roads looked like lava flows, ribbons of red and orange fire. The sky above was deep black and the stars brilliant; for a moment I felt that I was on a slope between heaven and hell. Far below me a cluster of torches marked the progress of the 1am starters and beyond them lights around the hut showed the next group were getting ready. I carried on upward.

Gradually the pure black of the night lightened and the bulk of the mountain became visible. It daunted me. Mick and Tony were already far ahead; Bernie's torch was a few hundred yards above and Mike and Sue were just behind. Life became a matter of placing one foot in front of another, of concentrating on moving forward. I remember thinking that this was one of the easiest routes in the Alps and feeling momentarily depressed. But then I knew it didn't matter – I was doing as much as I was able and enjoying the experience, that's what really counts.

A lone Japanese climber passed me and we grunted greetings. Bernie held a one-sided conversation with him for an hour before realising that the figure wasn't me; so much for his opinion of my conversation. The three of us reached the summit close together, shook hands and hugged each other. The summit was ours, the roof of Europe spread out before us, rows of peaks silhouetted against the orange streak of the sky. We pulled on down jackets and sat on our ropes to wait for the dawn.

GEORGINA CARRINGTON

# ART EXHIBITION

The tourist coaches disgorge their contents into the forecourt of the Jinling Hotel, Nanjing. The colours and shapes of middle-class Europe, America, Japan, Australia, stream through plate glass doors and stand in dazed clusters among their luggage, whilst tour leaders complete yet another set of check-in formalities.

Polished chrome and marble reflect luxuriant indoor gardens. A pianist's vacuous tinkling drifts from the intercommunication system. It could be the foyer of an international hotel anywhere in the world.

Outside, late autumn sunshine filters through the industrial haze. A complex of fountains makes dark splashes on patterned paving. The white-painted concrete fence marks a boundary, on the far side of which the other China, in sober-suited rows, peers with impassive curiosity at this world within their world, as we stand before cages at a zoo. We are aware of another China. It flows past endlessly on jangling bicycles; it smiles from doorways and factory workbenches when we are shown round. But in the restaurants we are segregated; even our Chinese guides eat separately. We shop in Friendship Stores for tourists, where they speak English. The other China is always just beyond reach.

Mary's padlock had broken, and she needed a replacement before we moved on tomorrow. Reception couldn't help. Neither could the girls in the hotel arcade, with its jade, cloisonné and mirror-smoothe laquerwork, all bargains to the wealthy. So I sketched a padlock on an envelope, and three of us ventured into the streets.

China goes to bed early. At 8.30pm the cyclists were thinning out and shops were closing, but delicious smells wafted from the stalls selling hot snacks, and there were people round these and the bookstalls. Orange sodium lighting freckled the pavement between shadows of plane trees bordering the road. Some shops re-opened at our approach. Their proprietors were anxious to help, but nobody had a padlock. We were about to abandon our search outside a shop displaying a plastic bowl of water in which a tangle of striped snakes writhed terminally (was *that* what we had for dinner?) when someone said in English:

"Excuse me, do you have a problem? May we help?" We explained about the padlock to the two young men. They looked doubtful, but one thought he knew a place, if we could catch it before it closed. They came from Bejing, we discovered, where they had studied English for two years at college, and kept it up since with a programme on Radio Bejing . . . "but it is wonderful to talk to English people!"

The younger man, with the fine-boned build of the northern Chinese, told me that he made his living as an artist. I was impressed. I had heard that only the specially talented could achieve this in China. I told him that my hobby was watercolour painting. His face lit up.

"My studio is very near. Please come and see my work. It is my home too." Then, seeing our hesitation: "My wife will be there." So we discarded caution and accepted.

We left the wide main street and found ourselves in an unlit alleyway. The ground was rough, and our companions produced torches to guide us. On each side concrete apartment blocks soared, with the sky a jar-edged patch of lighter darkness far above. Curious people looked from lighted doorways at the sound of our voices. We climbed a staircase outside an apartment block, and halted on the tenth floor, a narrow landing, onto which opened several iron doors with reinforced glass panels. Our friend opened the nearest door. We had arrived.

The harsh fluorescent light made us blink. Yuhang's wife, a frail looking girl wearing a floral shirt and black trousers, looked startled. She spoke no English, but shook our hands and smiled shyly. The room was about thirteen feet square. The walls and ceiling were white, the uncovered concrete floor was painted maroon. Opposite, a window stared like an unlidded eye into the night. The window wall was almost entirely occupied by a large double bed with a pink candlewick counterpane. Down the centre of the room was a long table covered with felt, and at one end of this was a collection of paintbrushes and ready-mixed pigments in ceramic jars. Along the wall with the door in it stood an enormous yellow-and-black tartan settee. The fourth wall was filled by a wooden dresser, behind whose sliding glass doors could be seen various personal items – photographs, a spray of plastic flowers and a toy panda. There was just room for a Chinese-sized person to squeeze between the furniture. We sat on the settee. We saw no sign of heating or air conditioning, nor cooking and washing facilities, which we assumed must be communal. Paints on scraps of paper, vibrant with colour and life, brightened the walls.

Yuhang showed us his photograph album.

"Here is my art teacher": short, sturdy, unsmiling, in a Mao suit and rimless spectacles.

"He is a very famous Chinese artist," interjected Zhiqiang. It appeared that Yuhang was considered quite a protégé: several photographs were of him and his mentor beside various paintings.

"Here is our wedding." They were still unsmiling, standing in a formal line before somebody else's dresser. "We have been married for a year now. Maybe in two years . . . maybe three . . ." his voice wished the time away, "we can have our baby." One child. The focus for all the love, unfulfilled hopes, unrealised ambitions; a great burden for small shoulders. The pages turned.

"These are paintings from my first exhibition." Many were traditional, in monochrome, but with his individuality clearly showing. Some were more modern, still very "Chinese".

"These are of Tibet. I went there recently. I am fascinated by the Tibetan women!" One picture caught my attention. A girl's profile, with an enigmatic eye fixed upon some distant point, but among the dark fronds of her hair a miniature cameo of a moonlit ruin like a Greek temple, with people casting long shadows. The base of her neck blended into a landscape.

"Yes, that is different – an experiment, a kind of fantasy." He laughed apologetically. "But I sold it, to a Canadian."

"I should have liked to buy it if you hadn't," I said.

Soon the table was covered with his paintings. We all bought one, at a ridiculously low price for work superior to anything else we had found. However, he was obviously delighted, and on a sudden impulse pressed a 50 yuan note (about £10) into his friend's hand.

Pride was hurt. Anger crackled in the confined space as the older man tried to return the note and, meeting resistance, grabbed hold of Yuhang's shoulders and shook him, speaking vehemently in Chinese. Yuhang's wife, who had been seated on the bed, jumped up in alarm. Afraid that their dispute would become really physical, I caught their arms.

"Please don't fight, it will spoil a wonderful evening!"

"No – don't fight." They backed off, anger simmering.

Later, as we walked back, carrying our paintings wrapped carefully in pages of the *China Daily,* Yuhang explained.

"You see, my friend is a talented photographic designer, but he works for a State Company, for a low wage. I wanted to share my good fortune with him. Friendship is more important than money, would you agree?" I hoped that the anger between them was short-lived, and that he found some more diplomatic way to share his largesse. We stopped a hundred yards from the floodlit tower of our hotel.

"Come inside. We will buy you a drink." They declined reluctantly.

"No, we cannot enter tourist hotels. If we come in with you, very soon someone, maybe a policeman, would come over. He would not be polite." He made his voice rough. "'What is *your* business *here?*' He would take our names and addresses, and we would know that if we did not leave immediately things may be difficult for us in the days ahead." I asked him why. He shrugged.

"I think they believe if we fraternise too much with western people we may want to be like them. We may even try to leave and go to the West." His smile was ironic beneath the street lamp. "Did you not notice? There are not enough people in China!"

As we parted, he handed something to Mary. "You were looking for this, I think." It was a small padlock.

Back in the Jinling we treated ourselves to a nightcap in the Revolving Restaurant. A band played an up-tempo version of *You are my Sunshine* and a few couples bobbed primly on the dance floor. A group of Japanese men pursued the serious business of getting communally drunk. Outside, Nanjing completed a slow revolution, serpents of sodium orange among vertical columns of lighted apartment windows, and above all the random geometry of the stars and a crescent moon. Behind one of those windows an artist may be working. Thank you for our look into your China.

PHILIP CLARKE

# TRIPLE ALLIANCE

I do not recall how much my memories of that night-time journey were the creation of fitful dreams or the stuff of actuality. The blackness of the night and my own fears were real enough as the lights of the bus probed the landscape, revealing steep escarpments and the outlines of vertical cliffs. Sometimes, peering over the side of the bus, I caught sight of the ghostly white caps of Pacific rollers coming to spit their fury at a continent. The bus swept down the hills and then ground its way up another hilltop through a succession of sandy switchbacks. I kept thinking of the drunken Cary Grant in *North by Northwest,* as he strove to bring his car under control. Was our driver chewing coca leaves, as so many long distance drivers did in Peru, to ease the burdens of an eight-hour journey? I looked around the bus at the crumpled figures managing some sleep. Two rows in front of me a Japanese man slumped against a girl with a shock of auburn curls. A strange couple, I thought.

The first tendrils of light spawned a mist, which hung over the desert. In my half-sleep I thought the sand was snow for it had the thick texture of water-colour paper. It felt very cold.

The sun was already bright as silver on our arrival in Arequipa, a large city but untouched by ugly tall buildings. A colonial city with a sunny disposition. I found my bag and smiled at the Japanese and the girl with auburn curls. I produced my guidebook as an invitation to treat.

"Which hotel?" I asked. We introduced ourselves. The girl was German: a student dressed in ten different colours but unsmiling. Kazuo, a tall peering Japanese, was smiling, but smiling with the fixity of the nervous. There was an instant unspoken bargain struck. Travelling alone in Peru was a nerve-racking business. We would find a hotel together. One minute later, as we strode through the streets of Arequipa to the racing pace set by Regina, we found that our plans for the next week were almost identical.

"It would be nice to travel together," I ventured.

Over breakfast in our modest traveller's *pension,* with its sunlit courtyard full of cardinal red geraniums, we traded our identities in English, which was the only language we understood in common. The petty deceits that circumscribe our contact with other people become redundant in the fleeting moments one has with other travellers. Family bereavement had bred in Regina a sense of independence and toughness, akin to isolation. At eighteen she had felt the call to move away from home, a state of affairs accepted with stoicism by her mother. She had been travelling for three months in the Americas, but a recent illness, she confessed, had made her very vulnerable. Regina had a very clear idea what she wanted to see and to experience, and a buoyant belief that nothing bad could befall her.

Kazuo always expected the worst. He was travelling around the world and was sceptical of everybody and everything. His itinerary was frenetic, as notions of travel seemed to be based on seeing and recording a certain number of spectacular sights. His schedule gave him security, I smugly conceded, but given his language difficulties and the Japanese ambivalence towards travel, he was brave enough as it was. When he returned home, he hoped to secure employment where he could take three weeks of holiday every third year.

"We Japanese are an undeveloped people," he lamented. "I have brought discomfort to my parents," he added even more wistfully.

We spent three days in Arequipa. I learnt to adapt to Regina's pace and to Kazuo's sharp cries of pleasure at seeing any Japanese goods. As nearly every car in Peru was Japanese, these cries would punctuate any long silences. Conversation, under these circumstances, is a bit of an effort, as bonhomie can be taken only so far before familiarity makes it both superfluous and a little ridiculous. We did, however, share one common characteristic – we were all introverts, but that was about as far as it went. For a start, we must have looked an unlikely assortment: a German hippy with flowers decorating her trousers; a tall Japanese continually grimacing and emitting cries; and myself, wrapped against the sun and locked into my duty to promote conversation.

The train to Puno is regarded as one of the most spectacular rail journeys in the world. It is also one of the most dangerous. The guidebooks all suggest that there is an eighty per cent chance of having something stolen. The station at Arequipa has a particularly unpleasant reputation for bag-slashing, petty theft and daylight robbery. I remember sleeping fitfully, working out how I would deal with my attackers and protect my companions, but these plans were unnecessary. We took a taxi into the station, where it rapidly became apparent that the spectre of the bad guys hanging around in gangs like *West Side Story* extras was the stuff of dreams. Instead, traditionally-dressed women waddled along the platform carrying mountainous baskets.

The train pulled its way up onto the altiplano with its stunning emptiness and its snow-capped mountains beyond. Whatever pleasure one has in the newness of it all, the harshness soon becomes apparent. For the spectator the coruscating sodium light and the pounding of one's temples from the 15,000-foot altitude are not conducive to appreciation. For the Indian there is a bleakness that their bright clothing cannot efface – dun-coloured landscapes, an absence of trees and shrubs, and a piercing wind setting up miniature whirlwinds which bob across the tableau. Three or four adobe houses cluster near the railway, where a dog may raise himself to give sporting chase to the train. In fixing such a picture in time, one had mood in plenty but no focal point – no dominant feature that would lead the eyes into the rest of the scene. Puno, a frontier town in both senses, on the shores of Lake Titicaca had both mood and focal point.

All through Puno, women, with hair plaited in pig-tails and hats perched uneasily on the crown of their heads, sported themselves under great bundles of cloth. I suppose the town must be the knitting capital of the world, for at every turn these women pursue you to sell pullovers, socks and ponchos. You are invited to try on a whole array of richly hued garments. "Ah Señor, jumper," they would mew in the sing-song style of imitation subservience. If you want to dress like a canary, this is the place for you. Regina was in her element here, and rather unheeding of male boredom.

When we arrived, it was dark. Regina grabbed the key for the last room in the cheapest hotel in town. Fortunately it had three beds in it, but that was about as far as comfort went; it was small and cold, but for a dollar a day it was acceptable. Our *ménage à trois* did not have the sporting connotations that the term suggests. The marriage of convenience was simply that. It was difficult enough to sort out three lots of clothes, to adjust our points of demarcation and to ward off the cold without having to worry about potential embarrassments. National characteristics, as I like to think of them, rather than mere idiosyncracies, were paraded for each of us to see. In the Japanese world to my right, everything was arranged "just so".

To each object its allotted place – the pad for origami, the box for shaving gear, a diary full of pasted tickets, along with paste, Sellotape and pencils in another bag, the calculator and a camera in another compartment. Clothes were placed as if they had been left by a valet. The detail of routine brought order into the unpredictable world. On coming into our bedroom, Kazuo's first act would be to close the window, whilst Regina's would be to open it again. At such times Kazuo took on the muted solemnity of an afflicted Thurber husband. He lived his life by a different code. "I could not marry your Western girls," he once confided to me.

And to my left was Regina, who shattered my preconceptions about German order. Clothes were thrown everywhere, and added to with fresh purchases of woollen garments from the market stalls. Where she did conform more clearly to the national stereotype was in the continual use of the imperative. "We vill be having a shower this morning – yes?"

"We vill," I sang back. However, we both shared a fascination for the quiet rituals of the Japanese – the gentle massage of his face and the toning of each muscle as he got up, the clasping of his hands in prayer at the end of each meal – embodying all the gentility that our harsher Anglo-Saxon cultures had lost.

The train journey to Cuzco, the imperial capital of the Incas, was wearisome – like passing through an endless corridor in which small boys kept hitting your head with books. We stopped at a series of villages and small towns, all with the same harshness of colour. At one stop, where we spent no more than a minute, a middle-aged man slipped out of a doorway and leant against the adjacent wall. A small child approached him with a bottle in one hand and money in the other, but dropped the bottle at the moment of transfer. The man cursed and staggered away, leaving the child standing stock still. The train moved off.

We had begun to get to know each other, and with this understanding came the explanations of what it was like to be German, Japanese and English. We teased each other about our idiosyncrasies and our pretensions. Kazuo admitted that hard work blinded many Japanese to the potential of life. On his travels he had felt more at home in Germany than in any other country. He had found the British rather disdainful. Regina spoke with pride about her love for Germany and about her irritation with questions concerning Hitler. Little failures were confessed and hopes expressed. The common chords of isolation and uncertainty were gently touched. I had the advantage of language and taught Kazuo idioms. "What is this 'bright-eyed and bushy-tailed' that I am this morning?" he kept muttering.

"'Danger of homosexual rape' the guidebook says," I read out, as we got up and started planning our day. Kazuo reached for his dictionary, found the appropriate words and shook his head in dismay. "Very strange, very strange." We would then march off to find breakfast, making it clear to Regina that muesli and yoghurt were not our idea of breakfast; but she always won because she knew precisely what she wanted. Inadequately fortified, we would follow her to see some imposing Incan ruin with its perfectly-shaped rectangles of rock fitted together with mortar. Regina would lie in the sun catching the atmosphere, while Kazuo and I would trot around every nook and cranny in case we missed anything. "No rape today – very good day," Kazuo would comment and then slyly smile.

I watched them pack early on our final morning together. Regina and Kazuo were continuing on to Macchu Picchu before Regina returned home, while I was going into the interior. Our farewells were brief as we noted the happiness of the week and the fact that we were sorry to be parting. Yes, of course, we would try and meet again. I heard them close the front door and move out into the darkness.

# FRANCES ROBERTSON

## HIDDEN RIVERS

As I climbed up out of the station the street stretched away uphill, shining under the lights like an old trouser seat. There were houses everywhere and scraggy trees, but I couldn't see a pub anywhere. Thin drizzle peppered the thirsty pavements and I realised this was a hopeful start; I'd found a real, if repellent, suburb in an elusive city. I was standing in Salusbury Road, in Queen's Park, in London.

Some of the shadowy nature of London is that one feels it ought to be well known. Anyone who can read can know London; from Dick Whittington to witty Dickens and beyond, every view is veiled with reference.

This time, in my search for the real London, my only literature was the A-Z street guide and the Underground map. But even the Underground, although picturesque, is not suitable for an *entire* holiday, although I am convinced that many travellers are diverted to this stratum. It is so easy to bolt down a hole into the roaring maze and follow the red, the brown, or the stripey thread of the map; following that thread along the acrid windy galleries and moving stairs becomes the real adventure. To be sure, you can pop up at the V & A or Madame Tussauds, but how are they connected except by this bloodless Tube filled with the sound of sighs? There is no real evidence that these sights are on the same planet, never mind in the same city.

On this holiday I was determined to discover what else was possible. I had a pretty good chance on two counts: I was to stay in Queen's Park, an inkwell into which no writer's pen I knew had ever dipped, and I was on a working holiday, to study costume cutting. Between the artisans' dwellings and the crash of shears on calico I was out on my own, gathering raw experience as the baleen whale sucks in slime. That was my plan.

I soon found Queen's Park to be inhospitable; intended by philanthropists as a suburb to encourage workers to be thrifty, not thirsty, there are no pubs at all and scarcely any other comforts.

But Soho, where I tubed to my studies, is the opposite. Sandwiched between the drinking establishments are crammed shops for food, sex, clothes of every description. It is a black sun to the asteroids of the entertainment industry. To a seamstress from the provinces like me, this area bulges with every conceivable oddity and commodity such as iridescent diamond buttons and leather knickers. In my lunch breaks I bought bread and cheese in Brewer Street, and what *lovely* bread and cheese – rubbery Italian bread, salty *pecorino* and mammoth olives as large and pungent as ancient eggs.

The Association of British Theatre Technicians in Great Pulteney Street, where I pursued my studies, is a kind of temple to artifice, dedicated to the mechanisms of theatrical illusion. One steps through a plain door off the street and up the wooden stairs. There are offices and a small lecture room, the ceiling of which is crammed for teaching with more lanterns than could light a small theatre. I imagine a weekend lighting course with the enthusiastic lads and girls rushing up and down steps, focusing the lenses.

But this weekend is for costume cutting and we are all girls; pinning, measuring and sewing, lashed on by our two teachers. There is so little time and so much to learn. There are twelve of us from all parts zf the country – I came down by bus from Scotland. Only the thirst for knowledge will ever force me to travel that way again, but it's the cheapest when you're unemployed. There's another girl there as skint as I am, Izzie from Oxford. She's wearing a leather mini-skirt which unzips entirely into shreds and is quite obviously pilfered from some bygone production.

Izzie's made a special corset for one of our teachers and laces her into it at the end of the day. The peristalsis of sprung steel and canvas half swallows her down and displays a heroine of the *belle époque;* tiny waist and huge trembling bosom. Shrieks! – Is there a man looking in from across the road?

Then we close the windows, consult the maps and leave our dressmakers' dummies standing in the darkening room. Twelve of them, in their calico finery.

That evening my hosts were to sing in a concert in Highgate, and I might join them if I was early enough. By the time I'd won through to Archway Station (which sounded cryptic) and started up Highgate Hill (which did not) it was too late, the concert had already started. But by this time my A–Z had become like one of those magic painting books children have, where a few strokes with a wet brush make the colours appear between the lines. London was growing up around my eyes and under my exhausted feet. To colour in some more of the network of streets and names I would walk right over the hill and down to Highgate Station.

After a steep climb I came to a park, where the ponds lie in levels under the hilltop and trees hang in curtains above. The smell of earth and new leaves rose up as the rain dropped in rings. Water gleamed in veils on every bank and I soon realised this was not a passive wetness, but that the whole area was alive and springing with moisture.

Later, back at home, I described where I had been to my hosts. Where does that water *go to,* I wondered?

"Aha!" cried my hostess, flourishing a book out of the shelves.

"You have observed the source of one of *The Lost Rivers of London.* [This is the title of the book, by Nicholas Barton.] You were in Waterlow Park, and right across the hill (which lies like a soggy sponge on a draining-board), through Highgate Ponds to Hampstead, spring up streams that feed the river Fleet, once an important tributary of the Thames and sometime known as the River of Wells. It is now a gigantic sewer culverted away underground and pours into the Thames below Blackfriars Bridge." She paused for breath and resumed:

"To where Fleet-ditch with disemboguing streams
Rolls the large Tribute of dead dogs to Thames".

This, I discover, is a quotation from Alexander Pope's *The Dunciad.* After this impromptu lecture I took the book to bed and coloured in courses of the hidden rivers in my A–Z with a blue felt-tip pen.

I was fascinated. The water I had seen today was now running down from Kentish Town to Pentonville, Clerkenwell and Holborn, gurgling secretly under houses and unknown to the sleepers above except the lucky few (as I read) with observation trapdoors in their cellars.

I told myself there was no real mystery to it; that any great city needs, and pollutes, water on a massive scale. But all the next day, in the lecture room, and on the bus home with a stiff neck and a bad temper, a trickle grew and grew in my inward ears into a silently roaring flood which swept away all I had known before.

The imprisoned rivers vaulted over with streets and houses seemed to me the most real thing I had found on my journey.

MARGARET HENDERSON

# ONE DAY ALONG THE GOLDEN ROAD

It was only on the way to Samarkand, the real pearl of ancient Central Asia (now the pearl of the Soviet Socialist Republic of Uzbekistan). But the memories of that day in little Bukhara are more vivid, more persistent, and looking back I think I understand why, through the centuries, merchants and pilgrims and assorted adventurers, guided by nothing but the stars, were prepared to brave the Red Sand Desert, the Celestial Mountains, the look-outs on the Tower of Death and very likely the Black Pit of vipers and vermin for a look at the fabulous, forbidden town.

They say that only two Christians defiled Bukhara with their infidel gaze in the 400 years before 1840. That was the year Captain Connolly of the Bengal Light Cavalry crawled out of the pit with his flesh in tatters, to have his head cut off in the ceremonial courtyard for his pains.

I expect we must have crossed the desert, too, but it had been bedtime, mine at least, before we got airborne from Tashkent. Missed the desert stars, was my first thought as I woke to soft music. (Fly Aeroflot and you take off and land to the sound of the balalaika.) But that was silly, because you never see stars from planes, not in my experience anyway.

At the tourist hotel Bokhoro (it's the only one so far) my new floor lady rose cheerfully from a snooze in her armchair beside the lift and fetched some lemon tea from the electric samovar along the corridor. She giggled behind a modest hand as she helped me out of my light jacket to show me how I'd been wearing it inside out. I laughed along with her, then found my bed and flopped into sleep again for what remained of the night.

I was late in the morning of course, and the best I could do was to accept the kind offer from the Americans travelling Intourist de luxe in a curtained limousine.

"Gee," ventured Herb from Kansas City at the Tower of Death. "I guess this little minaret here must be nearly as tall as that space rocket at our Cape Canaveral. The one they take your picture beside. I have one. A pic I mean. Ever been to Florida? Nice. Everything brand new."

The Kalyan Minaret was 900 years old, 148 feet high, held together by an ancient mortar based on camel's milk. Herb leaned back as far as he could without toppling over to get it all on ciné.

In use, it had been what you might call a multi-purpose minaret. From its slender summit they must have watched anxiously for Tamerlaine, back specially from his Persian conquests to drive the Golden Horde from the town. In the intervals without strife they would read the starry constellations for signs of peace or war. It was also a sort of desert lighthouse. Fires were lit to guide the camel-trains through sandstorms to the safety of the caravanserais within the crenellated city walls. From the same minaret, muezzins had made calls to prayer and red guards proclamations of Soviet power. On bazaar days, not so very long ago, they used to push up the inside stairway and down from the top to a public death thieves, murderers, drunks, adulterers, seditionists and barren wives. That's how it got its second name, the Tower of Death.

The next building, the one with the majolica mosaics, was the Miri-Arab Madrasah, a seminary for the priesthood and the headquarters of the Spiritual Board of Moslems of Central Asia and Kazakhstan. Round the corner a couple of young fellows on scaffolding were sharing a joke as they restored the gold tracery on the old hospice for wandering dervishes.

For the Americans it was time for lunch de luxe. For me, the Lyabi-khauz which, according to local intelligence, was as good a place as I was likely to find for a bowl of green tea and kebabs. It was the old town centre, the watering hole, now a clear, terraced pool overlooked by the winter mosque and surrounded by *sofes* – divans set with low tables for food or chess.

Out of an acacia tree above my *sofe* a flock of little boys dropped down, hoping for a magic picture from my camera. Alas, it wasn't a Polaroid. I searched my bag for a souvenir. "Eenglish money," said the one with the biggest brown eyes, more mischievously than expectantly, I thought. The man from the next table had overheard. He was wearing an armband on his *khalat,* the traditional navy blue quilted coat of the Uzbeks which wouldn't look out of place in a London club as a smoking jacket.

"Please, Madame. They are not hungry. It is different now," he said. I could see they had a problem. At the crossroads of the Great Silk Route, the human instinct for trading has a heritage of thousands of years. I was relieved that stickers and postcards from home met with his approval, and theirs.

At the Ark citadel and residence of the emirs I discreetly infiltrated another English-speaking group of tourists with an excellent guide, Tatyana.

Time hadn't mellowed these emirs a bit. The last of them, one Abdul Said Mir Alim Khan, was as gifted in torture as any of his line. It was he who perfected the technique of the "sweet death", a concoction of boiling sugar poured down the throats of those of his harem who failed to please – women or boys, he wasn't too fussy. The boys travelled better when he fled before the Red Cavalry to a new life as a tea merchant, eventually, in Kabul, following a tip-off over the telephone still on display. That was in 1920.

On the way to the war memorial were the *taks* and the *tims,* the merchant domes and arcades of medieval times, still busy and in a fine state of preservation. The money-changers had gone, but not the hide-curers, nor the gold-thread embroiderers, the skull-cap sellers or the craftsmen in chased copper and alabaster. A sculptor worked on a terracotta statue of an Uzbek man wearing the *khalat* and baggy trousers stuck in high boots. The finely-modelled face was unmistakably Lenin's. Apprentices watched the masters at work or fetched glasses of water from the public drinks dispensers, fermented brown *kvass* or Pepsi-Cola (yes, Pepsi-Cola, it was written in Cyrillic script on the labels).

At the memorial to the Great Patriotic War, a large wedding party was stepping out of several decorated Ladas to leave the bridal bouquets at the tomb of the Unknown Soldier. Before I could ask for permission to snap them, they had pulled me into the family group and filled my arms with flowers. Two little sisters took charge of me as if I were a favourite auntie and shunted me around the memorial complex as the young photographer posed us like a real professional for his once-in-a-lifetime shots. At the end of the session the little girls patted me on the back as if I'd done rather well, considering.

It was noisy back at the hotel. Fireworks were popping to mark an announcement by Mr Gorbachev of a further moratorium on nuclear testing. They must have been hearing the music from the loudspeakers on the wall of the hotel's al fresco ice-cream parlour all over the town. And coming from the other side of the square was pop music from an open-air "youth café".

I sat down. Toddlers in the area with child-sized tables and chairs were attacking mountainous cream ices in three shades of pink. Our coach was back from the excursion that I'd missed. The trade unionist from Scotland joined me. He was someone quite well known at home. I'd seen him on television. You meet interesting people on package holidays.

Two tiny boys with curly hair slid from their seats and started jumping and jigging together. A father snatched his little girl from her startled *babushka* to get her on the pony ride just leaving the hotel gate. The fluffy dog stretched under my table was much more interested in sleep than food until the peace parade started to move off and he rushed yapping into line behind the red banners. "No star wars," said the slogans. "Outer space for peace." "Children, the future of the world is yours."

"Aye," said the trade unionist as he surveyed the scene. "So this is it. Reagan's evil empire. The trouble is, nobody listens to you when you get back. D'ye ken, there's some of my mates at work still think they eat their own bairns."

"That little place sure must have been wonderful in its hey-day." It was Herb again, having a last look at Bukhara from the night express to Samarkand.

"Now isn't that just typical. I've said it before, Herb, and I'll say it again. You really are the original male chauvinist."

I hadn't realised there was a Mrs Herb.

"My Herb, now," she turned to me, because I was there, I supposed. "His aesthetic sensibilities were so offended by the television aerials on all these cute, mud-walled houses we passed on the way to the collective farm."

"Just don't forget, Herb," (it was his turn) "when it was all so picturesque, it was the women who carried the burdens. Who was it that walked miles to bring back the pitchers of dirty water on their heads? You wouldn't do that, Herb. Now would you, Herb? I'm speaking to you, Herb."

"No, honey. I mean, yes honey, of course I would."

He wasn't really listening. Nor was I. The tray of tea-glasses in filigree holders had just gone past us to the sleepers. They had a real, charcoal-burning samovar on this train and plump lace-edged pillows on the bunk-beds. On the trains they have music too. I did Leningrad to Moscow once and the Red Arrow slid away to a rather catchy, if somewhat martial tune. It was a night for the slim volume of poetry I'd brought with me and maybe some star-gazing as we continued the Golden Journey eastwards across the Hungry Steppe.

*"Away for we are ready to a man.*
*Our camels sniff the evening and are glad."*

James Elroy Flecker, of course. There must be something more appropriate further on.

*"But surely we are brave.*
*Who make the Golden Journey to Samarkand."*

I wasn't feeling particularly brave. There wasn't any reason. Just awfully sleepy.

I saw no stars that night either. I didn't even hear the music of the train.

# MEMORIES

They met at sunset on the banks of the sacred Ganga, at Shamshaan Ghat. Shamshaan Ghat, the Ghat of Death, where Hindus of all castes, rich and poor, burn their dead, convinced that the deceased will obtain instant salvation from the cycle of birth and rebirth that is the lot of all men. Above them, the giant stone steps mounted majestically from the kingdom of the dead up to the city of the living. Around them spiralled acrid fumes from the rows of corpses laid out on blazing funeral pyres. At their feet lapped the waters of the sacred river, midnight black with the putrid refuse of the city. The last rays of the setting sun illumed with an odd clarity the golden marigolds flecking the river surface and bedecking the bodies of the dead awaiting their final immersion in the Ganga before being set ablaze by the sacred flame gifted by Shiva.

They sat a few feet apart, two women from different worlds. The long straight tresses of one, partially shrouded by the *pallav* of her white sari, contrasted starkly with the cropped curls and dark dress of the other. They watched in silence as a huge shaggy ram passed between them and, straddling a waiting corpse, began to chew mouthfuls from the garlands draping the body. As the keepers of the cremation ground pierced the unburned remains with long poles and hurled them into the river, they exchanged glances. As the dogs, reared from infancy on a diet of human flesh, fought the circling kites for the remains, they began to speak, hesitatingly, each groping for words in the language of the other.

The roads that had led them to Varanasi, to the Ghat of Death, were different. For Sita, the journey had begun in a remote hamlet. In a midnight ceremony she had stumbled, a bleary four-year-old, circumambulating the sacred flame of matrimony behind her eleven-year-old groom, Raja. She remained, however, a child in her parental home, her life unchanged until, mature at thirteen, she was despatched to her husband's house. Even there, her existence did not alter; only the nights were spent with the husband ordained for her by fate. And in a few months her husband left home to seek work in the city. She remained with her mother-in-law, performing her daily chores, waking in the morning before sunrise, lighting the fire for cooking, and fetching water from the well with the other village women before going to work in the fields. At sunset she returned home to perform the evening tasks before sinking onto her straw *charpoy* for a few hours of rest before sunrise and the monotonous grind of another day.

Then one hot, bright afternoon, her husband arrived home from his sweeper's job in the city and announced that he had offered her services as a domestic to his employer. She had packed her few faded saris and well-scrubbed kitchen utensils into a cheap cardboard suitcase, and, trembling with fear and anticipation, had left the security of the village and the home she had known for years for the city in the company of the almost complete stranger she called her husband. In the city, she came to know him. A simple man, an affectionate man, a hard-working man, saving his meagre salary to buy her gifts and brighten the whitewashed walls of their one-roomed apartment. Slowly, by degrees, she came to love him. The only shadow darkening their life was the fact that they had no children.

And then he died. Quite suddenly, on another hot bright afternoon, he came home, ashen-faced. He had clutched his heart, complained of a burning sensation, and, quickly, within a few moments, had died, holding her hand.

She had buried him, with little pomp and less ceremony, in the city. He mattered so little to the world; only a few co-workers attended his last rites. Even his employer was more concerned about losing her services: a sweeper is easier to find than a good domestic. She had remained, therefore, in the city on an augmented salary. What did life hold for her in the village, in any case? She would be a widow, the harbinger of evil, the unlucky one, permitted to wear no colour, permitted to have no colour in her life. She would live out the remainder of her life, unwanted, as the lowest of the low within the shadows of the walls of her husband's home. Here in the city she could at least cloak herself in anonymity among the teeming millions.

She worked and she saved. Gradually she hoarded enough to make the long journey to Varanasi in her thirty-ninth year, to fulfil a promise made to her husband on his funeral pyre: to immerse his ashes in the sacred Ganga and, hopefully, obtain *mukthi* for him.

For Carol, the journey had begun a quarter of a century ago and a continent away, in a small village in the English countryside where she had lived out a tranquil existence as the daughter of the local parson. The son of the village doctor, Mark, her first and only love, had been part of the fabric of her life from her earliest years. Together they had explored the magic realms of childhood and experienced the uncertainties of adolescence. They had married at twenty-one, one summer morning, in a quiet ceremony in the village church. They had filled the small church with roses, and the scent of roses always brought back memories of the ceremony to her: her father fumbling with emotion as he turned the pages of his prayer book, Mark standing tall and straight, the sunlight from the stained glass window spilling a rainbow of colours on his blond head.

She had gone to work as his father's receptionist; he had joined the local solicitor. The even tenor of their days had been punctuated by routine happenings: afternoon tea with scones and wafer-thin cucumber sandwiches, an occasional beer in the local pub, weekend cricket on the village green, evensong on Sundays. No children had arrived and, after a while, they had given up hoping.

And then, quite suddenly, on Christmas eve, in an almost identical fashion to Raja, he had died, clutching his chest and complaining of heartburn. All that winter she had been depressed, haunted by the lyrics of that Beatles' melody, *Eleanor Rigby*. In spring, impulsively, she had taken their little nest-egg, sent telegrams to a friend in India and bought a ticket to Varanasi, to the city of the Ghat of Death.

And now both of them sat together among the living dead, wrapped in memories of their dead. They sat a long while, motionless, watching the brutal simplicity of the ritual of death. Bodies arrived, one after the other, carried by pall-bearers chanting the name of Rama. Distinctions between the living and the dead vanished as all were subjected to the traditional rites. As the flames licked away at the corpses, silk-bedecked, bejewelled forms, drenched in expensive ghee, heaped high with propitious coconuts and laid on pyres of fragrant sandalwood crumbled into the same ashes as cotton-shrouded corpses lashed with rope. The little children, too, were no respecters of mortal differences, as they swarmed out of the serpentine city alleys to scavenge, indiscriminately, the coconuts placed on the dead. As the funeral embers lost their glow, the children came armed with earthenware pots to collect coal to cook their evening meal. The cycle of life played out around the pyres of death.

Night had long since fallen when I went in search of Carol and found them mounting the steps together, an incongruous pair, but touched by the identical sorrows and struggling with similar emotions. I spoke only briefly to Sita as she folded her hands together in the age-old gesture of greeting and farewell. Then, in an awkward motion, she thrust the urn that had contained the ashes of her husband into Carol's hands before slipping away into the darkness.

It was a year later, on the Fourth of July, that I stood with Carol, on the deck of a ferryboat, one of the thousands celebrating at the foot of Lady Liberty. Silently, under the cover of darkness, she slipped her wedding ring, the tangible symbol of bondage to Mark, into the urn before sliding both into the water. At the festival of freedom, she loosened her ties to the dead and turned to me with a smile.

They had met at Shamshaan Ghat, two women from different worlds. They had spanned the light years separating their cultures and derived strength and solace from each other. In identical gestures of renunciation, they had closed the pages of the past and begun life again.

For the Colonel's lady and Judy O'Grady are sisters under the skin . . .

JACKI POLANSKI

# NAKED AMONGST THE GUZERAT

Juan turned on the generator at 3am. The slap of light catapulted me towards the obligatory shower. By three-thirty Señor Sanchez had arrived to take us on the long journey to Caracas. In air-conditioned blackness we drove past the fan-shaped traveller's palms screening the swimming-pool, past the banana plantation where every day old Eduardo listlessly dribbled the hose over the tall leaves; through the iron gates of the hacienda to cross the wide, lush valley of African stargrass. The herds of Brahman cattle recently delivered from the Llanos plains for fattening stopped grazing momentarily to walk away from the assaulting headlamps. Already their vivid black noses glistened with good health, their silvery hides hanging in draped bands like velvet necklaces swaying gracefully as they munched.

The immaculate Lina placed the bag of tangerines, gathered yesterday from the two big trees by the wash-house, on the seat between us. I decided that in a few minutes I would ask for one.

We shuddered over the cattle-grid onto the common land beside the lake. No grass here, just prickly shrubs and baked mud.

The dry season lasted from January to April, and at night threatening bush-fires lit the surrounding mountains to a fierce red. Don Juan and his herdsmen were skilled in the art of "back-firing". They would light a strip of scrubland below the length of the bush-fire, so that on meeting the two fires exploded and burnt each other out. Sprawled over the track lay the cattle and horses belonging to the Indians. Juan shouted, drumming his palm against the door until the scraggy animals rose up and moved painfully aside. Lina, being used to this procedure, handed around the tangerines. But in the artificial light the look of hopelessness in the eyes of the animals became distressingly accentuated. It was a look I had witnessed constantly amongst human- and animal-kind during my weeks of travel in South America. And not least here in Venezuela, considered the most Americanised of Latin American cultures.

During my first evening Lina graciously asked, "What would you like to see in our country?"

"Angel Falls please."

"But dat is just a long streak of white!"

I shrugged. "Then I shall walk to the mountains to paint."

"No!", wagging forefinger. "You do not go anywhere beyond de wire fencing. De Indians carry machetes and you with your little brush, what do you think you can do? You can get bitten by mapanari out dhere and dat snake-bite is lethal. This is not Kew Gardens, my dear."

I was silenced into appreciating the black bean soup.

So, every morning I accompanied Juan to his offices by the breeding-pens and from there I walked, equipped with drinking-water and reeking in Autan, to look for pictures to paint. I learned not to sit on the track where passing vehicles whipped up dustclouds to smear my brilliant colours. Instead I braved the immensity of space, fighting to keep my brush steady when seven Nelore bulls encircled me, their combined tonnage an awesome counterpoint to the lightness of their tread. They disappeared mysteriously to drown in extensive pastures. I heeded Juan's advice when three barefoot cowboys rode up swiftly, laughing in curiosity, and inclined my head in a formal nod of greeting. These tough Llaneros can write their names and are the fathers of schoolchildren, yet they feel excluded from the modern world. They assemble in their best suits on pay-day to see The Don Juan because he can explain what is written, otherwise the bank clerks may not honour their cheques. For it was he, the fair and courteous *el mister,* who had talked his way out of danger when the military, without notice or explanation, invaded his hacienda. The Don Juan ruled O.K.

I had fallen for the young champion Brahman bull, which always greeted me fluttering endless black eyelashes. I had seen him give sperm for freezing, so I suppose we were on rather intimate terms. "Juan has gone over to the electric ejaculator," Lina announced coquettishly. For reasons of economic progress, Juan had been advised to limit the natural servicing methods of breeding and adapt to artificial insemination. Little realising that I was to witness a ceremony normally forbidden to women, and which few foreigners see, I accepted an invitation to watch my beautiful champ perform. The animal was roped and harnessed within a secure pen. Hector's arm then disappeared to the elbow to clear the animal's rectum of faecal residue. Into it he inserted a metal objected shaped like a toy submarine which was attached to an instrument-box by two long wires. Champion suffered this invasion with calm professionalism. Whilst Hector held fast at the rear, Tiburcio crouched under the penis ready to catch semen in a scrupulously clean plastic cup. Juan began to administer gently escalating doses of electric current. The mounting frequency of his breathing sucked the bull's haunches inwards and pushed his belly outwards like a huge pair of bellows at work. After some fifteen minutes the sugar-pink penis slowly emerged from its tube of muscular, hairy skin making short contractions. Juan, expert at reading bull signals, shouted *"Ahora! ahora!"* and in a delirium of spasms Champ ejaculated his valuable high-progeny-count semen neatly into the cup. Then, with eyes cast ecstatically heavenward, his body slumped into the cradling harness. Upon recovery he was patted and praised and hosed down.

The next bull, a promising Nelore of good growth and scale of muscling, was a virgin. Not only did he resist the rectal washout but he fought the toy submarine hard with heaving haunches and persistent head batterings. It took more than thirty minutes to achieve success, and then Tiburcio nearly missed his catch. There was no discernible moment of ecstacy, only tendrils of streaming blood and saliva from the wounded muzzle. But after the microscope reading Juan pronounced an exceptionally high progeny-count, so young Frisky was in for a long term of ecstasy-training.

I had formed the habit of swimming an increasing number of lengths before sundown, and was in the water when Lina called out flourishing tickets to Angel Falls. To her surprise there was a Tourist Camp down there, primitive but operational. So we flew in a small jet southeast from Caracas for several hours. We covered vast patterns of land, now dazzlingly flat, now sharply undulating, until we landed at the newly constructed town of Puerto Ordaz on the mighty Orinoco Delta. The relief pilot stared at us for some moments. Then he approached with an invitation to share his view from the cockpit. Within twenty minutes the plane had become a silver-winged dragonfly skimming over jungle flanked by giant mountains. The presence of these flat-topped Tepuy created one enormous sweeping canyon. I understood the excitement Jimmy Angel must have felt in 1935 when he discovered the 3,000-foot high falls. Suddenly we were flying against a great streak of gushing white. The plane had shrunk to a gnat. Brushing spray, we circled the summit and doubled back. Now the viewing passengers on the other side could have their shrieking, swooning fainting-fits.

Our thatched cottage at the pretty lakeside village of Canaima provided unaffected comfort. To escape the bugs we moved the beds well away from the walls and sprayed everything. Two Indian guides in scarlet loincloths and feathered headbands took our small party by canoe along the Rio Carrao. After chasing over rapids and passing countless waterfalls cascading from the tops of the Auyan-Tepuy we landed at Orchid Island. There we swam in fresh bronze-coloured waters and sat on coral sands to eat barbecued chicken and *tequenos*. Soundlessly from out of the jungle there paddled an old "Dutchman". He had lived with the Indians for over forty years and would not talk about himself. He wanted food. Pointing out Vei-Tepuy, the Sun Mountain, he told us that during May and June the sun rises between the cleavage of its two breasting peaks. Then tribes, as yet unknown to the white man, make their sacrifices.

On returning to the hacienda I made my final swim and sprang dancing from the pool. It was then that I noticed them. The herd of newly delivered Guzerat had stopped chewing and were gazing at my swirling nakedness. I could read nothing from their eyes. But the shape of their high circular horns skirting the bougainvillea hedge spelled out a long OOOOOOOOOOOOOOOO!

Like the night, the dawn was now arriving quickly, revealing the horrors of Los Ranchos, the shanty-towns on the mountainsides framing Caracas. I handed Juan a card.

"Could Señor Sanchez please take me to this address?"

Lina glanced at me. "What about your trip to Rio?"

"I have to go down to the Guyana, the land of Green Mansions."

"But dhere is nothing to see! Just a lot of tall grass . . ."

TOM MEINHARD

# "IN THE BLUE RIDGE MOUNTAINS OF VIRGINIA ON THE TRAIL OF THE LONESOME PINE . . ."

The Blue Ridge Mountains are the first ridge of the Appalachians as you cross the coastal plains from the Atlantic and step up off the Piedmont plateau. Famed in the Laurel and Hardy theme song, they rise fold on rounded fold of thick hardwood forest, to some 6,000 feet.

Three hours' drive from the steaming sauna which is Washington in the summer, and 3,800 feet up in the clear air of the Blue Ridge Mountains, lies the Wintergreen Mountain Resort. Perched a few miles west of Thomas Jefferson's Monticello and the University of Virginia which he founded, the resort is stamped by a distinctive feature. The facilities are owned and controlled by the property owners, who have bought sites and built second homes within the Wintergreen area. The owners underwrite a management company for the resort, securing it against insensitive over-development and downmarket pressures with a degree of success which has made them keenly studied and imitated by leisure resorts elsewhere.

Wintergreen covers 11,000 acres of mountain forest, with recreation facilities of general range and quality. A par-70 golf course has been cut out of the forest and winds for 6,500 yards across blue grass fairways and watered greens, with sudden mountain vistas fifty miles across the Great Valley to the Alleghenies. There are sixteen tennis courts, outdoor and indoor swimming, pony trails and lakes for swimming and canoeing in the valley below. There are twenty miles of marked tracks through the forests, and guided nature trails to study plants, trees, fungi, wildlife, geology. Ten ski slopes, including 1,000-foot vertical falls and snow-making equipment, provide for a three-month ski season, with lifts and floodlit skiing.

And yet, all this is lost within the vastness of the mountains and the forests. Nature overwhelms man. Rocks formed 1,100 million years ago fold into mountain ridge lines, valleys and rock faces, where plant and animal life have found their niches. Variations in slope direction, altitude and moisture give shelter to different forms of wildlife. Natural gardens have established themselves, in different microsites, with different plants. Springs rise, streams are fed, waters tumble down mountainsides, over rock slides, through trout pools. Deep gorges are cut. Shamokin gorge (a Monocan Indian word meaning "land were the antlers are plenty") at Wintergreen drops almost 3,000 feet from the top of the rocky slide down into the creek bed.

The main trees I see are shagbark hickory, red oak, white ash, yellow birch. Also chestnut oak, with their gnarled twisted trunks, table mountain pine and huge Canadian hemlock up to six feet in diameter. These form the leaf canopy overhead, and insulate the forest floor from the hot sun. By late September the hickory leaves have turned bright yellow, and Virginia creepers add blazes of vivid red. Very soon now the forest will turn, and the trees take on their autumn colours. At head height, rhododendron, azalea and mountain laurel abound, promising brilliant colour in early summer. American chestnut, reduced by a disastrous blight at the beginning of the century, struggles cyclically back to shrub height before disease cuts it down to the roots again. Underfoot meanwhile, my scant botany cannot keep pace with the profusion of wild flowers and fungi. On one short trail I count twenty-one different plants in bloom. Yellow lady slipper is in flower. So too is ginseng, with its red berry fruit, a protected plant whose dried root fetches $300 a pound for export to the Far East. There are oxeye daisies, yarrow and crown vetch; numerous varieties of fern; wood nettle and its antidote, jewel weed; wild vine, wild orchids and lilies.

I walk in the forest all day without seeing or hearing a soul. Now the going is flat; now I am scrambling over large rocks, across streams, up steep slopes. The forest is wide awake and I hear the continual muted plop of falling acorns, the piping squeaks of the chipmunks, the whistling of jays, the raucous bark of the slope-soaring ravens. Sound carries in the mountains. Now and again a heavier thud denotes the falling of dead wood, perhaps close by, perhaps way over on the opposite slope – the forest sheds twenty-five tons an acre every year. When I sit quite still, for several minutes, the wood mice emerge to explore me. The chipmunks, jaw pouches grotesquely distended with freshly garnered acorns, scamper stiff-legged and tail erect to where I watch; but they never look me in the eye. Water-thrush sit in the ninebark by my head. Bear, deer, bobcat and the emblematic wild turkey, are lurking in these forests unseen.

Without the trail-blazes painted on the trees I would soon be lost. Outside the marked track I am following, the forest is trackless. It is as Roman and medieval Europe must have been, a place of danger, where bandits could lurk, where Arminius could ambush Varus and slaughter three legions, where Robin Hood could hold the Normans at bay. Safe in the twentieth century, I note that the forest is impenetrable, that I can discern virtually nothing beyond about a hundred yards, and I understand how ancient forests could dominate the imagination, breeding fear and mystery, fairy tales and folk myths, dragons and witches.

For some hours I follow the Appalachian Trail. This footpath runs for 2,000 miles from Georgia up to Maine, and as it passes through Wintergreen it follows the high mountainside through the trees, emerging now and again at spectacular rocky escarpments. On one of these I sit for an hour in the hot sun, high out on a projecting rock, and look down across the rolling forest carpet and out to the Shenandoah valley below me. On the facing slope I see large white scree slides of antietam quartzite, which the Indians sought out for its special hardness and used for their arrow heads, scalping knives and tools. Hawks and ravens circle below me, lazing on thermals, hiding in haze and mist banks, waiting to thunderbolt their prey. I note that clichés, even while being clichés, can be true, that the endless treetops *are* a carpet, that the forest *does* shimmer with energy, that the mountains *do* slumber, that the heat *is* drowsy, that this is a Big Country.

After nightfall I sit in my luxury "condo" and sip a Virginia riesling. Suddenly the peace is ambushed by rushing volleys of rain arrowing down. Windlessly, huge drops plunge on to the trees and the leaves, overflow the gutters, splash on to the balcony and roll on down the forest slope. After an hour, just as suddenly, the storm stops, but it continues to echo, dripping from leaf to leaf, from leaf to ground, from eaves to gutter, each note different. The spring peepers have taken over, small green tree frogs emitting a ceaseless and unvarying shrill note like a million small whistling alarms in the liquid night. Framed in the open window of foliage above my head, stars are undraped, and I discern part of the Great Bear, Cassiopeia, the Pole Star, and a brilliant Jupiter loudly proclaiming his mythic role as king of heaven.

Nineteen-eighty-seven is the bicentenary of the American constitution – that nimble document crafted by wealthy slave-owners and disciples of Hobbes, as they convened through the summer of 1787 at Constitution House in old Philadelphia. This was while King George still ruled, and the colonists were anything but victorious. What better pretext – if pretext were needed – to visit the founding fathers at Monticello, at Ash Lawn, in Philadelphia, in Washington, and (mindful that the first president took all of four days to travel from his Mount Vernon home and take up office in New York) to temper unalloyed history with a diversion into nature, by paying a visit to Wintergreen.

## HELEN BLACKMORE

# HOLE IN THE SAND

It is just an ordinary hole, as holes go. Dug in the sand. About six feet by eight feet. Fairly shallow. Just deep enough for four bodies. The beaches of the Côte d'Atlantique, west of Bordeaux, are pock-marked with similar holes.

Occasionally a black Mirage fighter streaks low across the blue sky. A reminder of other times, other beaches, when men crouched, helpless, among the dunes and craters. But these French pilots are probably on the look-out for nothing more sinister than well-oiled, succulent, brown breasts. And the only threat from the Germans comes when, naked and ruthless in pursuit of their volley-ball, they bound over your hole, spraying their recumbent fellow-holiday-makers with sand.

There was a time when naturists and sun-lovers were confined to securely-fenced anthropological straw villages amongst the sand dunes, but now they frolic the length of the coast. ("For goodness sake! Take your swimming trunks *off,*" you whisper, embarrassed, to your eight-year-old. "I don't care what the boys say at school. Bums aren't rude!") But, however powerful the sun, a malevolent wind off the Atlantic can chill the naked body to a pattern of goose pimples or flagellate it with a whirl of sand. And so, calling upon an instinct almost eradicated by mortgages, dry rot, loft-insulation and damp-proof courses, urban man digs his private sun-trap in the sand.

Of course, nothing much happens when you spend your entire holi-day in a hole in the sand. Afterwards you have no entertaining travel-lers' tales of man-eating elephants or cracking ice floes. You cannot claim to have been winched to safety by a helicopter or marched away at gunpoint by freedom fighters. But you do discover that quite ordi-nary people take on a surreal quality when nude among strangers.

Look at those three retired stockbrokers paddling ankle-deep in the lace-patterned shallows of exhausted breakers. Modesty has obvi-ously driven them to a joint investment in a single outfit. One wears the jaunty red-and-white striped T-shirt, one the denim shorts and the third the straw boater. The heat shimmers, and for a moment tricks you with a glimpse of three curly-haired Edwardian boys with shrimping nets. But then you see the wrinkled necks, the self-satisfied bellies, the shrivelled scrota and the spindly legs. More like indolent, basking reptiles.

And what about that mountainous woman? Did you ever see the American Circus? The drums roll, the Ringmaster pronounces, the trumpets bray and the butch Fraulein Heidi stampedes through the curtains. Muscles rippling, she lifts her dainty white- and silver-clad companion in one hand and places her in a sparkling globe which she rotates, nonchalantly, on her nose, to thunderous applause. That woman, over there, picking sand from her nipples, she'd be transformed by Fraulein Heidi's spangled costume.

"*Glâces! Boissons!*" Alas, fame and glory escape her as the ice cream vendor, discreet in black swimming trunks, distracts her with a quid's-worth of ice-cream to share with her drooling, sand-clogged Scottie.

The portion of sea deemed "safe" for bathing and surfing is marked by blue flags and an umpire's chair. Does the immaculately-white-clad, handsome-but-unintelligent umpire decide whether each death by drowning was fair play? He watches black frogmen emerge from the sea; soon they will haul in their golden treasure chests, spraying the worm-bubbling sand with ingots and ducats. Ah! It's only surfboards they're groping for. They are just the unchic relatives of those lemon, turquoise and sugar pink rubber-clad surfing super-heroes; those men who crouch, crest, lurch, then swirl in with the spent breakers and scrabble ignominiously at your feet.

Meanwhile the children have found their second jellyfish. "Is it still alive?" they ask hopefully. You stare at the beached, transparent mound. "Well, I'm sure it's dead," you lie, remembering childhood stories of idyllic summers, invading Portuguese Men-of-War and infants killed by these floating plastic bags; "but perhaps we won't swim today." The protests start. "How about beachcombing? A bit further from the sea? In the dunes perhaps. See who can find the most unusual bit of metal or wood." An hour later, you realise you could start your own scrap metal business from the debris in the dunes.

All afternoon an old man with the face of Picasso stands on the dunes, hands behind his back, staring out to sea. He's still there as the sun sets spectacularly and you come panting back. Just standing by the rubbish bin. Staring profoundly at the sea. "*Pardon!*" you mutter, throwing Nivea bottles, apple cores, punctured balls and Camembert boxes wildly out of the bin over his feet. His gaze shifts as you locate a stained Sainsbury's bag. His wise blue eyes fixed on you, he discourses on art, philosophy and death. Or could he be inquiring how your car keys came to be at the bottom of the bin, covered with sticky melon seeds?

Car keys? Well, of course, no realist these days actually *sleeps* in the hole in the sand. At a safe distance of twenty minutes is the car and the family tent, surrounded by pine trees, several hundred other cars and tents, and all the trappings (including toilets that don't even smell French) of a 3-star Municipal Campsite. At the campsite you leave behind the flights-of-fancy of the beach. Here everyone is modestly dressed and cautiously behaved – even the family poodles. French social etiquette is best observed in the areas assigned for washing-up. The brow-beaten small man with two bowls of crockery (plates for first course, dinner-plates, side plates, salad bowls, fruit dishes, wine-glasses, coffee cups, pans, and extensive cutlery to match) might well commence a conversation with an attractive young woman, "Yours, I believe, is the charming dog three tents from ours?" They will be engrossed in details of the sleeping patterns and nocturnal walks demanded by their respective dogs, before his wife comes to reclaim him.

And beyond the campsite lies a small town. It looks like a cardboard model in lemon and pale blue, which can be folded flat and stored during the visitor-less winter months. The pharmacy is the most prosperous establishment, filled with exotic gilded perfumes and expensively packaged remedies for all ailments. The rest of the town comes to life when the market arrives. Traders ply you with their wares. You sip almond cognacs and taste the cheeses, Basque cakes, Vietnamese crisps and the pancakes, whilst declining to buy the amazing (look no butter!) pancake-pan.

Between the stalls of Indian and African fabrics you glimpse the bread, vegetables, fish and exotic cardigans. You perch on a stool at one of the busiest stalls and take a light lunch of champagne and local oysters.

But too much jostling can be fatiguing. You gather up the buckets and spades and head once more for the beach. You excavate two sand boats along the high-tide line from which the children can defy the incoming waves, then glance towards the dunes to check that Picasso is still meditating on the transcendence of the Atlantic. Reassured, you sink happily into your familiar hole, apply the ritual lotions and creams, place the token paperback on your stomach and stare vacantly at the blue sky, oblivious of all except the occasional roaring, swooping Mirage, mis-hit volleyball or hopeful shout of *"Glâces! Boissons!"*